Date Due

How to CREATE Effective TV Commercials

How to CREATE Effective TV Commercials

Huntley Baldwin

Second Edition

NTC Business Books
a division of *NTC Publishing Group* • Lincolnwood, Illinois USA

Cover Photo Credits:

Left photo: Photo courtesy of BBDO / Chicago

Right photo: Photo courtesy of J. Walter
Thompson, Inc.

Published by NTC Business Books, a division
of NTC Publishing Group, 4255 West Touhy Avenue,
Lincolnwood (Chicago), Illinois 60646-1975 U.S.A.
© 1989 by Huntley Baldwin. All rights reserved.
No part of this book may be reproduced, stored
in a retrieval system, or transmitted in any form
or by any means, electronic, mechanical, photocopying,
or otherwise, without the prior permission
of NTC Publishing Group.
Manufactured in the United States of America.
Library of Congress Catalog Card Number: 88-62119

9 0 ML 9 8 7 6 5 4 3 2 1

Contents

Part Two: Strategy to Idea

Part Three: Idea to Execution

Foreword

In the preface to the first edition of this book, published in 1982, Huntley Baldwin noted that *Time* magazine once characterized TV commercials as an "American art form," and he asked, "how often can you go to the office and create an American art form. . . ?" But, he continued, "the people who pay the bills—the advertisers—do not view themselves as patrons of the arts. They expect those cute little spots to move some product."

As one of those who "pays the bills," I can assure you that most advertisers define good advertising the same way: good advertising is advertising that works, period.

This book is a comprehensive, stimulating, amusing, and—after all—very readable book about how to make television advertising that works. Its author, Huntley Baldwin, is among the most qualified people I have ever known to write such a book.

An advertising professional for nearly 25 years (almost all of them spent at the Leo Burnett Company), Huntley is a rare bird among "creatives," for a couple of reasons. First he is expertly and equally skilled as a copywriter and as an art director—a true one man creative team. Second, unlike many agency creative people, who think that the creative process must proceed unfettered by "business considerations," Huntley understands the critical importance of sound strategy as the basis for creating advertising that moves product.

Among his particular strengths is Huntley's ability to keep the "classics" fresh. Noting that Burnett is perhaps best known for such long-lived campaigns as the Jolly Green Giant, the Marlboro Cowboy, and the Keebler Elves, Richard B. Fizdale, president and chief creative officer of Burnett says, "their endurance is a testament to the power of the original idea. But, sometimes it's even more challenging from a creative standpoint to keep these campaigns fresh and relative. Huntley Baldwin is a master at this."

Whether to an old favorite or new campaign, Huntley brings to his work, and to this book, a straightforward, no-nonsense style, a wonderful sense of humor, and the ability—becoming more and more rare in America—to say things in simple declarative sentences.

I have read the first edition of this book three times, and this second edition once. I have learned something new and useful with each reading.

To anyone with an interest, professional or casual, in the process by which effective TV advertising is created, I recommend this book enthusiastically and without reservation.

Michael A. Miles
President and Chief Operating Officer
Kraft General Foods

Preface

In 1968, during what is remembered as the Golden Age of Advertising, *Time* magazine paid this tribute to television commercials: "Commercials are infuriating. They are also irresistible. Commercials are an outrageous nuisance. They are also apt to be better than the programs they interrupt. Commercials are the heavy tribute that the viewer must pay to the sponsor in exchange for often dubious pleasure. They are also an American art form. A minor art form, but the ultimate in mixed media: sight, sound and sell."

That's heady stuff. How often can you go to the office and create an American art form, even a minor one?

Many commercials are artistic, but the people who pay the bills—the advertisers—do not consider themselves patrons of the arts. They expect those creative little spots to move some product.

Today's mass marketers play for high stakes. They do not like to be wrong. A commercial that costs more than $100,000 to produce and even more to put on the air is no place to take unnecessary chances. Everyone would love to be sure, before all that money is spent, that the commercial is going to do its job.

This explains the popularity of copy testing. Everybody is looking for a simple, inexpensive, foolproof method of spotting which commercial will be a winner and which will be a dud. Storyboards are analyzed to within an inch of their lives. And yet the secret formula for success still eludes us. Duds keep sneaking through. Commercials do not automatically keep getting better and better. Creating effective commercials remains more art than science.

This book looks at commercials through the eyes of the creative person—the copywriter or art director—whose job it is to think up, write, design, and produce television advertising that will do its part to increase sales for the advertiser. It describes the process of solving advertising problems, creating ideas, and translating them into commercials. The focus is on all the things that go into a commercial *before* it is produced.

Writing about how to think up a commercial is only slightly easier than actually thinking up a commercial. There is no orderly, standardized procedure. With the disclaimer that the creative process does not always work the way it is supposed to work, this book attempts to pull together the ingredients of advertising ideas and executions. It is a "rule book" for a process that has no rules.

Although this book is written *to* the copywriter, it is written *for* others as well. It is for anyone who works in marketing and advertising and wants to better understand how commercials work and what things contribute to their effectiveness. By better understanding the creative process and the creative values of commercials, marketing people will be better equipped to judge and evaluate advertising. It is also a book for students of advertising and for anyone who has watched commercials and wondered, even briefly, how and why people make them.

No one person ever made a commercial. And no one person ever made a book about commercials. Many people have contributed heavily to this effort, either willingly or unwittingly. For their ideas, inspiration, and assistance, special thanks are due Milt Schaffer, Dr. Vernon Fryburger, Dr. John Maloney, Lelia Green, Mary Ann Gordon, Carol Foley, Dave Mortimer, Donald Gunn, Rick Fizdale, Carla Michelotti, Barb Rowan, Marla Johnson, and most of all, Sandy Panozzo and her amazing word processor.

Part 1

Commercials in Perspective

Chapter 1

A Short History of Commercials

It is a short history as histories go. The first commercial, a ten-minute pitch for apartments on Long Island, was broadcast over the radio as recently as 1922. Commercial television did not begin in earnest until after World War II. A TV copywriter could have begun his career in those very first days and still be looking ahead to retirement.

But a lot of change, both technical and social, has been packed into the past four decades. Television commercials were born in the innocence of the Eisenhower years, when the biggest problems seemed to be dingy laundry and perspiration odor. But as times changed, so did commercials. The housewife became a career woman, with commercials no longer portraying her simply enduring the drudgery of wash day, but taking a man to dinner with her American Express card. Exit Ozzie and Harriet, Betty Crocker, hula hoops, and Speedy Alka-Seltzer. Enter the Woodstock generation, civil rights, Viet Nam, moon landings, Watergate, yuppies, and Max Headroom. Enter the technical advances of color, videotape, and computer graphics.

The cost of both producing and airing television commercials increased each year like clockwork. In response, the standard length of commercials shrank from sixty seconds to thirty seconds, and advertisers are currently flirting with fifteen seconds. And as commercials shrank, they multiplied. Increased clutter has made the competition for viewer attention tougher.

In their relatively short lifetime, commercials have been assailed as the corrupters of youth and morality and hailed as a minor art form. Some have been honored at Cannes. Others, for cigarettes, have been banned from the airwaves. These have been busy times for broadcast advertising.

3

The Beginnings: Radio Days

In the beginning there was only space.

The first advertising agencies existed to sell space in newspapers and magazines to advertisers. They were agents for the media and were paid a commission. Life was simple. Then, sometime between 1880 and 1900, agencies began to prepare the advertisements that went into the space. Creativity had come to advertising. While these early admen were busy creating newspaper and magazine ads, inventors were tinkering with devices that would have a bigger impact on mass communication than anything since the invention of moveable type.

In 1895, Guglielmo Marconi was conducting experiments in Bologna, Italy, with something called radio waves. That same year, inventors like Edison in America, Lumière in France, and Robert Paul in England were fascinating audiences by projecting a moving picture onto a white sheet. Radio pioneers envisioned a time when they would broadcast visual images as well as sound. And early filmmakers dreamed of the day when their silent movies would talk. But meanwhile, people tried to decide what to make of this new wireless device.

> At first people simply talked over the radio through microphones and headsets. It seemed most like a telephone, not like a magazine or newspaper so it was called wireless telephone or radio telephone. Radio added a new transforming dimension when the headset became a speaker, with better fidelity and more volume than a headset designed for one pair of ears. Radio now could reach a *group* of people— a whole family, not just a teenage boy tinkering with a crystal set.[1]

As Americans built and bought more and more receiving equipment, and as more and more radio stations rushed onto the air, the question of how to finance broadcasting arose. Proposals included an endowment of stations by wealthy donors, support by local government, or a tax on radio receivers. Few considered the concept that eventually took hold—advertising. It was AT&T that introduced the idea of toll broadcasting.

"On August 28, 1922 at 5:00 p.m., WEAF (New York) finally broadcast the first income-producing program: a ten-minute message to the public from the Queensboro Corporation to promote the sale of apartments in Jackson Heights, on Long Island."[2]

Another notable event in the history of commercials occurred in January 1923. An advertising agency arranged for Mineralava cosmetics to sponsor a talk by movie star Marion Davies entitled "How I Make Up for the Movies." An offer of a free autographed picture brought thousands of requests. This success attracted other advertisers to the potential of radio.

But the future of broadcasting and broadcast advertising depended upon two things: better programming for the listeners and broader coverage for the advertisers. Both were accomplished in 1926 when RCA announced the formation of a new company, the National Broadcasting

---

1. Stephen Fox, *The Mirror Makers* (New York: William Morrow and Company, 1984), 151–2.

2. Eric Barnouw, *Tube of Plenty: The Evolution of American Television* (New York: Oxford University Press, 1975), 45.

Company (NBC). NBC was so successful that it formed a second network in 1927. (The two were called Red and Blue. In 1943, the Supreme Court required that one be sold. NBC Blue later became the American Broadcasting Company.) That same year, 1927, rival network CBS was formed.

Just as network radio was gathering momentum, something happened that intensified interest in television. On October 6, 1927, Warner Brothers premiered the first talking film, *The Jazz Singer*. Sound and pictures had finally come together. The resulting upheaval in Hollywood was felt in New York's broadcasting circles.

"A vast changeover of theaters and studios was under way. Dramatists were frantically imported from the Broadway world. Stars with squeaky voices were set adrift. The mood of revolutionary change communicated itself to the broadcasting world. As film moved to sound, broadcasters reached for the image. The two industries had largely ignored each other, but now saw a convergence—or a clash—of interest."[3]

RCA's David Sarnoff foresaw a time in the very near future when television, still in the experimental stages, would be "as much a part of our life" as radio had become. Optimism reigned. RCA stock soared. Television's future seemed right around the corner.

Then, in 1929, the stock market crashed.

Because of the Great Depression that followed, Sarnoff's optimistic timetable for television was delayed. Experiments and demonstrations continued throughout the 1930s, but it was radio that really prospered during these hard times. Radio became people's link with humanity. President Roosevelt's radio fireside chats helped many Americans through those dark days. Listeners sought guidance from the daytime serials and escape in the free entertainment provided by such new talents as Ed Wynn, Jack Benny, Fred Allen, and Eddie Cantor. And the sponsors of these popular programs prospered.

Meanwhile, television continued to make steady progress. RCA staged a demonstration of television at the New York World's Fair in 1939. The Republican and Democratic conventions were televised in 1940, as were the election returns. But when America entered World War II, television schedules were curtailed and the manufacture of receivers was halted. The heyday of commercial television would have to wait.

Television Takes Over

1945. The war was over. Television historian Erik Barnouw describes the times:

> Electronic assembly lines, freed from production of electronic war material, were ready to turn out picture tubes and television sets. Consumers, long confronted by wartime shortages and rationing, had accumulated savings and were ready to buy. Manufacturers of many kinds, ready to switch from armaments back to consumer goods, were eager to advertise.

---

3. Barnouw, 63.

Returning servicemen with radar experience, whose knowledge was convertible to television, were snapped up by many stations. Advertising agencies were ready; many had already formed television departments and had experimented with television commercials and programming.[4]

In the summer of 1946, RCA entered the market with black-and-white sets and that fall demonstrated a crude but compatible electronic color system. Television stood poised on the brink of a boom.

Then, in late 1948, the Federal Communications Commission declared a freeze on new television licenses. What was to have been a temporary hiatus, while it coped with the proliferation of stations, ended up lasting 3½ years. This proved to be a temporary shot in the arm for radio. Although television had pockets of strength for advertisers, radio remained the dominant national medium. Those cities with strong television coverage were watched closely by advertisers, and what they saw was impressive. In one instance, Hazel Bishop lipstick, which began advertising on television in 1950, saw its sales rise from $50,000 to $4.5 million in 1952. Movie attendance in television cities dropped. Even sports events, restaurants, and night clubs felt the impact of this new medium. "Even under the FCC freeze the industry's total TV business went from $12.3 million (1949) to $40.8 million (1950) to $128 million (1951), a level that radio had taken 16 years to reach."[5]

In 1952, the FCC lifted its freeze, and hundreds of television stations rushed to reach the air as more and more advertisers turned to it for their audiences. And the role of radio changed to that which we know today.

Radio reeled from the competitive impact as advertisers traded their broadcast dollars with almost dizzying speed. Although in absolute terms radio gained almost $90,000,000 in annual revenue (from 1950 to 1960) its share dropped sharply, from 13% to 7%. But the big change in radio as an advertising medium was not so much in this considerable loss of dollar share as in its dramatic reformation from an all-family, prime time, mass medium to a highly localized, individual companion—traveling with Americans from room to room, in their cars and to their places of work or play.[6]

TV Commercials: The Early Years

As television commercials began to appear in American homes after 1948, the country was emerging from wartime shortages to discover a newfound affluence and an abundance of consumer goods. Food shopping shifted from the corner grocery to the supermarket, where a succession of convenience goods appeared. There were big family cars waiting to be filled with cheap gasoline. There were appliances and cleansers and detergents to help

---

4. Barnouw, 99–100

5. Fox, 210.

6. *Advertising Age* (April 30, 1980): 148–55.

the harried housewife—all waiting to be made irresistible in sixty seconds of glorious black-and-white.

During the fifteen years after the end of the Second World War, American advertising parlayed this expansive cluster of circumstances—cars, highways, new patterns of suburban consumption, and the explosion of the ultimate ad medium—into its greatest prosperity since the 1920s. Breaking away from the long drought of Depression and wartime austerities, the gross total of advertising expenditures doubled in only five years from $2.9 billion in 1945 to $5.7 billion in 1950.[7]

Commercials in these early days introduced techniques and formats still in use today. There were presenters, from the easy-going Arthur Godfrey to authoritative experts who talked at the viewer. There were slice-of-life dramas in which a helpful friend or neighbor would introduce the product in time to save a domestic or social crisis. There were testimonials in which "real people" or well-known celebrities testified to their personal experiences with the product. There were demonstrations, like the simple but dramatic commercial in which an electric razor shaved the fuzz off a peach. And viewers were introduced to a gallery of characters who identified, symbolized, and dramatized various products. Many of the most memorable commercials of the fifties utilized animation or stop motion, including some animation classics for Jell-O gelatin using the art styles of Maurice Sendak and Saul Steinberg. Among these pioneers, some of whom are still working, were such familiar characters as the singing pixies for "Ajax, the foaming cleanser," the Gillette razor parrot ("Look sharp! Feel sharp! Be sharp!"), the Kool cigarettes penguin, Speedy Alka-Seltzer, the Hamm's beer bear from "the land of sky-blue waters," Tony the Tiger for Kellogg's Frosted Flakes, Mr. Clean, and Bob and Ray's engaging Bert and Harry Piel for Piel's beer.

©1976 Miles, Inc. Used by permission

_____
7.   Fox, 172.

Viewed today, after thirty years of social change and technical advance, many early commercials seem clumsy and naive in concept and production technique. And because they were a mirror of their times, these commercials appear most outdated because of the life-styles they portrayed. The role model for women that commercials presented was that of mother and housewife, searching only for ways to make her own life easier while she made life better for her husband and children. The personification of the fifties woman was Betty Crocker, who moved from radio to television to offer helpful homemaking hints.

Women were for selling to, not for selling. A revealing trace of male chauvinism comes out in the following do's and don'ts for using women announcers that Harry Wayne McMahan offered in his 1954 book, *The Television Commercial:*

(Illustration: a woman in a large brimmed hat) DO give the woman announcer a "prop," if possible, to open her commercial. Women talk that way, for one thing, and a "prop" increases the opening interest in the commercial and diverts attention from her own personality until she can establish herself and win her audience.

(Illustration: smiling woman with hands on her hips) DON'T let your woman announcer be too aggressive. She will antagonize all men, and many women. She must, however, speak with authority, either from experience or special knowledge of the product. A woman announcer is always a hazardous risk and few can please all viewers.[8]

Women had not yet come a long way, baby. Father knew best. But men, too, were treated more as stereotypes than as real people. "Men were he-men in the commercials of thirty years ago. They were well-groomed, unemotional and happiest away from home enjoying the company of other men. . . . But along with this masculinity came an unnaturalness; during the fifties, men were constantly 'posing' in commercials."[9]

Men adopted a role in commercials that they continue to fill today, that of spokesman. Unlike the "risky" women that Harry McMahan cautioned against, men projected a credibility, be it authoritative or intimate. One of the most enduring early spokesmen was the former TV newscaster John Cameron Swayze, who put Timex watches through a variety of torture tests to prove, "It takes a licking, but keeps on ticking."

Jingles, which got their start on radio, made their way into television. "Winston tastes good, Like a (clap, clap) cigarette should." "Hey, Mable! Black Label!" "Brylcream, a little dab will do ya." And who could ever forget, "Use Ajax (bum-bum) The foaming cleanser (ba-ba-ba-ba-ba-bum-bum) Floats the dirt right down the drain (Ba-ba-ba-ba-ba-ba-bum!)"? While these ditties proved to be just as memorable (irritating?) on television as they had been on radio, their transition to this new medium was not easy. Fairfax Cone observed:

---

8. Harry Wayne McMahan, *The Television Commercial* (New York: *Hastings House,* 1954), 136–37.

9. Jim Hall, *Mighty Minutes: An Illustrated History of Television's Best Commercials* (New York: Harmony Books, 1984), 63.

Television turned out to be something quite different from radio-with-pictures, which was the way it was conceived, and it quickly became apparent that radio techniques and most radio people had no place in the new medium. Television belonged to the genre of the motion picture. Whereas radio depended upon the listener's imagination to picture people and places and most of the action, television left no more to the imagination than the moving pictures. It was a medium both explicit and complete. . . . Still, it took time to make the most of this and in the years immediately following World War II, television was little more than vaudeville brought into the country's living rooms.[10]

What was true of the medium in general was true of the commercials. Many were little more than televised radio. On "Texaco Star Theater," for example, a quartet of service station attendants simply stood in front of a painted curtain and sang their message. The video added little to the sales presentation.

In his book *Confessions of an Advertising Man,* David Ogilvy confessed:

In the early days of television I made the mistake of relying on *words* to do the selling; I had been accustomed to radio, where there are no pictures. I know that in television you must make your *pictures* tell the story; what you show is more important than what you say. Words and pictures must march together, reinforcing each other.[11]

Despite the technical and conceptual crudeness of early commercials, their sheer novelty was enough to command attention and interest (just as the mere presence of sound was enough to attract curious movie audiences to the early talkies). After years of hearing about products on the radio, it was almost a treat to actually see them. Today's production clichés were yesterday's marvels. A novelty like animation or stop-motion photography could assure the advertiser a captivated audience. Marching cigarettes or talking bananas could fascinate viewers. But like many child prodigies, commercials soon stopped being prodigies.

In 1954, Harry McMahan observed:

The television commercial has now reached adolescence and needs to face the facts of life. In the early days, this brash youngster never had to work very hard to earn a living. Even with hit-and-miss techniques, people liked him and people bought. Now comes the awkward age. The youthful charm is gone and familiar childish tricks no longer satisfy.[12]

Already technical advances were opening new doors. In 1954, color television made its public debut. It would be about ten years before prices for color sets came down and color programming increased to a point

---

10. Fairfax M. Cone, *With All Its Faults: A Candid Account of Forty Years in Advertising* (Boston: Little, Brown and Company, 1969), 20.

11. David Ogilvy, *Confessions of an Advertising Man* (New York: Dell, 1963), 160–61.

12. McMahan, xi.

where the broadcasting industry, advertisers, and the public finally converted, but even in television's infancy, color dangled tantalizingly on the horizon.

And from the moment an "easy-opening" Westinghouse refrigerator door jammed on embarrassed Betty Furness, advertisers and broadcasters dreamed of the day when they could avoid the surprises of live telecasts. That dream became a reality in 1957, with the introduction of videotape recording.

During the decade of the fifties, the dollar rate of advertising investment more than doubled, and television's share leaped from four to seventeen percent. In 1950, only about one in ten American homes could boast a television set. Ten years later, set penetration approached ninety percent. There had been a revolution in advertising media. The stage was set for a revolution in advertising creativity. Good-bye, 1950s. Hello, 1960s.

The Creative Revolution

"So there we stood," wrote Larry Dobrow in *When Advertising Tried Harder,* "after a decade of want, a decade of destruction and a decade of limited achievement—ready to greet the future. As people, we were younger than at any time in our history, better educated, growing more mobile and extremely restless, and most important, we were optimistic.

"As a result, it wasn't enough to merely enter the sixties. We exploded into this new era. We elected our youngest president, we adopted Britain's Beatles, we began the worship of youth and the exploration of space."[13]

The social change that swept over the country brought a breath of fresh air to advertising. "The post war baby boom was maturing leaving unsettled campuses and seeking jobs on Madison Avenue. These young people did not leave their disrespectful notions in school; some hoped to make the creative revolution serve the larger Revolution. They were the first generation raised on movies and TV, not books and magazines."[14] New creative agencies appeared, notably Doyle Dane Bernbach. Even established agencies began to place new importance on their creative product. Art directors no longer waited for copywriters to toss them copy like so much raw meat. Copywriters recognized the vital contribution of visuals. Creative teams emerged. Visual and verbal elements were integrated into a single, relevant advertising message.

If any one commercial can be singled out as having ushered in a new wave of television advertising, it is probably Alka-Seltzer's 1964 "stomachs" spot.

> For years, "Speedy Alka-Seltzer," cartoon imp with a tablet for a hat, insulted audiences by pushing the fizz as though he were conducting a *Romper Room* class. Then the Jack Tinker agency took over the account and decided to try for a touch of wit and realism: a film showing

13. Larry Dobrow, *When Advertising Tried Harder* (New York: Friendly Press, 1984), 8–9.

14. Fox, 270.

nothing more than a quick succession of people's midriffs being prodded and pushed, or just merrily jouncing along. The message was: "No matter what shape your stomach's in, when it gets out of shape, take Alka-Seltzer." Along Madison Avenue, the film became an instant classic.[15]

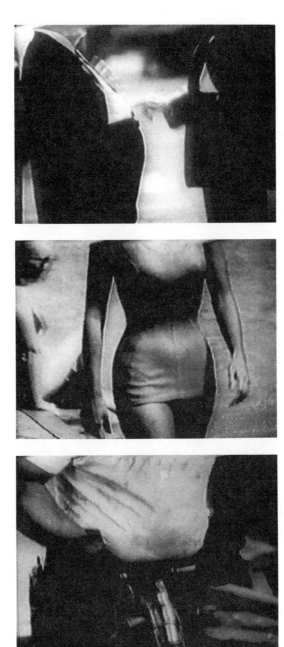

©1967 Miles, Inc. Used by permission

15.   ". . . And Now a Word About Commercials," *Time* (July 12, 1968): 58.

Commercials now had something for everyone: fun and reward for the viewers, bright ideas and polished production values for the creative people, and (hopefully) positive sales results for the advertiser. Commercials demonstrated that advertising did not have to bore or insult to communicate. They could be witty and direct, clean and simple.

Two automobile commercials produced in 1963 illustrate the shift in creative focus from technique to concept. The first, for Chevrolet, showed a 1964 convertible on top of a fifteen-hundred-foot pinnacle in the Utah desert. A nervous model waved cheerily to the camera as it circled overhead in a helicopter. This was the latest in a series of Chevy spectaculars (in 1961, a convertible drove on top of the water along a Venice canal) and typical of car advertising of the period.

The second, a Volkswagen commercial that aired that same year, showed a Beetle chugging through a snowstorm at the crack of dawn while the announcer asked, "Have you ever wondered how the man who drives a snowplow drives *to* the snowplow?" The Volkswagen stops, the driver gets out and drives off in the snowplow to clear the same road the Beetle drove in on. The announcer continues: "This one drives a Volkswagen. So you can stop wondering."

Copyrighted by, and is reproduced with the permission of, Volkswagen United States, Inc.

The Chevy commercial was highly memorable and interesting to watch. But it said little about the car beyond, "Hey, look at me this time!" The Volkswagen commercial drew you into an intriguing story and left you with a single, clear impression of how the car performed in adverse winter conditions. One dazzled with special effects, the other with its idea.

The sixties will be remembered most fondly in advertising circles for such creative, revolutionary campaigns as Volkswagen, Cracker Jacks,

Alka-Seltzer, and Benson & Hedges 100's which brought commercials to a level of excellence where they often seemed better than the programs they interrupted. But the sixties also had its share of silliness and exaggeration.

> Screwball fantasy situation comedies were in vogue on television in the mid-1960s. There was the best friend who was a talking horse, the wife who was a witch, the uncle who was a Martian, and the mother who was a car. Considering the times, it was perhaps not unusual that one of the most popular identifiable characters was the Ajax White Knight.[16]

Besides this stronger-than-dirt Lancelot who zapped citizens and turned their dirty clothes a dazzling white, there were swirling white tornadoes and people being dropped into cars as they were told, "Hertz puts you in the driver's seat." Some more likeable and more enduring characters were also born in the sixties: Charlie the Tuna for Star-Kist, Poppin' Fresh the Pillsbury Doughboy, Morris the cat for 9-Lives, the "I-hate-Quantas" koala, and the Dreyfus lion. Along with these fantasy characters, some familiar real characters made their debut: Josephine the plumber for Comet cleanser, Mrs. Olson for Folgers coffee, Mr. Whipple for Charmin bathroom tissue, and the lonely Maytag Repairman. And in 1965, a clown appeared on television in the Washington, D.C., area who would go on to become one of the best-known advertising characters of all time, Ronald McDonald.

One of the most widely discussed commercials of the sixties was not for a product, but for a candidate. It showed a little girl picking petals off a daisy. Her counting became a somber countdown until her image dissolved into an atomic explosion and Lyndon Johnson's voice began, "These are the stakes. . . ." The commercial was pulled from the air, but Barry Goldwater's image as a hawk had been seeded, and television commercials had proved they could stir up a political controversy.

Another controversy would have an even bigger impact on broadcast advertising. The Surgeon General's report in 1964 linked smoking to cancer and other health hazards. The FCC extended the fairness doctrine to require stations which ran cigarette advertising to devote reasonable time to antismoking spots. Finally, a law banned all cigarette advertising from both radio and television as of January 2, 1971.

As America headed into the seventies, the face of television was changing. Minorities were now common in TV dramas, newscasts, comedies—and commercials. Programs like "All in the Family" led to a new permissiveness in language and theme. Rowan and Martin's "Laugh-In" popularized a new kaleidoscopic comedy style well suited to commercials' need for shorthand communication.

The 1960s had been the time to be young and to be in advertising. Business was booming and creativity was king. Larry Dobrow describes the period as the Golden Age of Advertising.

> In the sixties, everything conspired favorably to increase the value of advertising to advertisers, the volume of advertising for agencies, and

---

16.   Hall, 26.

the vitality of advertising as a commercial art form. The creative revolution was aided significantly by a media revolution that was equally sweeping. Television was now the number one mass medium and the number one advertising medium.

The new technologies and the new creativity converged at a time and in a way that enabled art directors, copywriters, photographers and advertisers to conceive and successfully execute whatever their minds could imagine and their pocketbooks manage.[17]

But the party couldn't last forever. "As the decade ended, William Bernbach and Rosser Reeves (advocate of 1950s-style hard sell) found themselves in unlikely agreement. 'I worry about everyone trying to be different for the sake of being different,' said Bernbach. 'Young people coming in and mistaking the facade for the real thing.' 'During the 1970s, I predict that the advertising narcissists will wake up,' said Reeves. 'Big business will return to immutable advertising law that the agency must make the *product* interesting, and not just the advertisement itself.' "[18]

The Sobering Seventies

The swing of the pendulum was not long in coming. Early in the 1970s, the hottest agency of the 1960s, Doyle Dane Bernbach, lost its first major account. Ironically, it was Alka-Seltzer, and the loss followed two classic commercials—"Groom's First Meal," in which hubby's memories of his dinner and his young bride's ideas for future meals send him back into the bathroom for more Alka-Seltzer, and "Mama Mia, That's a Spicy Meat-a-Ball!" in which a commercial actor is undone by too many retakes of an eating scene. The account moved to Wells, Rich, Greene. "We will be more product oriented," Mary Wells announced, "and try to explain more clearly what Alka-Seltzer does." Her comment unwittingly set the tone for the decade.

The 1970s had begun ominously with the 1971 ban of cigarette advertising from television. Watergate forced the resignation of President Nixon and an Arab oil embargo forced American drivers into long lines at gasoline pumps. The economy sputtered. Television time and production costs continued to climb. Cost control collided with creativity. Advertisers looked increasingly to copy testing to assure them that their dollars were being well spent. An activist consumerism movement pressured government regulatory agencies to increase their scrutiny of advertising claims and demonstrations. The FTC ordered some companies to run corrective advertising. Action for Children's Television (ACT) urged limitations and improvements in commercials aimed at young people. And clutter, the number of commercials within allotted nonprogram time, increased as more and more advertisers moved to shorter, more efficient thirty-second lengths.

---

17. Dobrow, 201.
18. Fox, 271.

The 1970s most resembled the 1950s in copy style and management practices. Hard sell became appropriate for the tighter economic climate at the start of the decade. Creative awards no longer guaranteed jobs and promotions. Agencies instead sought marketing MBAs, people who understood the nuts and bolts of pricing, distribution, and packaging. Instead of rubbing their muses, artists and copywriters were handed the selling idea, with suggestions on how to present it.[19]

There were bright moments with marketing success stories and creative commercials. McDonald's established hamburgers and fries as a way of life by reminding Americans that "You deserve a break today." Soft drinks courted the youth market with lively music and quick-cut commercials, but two of the more memorable spots were atypical of the genre. The first featured a group of young people from many nations gathered on a hilltop in Italy to sing, "We'd like to buy the world a Coke." The other showed a boy offering his Coke to "Mean" Joe Green, who turned out to be not so mean after all when he tossed his football jersey to the boy in return.

The Women's Liberation movement of the late 1960s and early 1970s began to affect the way in which women were portrayed in commercials. Virginia Slims spoofed the change with commercials that showed Victorian-era women sneaking a smoke, replaced by modern women in the latest fashions and smoking "their own cigarette." A jingle proclaimed the advance with, "You've come a long way, baby. . . ." (Short-lived on TV, the campaign still thrives in print.)

Enjoli perfume celebrated women in her triple role of wife, mother, and working woman. Peggy Lee sang, "I can bring home the bacon, Fry it up in a pan, And never let you forget you're a man." Revlon's Charlie capsulized the spirit of the seventies woman as, "Kinda young, kinda now—Kinda free, kinda wow."

As women moved out of their housewife stereotypes, men began to shed the tough-guy image.

TV commercials, once again acting as social barometers, recorded the winds of change that were freeing men to be more open and tolerant. The traditional father figure could even risk looking foolish, a liberty no commercial maker would have dared to take in the fifties.[20]

In one commercial, inspired by a similar scene in the movie *Kramer vs. Kramer,* a young father messes up his kitchen trying to make French toast for his son because mommy is not around.

But the good ol' traditional sexist ways continued, too. There were plenty of hard-working, blue-collar, macho workers rewarding themselves with a Budweiser ("This Bud's for you") or a Miller beer ("Welcome to Miller time"). And sex continued in the steamy pace set in 1966 by Swedish blonde Gunilla Knutsen, the Noxema shave cream girl who urged men to "Take it off, Take it all off." Joey Heatherton sang and gyrated for Serta mattresses; Suzanne Somers teased Ace Hardware's "helpful hardware

---

19. Fox, 327–28.
20. Hall, 75.

man"; and Susan Anton showed up in a men's locker room wearing a slinky silk dress and singing about Muriel cigars.

Advertising, and television specifically, continued to prosper. Total expenditures rose from $19.6 billion in 1970 to $54.6 billion in 1980. Television spending climbed from $3.6 billion to $11.4 billion. Products still sold. Commercials still worked. But the exceptions proved the rule, and the rule was that, compared to the glory days of the creative revolution, commercials had become less charming and more combative. There were more naming of names, more side-by-side comparisons. 7-Up took on Pepsi and Coke, positioning itself as the Uncola. Avis revived "We try harder" to go after Hertz. Scope attacked Listerine for leaving users with "medicine breath." Federal Express overtook Emery with a comparative campaign (before moving to the humorous commercials it would later be famous for). Many commercials became more rational, sensing perhaps that consumers needed more justification to pay the higher prices brought on by the inflation of the period. "Value" became a frequent strategy as the specter of generics haunted the national brands. Although research cannot be all to blame, Stephen Fox assigns it its share as he comments on the state of advertising at the close of the 1970s:

> TV advertising relied on pretesting methods—especially the telephone inquiries of the Burke service—that favored hard, rational content and strong reasons-why. A commercial with a low Burke score would not make it to national exposure. As in the 1950s, advertising lost creative verve when it regarded itself as rational, quantifiable science. Ads came to resemble each other: vignettes and slices-of-life showing people enjoying the product; . . . take-off shots for airlines; . . . naked women in bath-oil spots; macho sportsmen in beer ads; pet-food commercials with a pet and a bowl of the product.[21]

"1984" and Beyond

The television audience of Super Bowl XVIII witnessed one of the most talked-about commercials of recent years: gray-faced, shaven-headed citizens of a futuristic city trudge through a glass overhead tubeway and shuffle into seats in a vast theater. On a giant screen a grim-faced "Big Brother" addresses them: "Today we celebrate the first anniversary of the information purification directives. . . ." In cutaways, a young woman athlete in red shorts carrying a sledge hammer sprints down the tubeway, pursued by helmeted security guards. She arrives in the theater and hurls her hammer at the screen, which explodes to the astonishment of the audience. An announcer reads the title that is left on the screen: "On January 24th, Apple Computer will introduce Macintosh. And you'll see why 1984 won't be like '1984.'"

The sixty-second commercial cost about $900,000 to air one time and between an estimated $400,000 and $1 million to produce. It stirred up opposing opinions in the advertising trade press. ("The spot makes a great statement with a simple objective," began one advertising executive. "I

---

21. Fox, 327–28.

Courtesy of Apple Computer, Inc.

think it was pretty much a waste of money," said another.[22]) And it was the Grand Prix winner in the 1984 Cannes Festival.

"1984" is far from a typical commercial of the 1980s. But it is indicative of the current high level of the state of the art of film production. It shows that breakthrough is still possible for the advertiser willing to buy top talent and spend top dollar (not that this is the only way to break through). It shows that in a world of short look-alike executions, a commercial that takes the time to create a mood and tell a story can, if nothing else, stand out.

It is difficult to say if someone writing about TV commercials from the perspective of the 1990s will point to "1984" or any other commercial of the 1980s as proof of another creative revolution. But it is safe to say that commercials were starting to look different.

One of the different looks actually began in the mid-seventies with some commercials for Federal Express. Gone were the pretty, plastic people filmed with flattering light and conformable camera angles. Instead we saw strange (ordinary, real) people, caricatures of types. The action was staged, contrived. And the commercials were very funny. They were the creations of Chicago director Joe Sedelmaier. Besides creating Federal Express spots (which included a parody of corporate buck-passing, as the

22. *Advertising Age* (January 30, 1984).

responsibility for getting the package there on time was pushed down the ranks; a hapless worker singled out at the annual meeting for failing to get a package delivered on time; and the incredible fast talker), Sedelmaier fired the loudest shot in the "burger wars" with his "Where's the Beef?" commercial for Wendy's. Many advertisers embraced this look and style of humor, but it was not the only direction commercials were taking. Another started on the West Coast for advertisers like Gallo Wine and Henry Weinhard beer. No two characters are further from the caricatures of Joe Sedelmaier than Ed Jaymes and Frank Bartles, the creations of Hal Riney for Bartles & Jaymes Premium Wine Coolers. Contrasting Riney's folksy style with the creative revolution of the 1960s, Art Kleiner wrote in *The New York Times Magazine:*

> At that time, small, independent advertising agencies suddenly rose to prominence in New York, fueled by Jews and Italians from the streets of Brooklyn and New Jersey whose sales pitches bounced with the patter of stand-up comedy. Such renowned campaigns as Volkswagen's "Think Small" and Alka-Seltzer's "I Can't Believe I Ate the Whole Thing" date from that period.

> This time, the new creative people are aggressively middle American. Following a hallowed advertising tradition, many of them left their small towns to escape the limitations of rural life, but brought along a common touch—a facility for selling to the folks back home.[23]

Bartles & Jaymes walked off with a gold medal in the 1986 Cannes Festival. More importantly, perhaps, "Dick Maugg, who plays Ed Jaymes in the wine-cooler ads, was even told by a clerk at his local welding shop: 'I've noticed that advertising is becoming less strident, more gentle and lots nicer since you started making those commercials.'"[24]

The same year Hal Riney won his gold at Cannes, the Grand Prix winner was a gritty, realist campaign for John Hancock life insurance built around the theme, "Real Life. Real Answers." Shot by hot director Joe Pytka, it represented a move toward realism and natural dialogue.

This cinema verité look and eavesdropping dialogue showed up in commercials for Apple Computer, Wang, and AT&T. Writing in *Advertising Age,* Bob Garfield cautioned: "This jarring cinematic style, like the washed-out film that is its hallmark, rapidly is approaching over-exposure. Think of it as a visual 'Where's the Beef?' racing from phenomenal to irritating, from novelty to cliche."[25]

Off in another direction from the humor of Sedelmaier, the folksiness of Riney, and the realism of Pytka are the visual tours-de-force spawned by the rock music videos of MTV and abetted by state-of-art computer graphics and electronic paintbox video tricks. These commercials almost assault the eye with stylish images jarringly edited to a driving music track. Chevrolet's "Heartbeat of America" is a tamed-down heir to this tradition. This school of commercials is further evidence of the high degree of film literacy

---

23.   Art Kleiner, "Master of the Sentimental Sell," *The New York Times Magazine* (December 14, 1986): 54.

24.   Kleiner, 56.

25.   *Advertising Age* (April 27, 1987): 52.

possessed by today's audiences. One can only imagine what it will take to visually surprise viewers who will have grown up watching "Pee Wee's Playhouse."

The creative advertising person of the 1980s and beyond has literally the whole world to draw upon and to compete with. Agency megamergers, multinational clients, and international film festivals have all tended to turn the advertising business into a global community. What began as a U.S. exclusive—the television commercial—is being practiced with such style and creativity in Europe, Asia, and Latin America that it often shames (and inspires) domestic work. Outstanding commercials in Great Britain or Japan or Brazil are likely to affect advertising styles in the United States.

The experience of watching television is changing, too. The humble TV set families ate their TV dinners in front of is growing into huge home entertainment centers. Besides home video recorders (VCRs), future sets will have ". . . attachments to plug us into such services as a home computer, two-way cable, and videotext. The set itself will have a much different look. Many of us will own flat, wall-size screens upon which the picture, now freed from the tube, will be projected. And the landscape of America, criss-crossed by TV antennas in the 1950s, will be dotted by dish-shaped receivers that will allow us to pick up programs and services from satellites cruising in space."[26]

Cable television, in which programs are transmitted through wires instead of through the air, permits much greater channel capacity. Advertising on cable, according to one cable entrepreneur, ". . . is going to be the great equalizer. Even mom-and-pop retailers will be able to afford time at the local level, adjacent to a special-interest program that relates to their product. And long-form commercials might just be a copywriter's dream. Just think of all the things that can't be adequately sold in thirty or sixty seconds."[27]

There will likely come a day when we will not only be sold to by TV, but will actually be able to buy. *Advertising Age* reported on ". . . J.C. Penney Co.'s highly significant $40 million bid to make interactive TV a viable marketing tool. No $600 home terminal to buy. With just a Touch-Tone phone, consumers control the shopping "show" and peruse the offerings from Penney and other marketers."[28]

The future of television advertising promises to be as interesting as its past.

What Is Past Is Prologue:
Some Conclusions

We have followed TV commercials from innocence to maturity. Before we plunge more deeply into the process of creating commercials, it is worth-

---

26. Peggy Charren and Martin W. Sander, *Changing Channels: Living (Sensibly) With Television* (Reading, Mass.: Addison Wesley, 1983), 120.

27. Charren and Sander, 142.

28. *Advertising Age* (March 2, 1987): 16.

while to pause and consider what lessons might be learned from their brief history:

- A television commercial is more than radio with pictures. When television was still a novelty, perhaps audiences would sit still and watch somebody talk at them. Today, the visual must do more. Much more.

- Technique alone is not enough. The fascination that early commercials held for their audiences has worn off. A commercial has to earn its attention. There has to be an idea.

- The prospect is a moving target. What people want and expect from products has changed over the years and will continue to change. The housewife of the 1950s is not the career woman of the 1980s. Successful commercials will continue to be those that break with stereotypes (or are the first to spot new ones).

- Commercials need not insult the viewer's intelligence. Volkswagen and Alka-Seltzer demonstrated in the 1960s that humor and humanity can play an important role. Bartles & Jaymes proved it again in the 1980s. The viewer deserves some reward. And the advertiser deserves relevant entertainment focused on a single, simple selling idea.

- Many current commercials are older than you would think. There are many enduring campaigns whose success and longevity are rooted in their ability to capture something very basic and compelling about their product and to stay with it consistently, evolving when necessary to stay fresh and relevant.

- Chances are your idea will have to work in thirty seconds or less. Sixties begat thirties which threaten to beget fifteens. With the exception of cable, there does not seem to be a trend to longer and longer commercials. It will be increasingly difficult to build mood, personality, and character.

- Thanks to current technology there is virtually limitless opportunity for innovation. From crude beginnings, film and video production have reached such a high level that it is now possible to produce just about anything you can dream up, as long as time and money are not factors.

- Time and money are factors. Production costs show no real sign of decreasing. And advertisers' timetables and demands for cost efficiency show no sign of relaxing. Weak ideas will not be able to hide under the glitz of production value.

- Audiences have grown increasingly sophisticated. High quality production is now the rule, not the exception. It is getting harder and harder to dazzle. Audiences are harder to attract and hold. Cable and VCRs compete for viewership. More and more commercials compete in the same time periods. Viewers come armed not only with hardened perceptual defenses, but also with remote control "zappers" to switch away from boring commercials.

- Just as advertisers look to stay current with changing consumers, so do advertising creatives look to stay current with "the scene." To spot the next commercial "look," look to what's happening in the movies, on television, in music, and in the world around you.

- A good commercial is one that works. The marketplace is not a film festival. The best commercials build business for the advertiser. This will be as true in 1998 as it was in 1948.

Which brings up some interesting questions: How do commercials work? And what makes a good one?

Chapter 2

What Makes a Good Commercial

Everybody Knows What a Good Commercial Is

The viewers at home know what a good commercial is. A good commercial is entertaining and fun to watch. They may not even remember what product it was advertising. They don't know anything about advertising, but they know what they like.

The copywriters and art directors who create commercials for a living know what a good commercial is. A good commercial is a clever idea, skillfully written and artfully produced to be rich in subtle imagery. The commercial won an award at a film festival, so it must be good.

The brand manager knows what a good commercial is. A good commercial communicates the strategic sales points and is rich in product information. The commercial received a high recall score, so it must be good.

Except for the consumers, who don't care about such things, everyone would have to agree that positive business results are the ultimate measure of any commercial's success. The disagreements occur over how important these other things—entertainment and likeability, imagery and production value, information and copy point playback—are to the bottom line—sales.

A direct link between a commercial and sales is difficult to prove. Advertising may indirectly affect sales by positively influencing consumer attitudes toward the product. But other things can affect attitudes besides the commercial. There are other advertising factors besides copy content:

media weight, scheduling, vehicles, timing. There are other marketing factors, such as distribution, price, packaging, promotion, point of sale. There is the effect of competitive advertising, editorial comment, word-of-mouth, and actual experience with the product. There is the time lag between exposure to the commercial and purchase of the product, during which people may forget either the good or the bad points of the commercial.

Recognizing the difficulty of pointing to sales as proof of a commercial's effectiveness, those who would seek such proof have had to look elsewhere. Most often they have looked to copy testing. An advertiser who is about to spend thousands of dollars to produce a commercial and thousands more to air it is not easily soothed by assurances of creative judgment. ("This *feels* right.") He wants some tangible evidence that a commercial is good. He wants a number—a high number. But the person searching for a foolproof, ironclad commercial test might be compared to Diogenes in search of an honest man. Everyone wishes him luck, but few hold much hope he will succeed.

Before you can measure how well a commercial works, you must first reach agreement on how it is supposed to work. And what has continually frustrated those trying to reach such agreement has been that lots of different kinds of commercials have worked in different situations and in different ways. Sometimes a commercial that scores high on some accepted measure of effectiveness will fail in the marketplace. Sometimes a commercial that barely limps through copy testing will break the bank when it airs. Sometimes an orderly presentaton of product features has done the trick. Sometimes it has been all mood and music. It has been very difficult to come up with that one formula for success. Not that people have not tried.

Hard Sell vs. Soft Sell:
The Line Is Drawn

One of advertising's most outspoken theoreticians was Rosser Reeves of Ted Bates & Company. His book *Reality in Advertising,* published in 1961, became the basic text for the school of hard sell, an approach to advertising usually equated with a high degree of irritation (by its detractors), but equally high persuasion (by its supporters). Historian Stephen Fox summed up the Reeves philosophy:

> He pictured the consumer as beset not by irrational drives but by a plethora of ad messages, engulfing him on every side, glazing his eyes and overloading his memory. To cut through this deluge, an effective ad had to offer a Unique Selling Proposition (USP), strong enough to pull in new customers, that a competitor did not or could not make. The besieged consumer could only retain one strong claim or concept from a given ad; any elaboration simply cluttered the ad to no effect.[1]

---

1.   Stephen Fox, *The Mirror Makers* (New York: William Morrow and Company, 1984), 187–88.

Find the product's USP and drive it home. This will command attention and communicate a persuasive point of difference. If, in the process of being persuasive and memorable, the commercial comes out a litle heavy-handed, it is a price well worth paying. As Rosser Reeves said:

> Now, we're not in favor of commercials that are in bad taste, or terribly ugly commercials. But sometimes a commercial that conveys the idea is not what other practitioners of Madison Ave. are looking for. There's nothing particularly beautiful in a TV screen with two fists stuck in the face of the television viewer and you say, "Which hand has the M&M chococolate candy in it?"[2]

Reeves pointed with pride to case histories in which this product-based, copy-driven, research-supported, no-nonsense, rational approach helped clients increase their penetration and sales. But not everyone believed that a unique selling proposition was, to paraphrase Reeves, the only road to Rome.

> One of the difficult problems that advertising is confronted with is the increasing standardization of products and services. Any actual differences in quality, price, packaging, or service have disappeared almost to the vanishing point.[3]

This observation which so well describes the challenge advertising faces today was made in 1957 by Pierre Martineau in his book *Motivation in Advertising*. Martineau became the voice of the soft sell side of advertising. He argued that visual imagery and symbols were often a stronger selling force than words alone, and that advertising must do more than simply present people with claims of superiority.

> Fundamentally, advertising uses the laws of attention and association. It hopes to set off the product as something pretty wonderful by draping around it as many activating and pleasant associations as possible, by attaching to it all sorts of meanings with powerful motivation value in addition to its bare functional-use meanings.[4]

The secret to successful advertising for Martineau lay in uncovering the consumer's hidden motivations and then creating a powerful brand image. He pointed to the case of Marlboro cigarettes, which had changed its image as a feminine high-style cigarette by ads which showed only rugged men with tattooed hands. Marlboro was not yet the largest selling cigarette brand in the world, so Rosser Reeves remained skeptical:

> What, then, is the secret of these campaigns? The answer, we are told, is that brand-image campaigns communicate with the reader in another way. They establish contact with the subconscious of the consumer below word level. They do this with visual symbols instead of

---

2. "Rosser Reeves Talks About How He Writes Copy," *Advertising Age* (April 19, 1965): 100.

3. Pierre Martineau, *Motivation in Advertising* (New York: McGraw-Hill Book Company, 1957), 4.

4. Martineau, 13–14.

words, Mr. Martineau says, because the visual symbols are far more significant. They communicate faster. They are more direct. There is no work, no mental effort. Their sole purpose is to create images and moods.[5]

Then he drew the line which divides the two camps still today: "To put it bluntly, the U.S.P. is the philosophy of a claim, and the brand image is the philosophy of a feeling."[6]

Although each side would begrudgingly concede a contribution by the other, somehow advertising had come to fall under one of two categories: either it was rational and claim-driven or it was emotional and image-driven. In the first case what mattered was how well the consumer *remembered* the advertising. In the second case what mattered was how much the consumer *liked* the advertising.

Today the terms *hard sell* and *soft sell* have dropped from fashion. No one wants to be accused of advocating advertising that sells softly if that means not seriously or aggressively. But the debate continues over which style of advertising works better and which elements in the commercial are those which contribute most to its ultimate success. Is it information or imagery? Is it logic or emotion? Should the message be explicit or can it be implicit? Are consumers thinking or feeling beings?

The modern day descendents of the USP hard-sell school advocate commercials that are logical, linear, explicit expositions of real product benefits. In doing so they implicitly perceive the consumer as a highly rational decision maker who goes to considerable effort to pay attention to, actively process, and evaluate information in advertising to make a purchase decision. And they assume that the success of such advertising can be reasonably predicted by how well viewers can remember the brand name and play back the message. Not surprisingly, these advocates are often the advertisers, who want only to sell product and want proof that a commercial is working.

Today's soft-sell advocates are no less interested in selling, but maintain that advertising operates most powerfully on a gut level. They favor commercials that touch emotions and feelings through visual, nonverbal imagery. This point of view assumes that consumers are not vitally interested in advertised products and that the activities of daily life do not permit lengthy cognitive deliberations over which brand of toothpaste to buy. Furthermore, the advocates of more feeling-oriented advertising challenge the ability of conventional copy testing to effectively measure the strength of such subconscious communication. Not surprisingly, it tends to be the agency people, especially creatives, who argue for mood and style and bristle at the use of recall scores as a measure of effectiveness.

There are enough case histories to argue for either side. And there is enough evidence to suggest that a more reasonable position would be to accept that either style may be appropriate under certain circumstances and that both rational and emotional elements are involved in consumer behavior. Advertising should appeal to both the head and the heart, or perhaps more precisely, to both sides of the head.

---

5. Rosser Reeves, *Reality in Advertising* (New York: Alfred A. Knopf, 1961), 79.

6. Reeves, 79.

Left Brain, Right Brain

Arguments over how advertising works and debates between thinking and feeling ads are strikingly analogous to recent theories of how people think and create. These suggest that different sides of the brain—the left and the right—control different styles or modes of thought.

The two major modes of human brain-hemisphere function . . . were first described by psychobiologist Roger W. Sperry in his pioneering work during the late 1950s and early 1960s. Sperry's research, which was honored by a Nobel Prize for Medicine in 1981, has shown that the right and left hemispheres of the human brain use contrasting methods of information processing. Both thinking modes are involved in high-level cognitive functioning, but each brain half specializes in its own style of thinking and each has its own special capabilities. The two modes are able to work in a cooperative, complementary way while at the same time retaining their individual styles of thinking.[7]

The left hemisphere of the brain is the side that specializes in linear, logical, language-based thinking. "Its preference is for clear, sequential, logical thought, uncomplicated by paradox or ambiguity. . . . The right half of the brain (for most individuals) functions in a nonverbal manner, specializing in visual, spatial, perceptual information. Its style of processing is nonlinear and nonsequential, relying instead on simultaneous processing of incoming information—looking at the whole thing, all at once."[8] These two styles of thinking operate simultaneously. There is no conscious awareness of separate and different functions. Dr. Betty Edwards describes the two modes of information processing:

. . . As each of our hemispheres gathers in the same sensory information, each half of our brains may handle the information in different ways: the task may be divided between the hemispheres, each handling the part suited to its style. Or one hemisphere, often the dominant left, will "take over" and inhibit the other half. The left hemisphere analyzes, abstracts, counts, marks time, plans step-by-step procedures, verbalizes, makes rational statements based on logic. . . .

On the other hand, we have a second way of knowing: the right-hemisphere mode. We "see" things in this mode that may be imaginary—existing only in the mind's eye—or recall things that may be real. . . . We see how things exist in space and how the parts go together to make the whole.[9]

The left hemisphere sounds tailor-made for the hard-sell style of advertising. The advocates of imagery and nonlinear communication seem to be appealing to the right hemisphere. Television commercials have a little

7. Betty Edwards, *Drawing on the Artist Within* (New York: Simon and Schuster, 1986), 10, 11.

8. Edwards, 12.

9. Betty Edwards, *Drawing on the Right Side of the Brain* (Los Angeles: J.P. Tarcher, 1979), 35.

something for each side of the viewer's brain. They have information (copy points) and they have images (settings, props, casting, and music). Some commercials are reasoned, logical, expository, and full of information about real *product benefits*. They are structured like a careful sales talk, with a beginning, middle, and end. On the other hand, many commercials are emotional, sensual, visual, musical, nonstructured, kaleidoscopic—conveying the essence of the *product experience*. The former include most stand-up presenter and slice-of-life commercials; the latter include most vignette life-style commercials for soft drinks, blue jeans, and perfumes. These different styles of commercials not only seem to appeal to different sides of the brain, they make different assumptions about how advertising works.

Left Brain Advertising: The Dominance of Cognition

Traditional models of consumer behavior reflect a left-brain orientation. They assume that cognition (thinking) is the dominant force and affect (feeling) is merely the result. They assume that consumers consciously and rationally weigh brand alternatives. Advertising, by emphasizing specific product attributes, can favorably affect consumers' attitudes toward the brand, which in turn will influence their purchase behavior. It is as if in living rooms all across the country millions of viewers sit glued to their television sets with their attention riveted on each commercial. They listen carefully, evaluate the message, and decide whether or not to rush to the nearest store to buy the advertised product.

The model for such a theory would look like this:

In other words, before consumers buy the product they must hold favorable attitudes toward it, and attitudes can be affected only if the advertising is carefully attended to and the message is comprehended and evaluated. If you accept these assumptions, the challenge for your commercial is clear:

- It must attract attention and make a memorable impression.

- It must communicate its intended meaning.

- It must stir attitudes toward the product.

But even if this were how all advertising must work, there are some problems.

The Problem of Attention

The problem of attention is really two problems: 1) getting viewers to attend to your commercial, and 2) proving that viewers attended to your commercial. Rosser Reeves does not think the first problem is much of a problem. "Let me tell you one of the essential things about TV. The audience is going to look at your commercial whether it's interesting or not. When you put a commercial on the air one night and you have 20 million people looking at the screen, how the hell can they *help* seeing what you put on?"[10]

So if your audience is in place in front of the set when your commercial comes on, and if none of them get up and leave the room before it is over, the first problem of attention is solved. Viewers have been successfully exposed to the commercial. It is the second problem—proving attention—that is the real problem. Proof of attention usually means proof of remembering what the commercial was about, specifically, the brand name and sales message. For this to occur, the viewer must first recognize what the commercial is about.

Psychologists refer to the way the brain classifies messages according to their tentative meaning as indexing. If a message about one thing (floor cleaner) gets classified as a message about another thing (kitchen decor), it is said to have been misindexed. Misindexing is often discovered when advertisers try to measure attention to a specific message.

One common type of misindexing occurs when the commercial is so engaging or entertaining in itself that the specifics of the message are forgotten. A common example of this is when someone loves the commercial but forgets what the advertised product was. (Right brain advocates who contend that communication of a different kind may in fact be taking place would have some comforting words for advertisers who create likeable advertising whose literal message is not recalled.)

Sometimes commercials trying to attract attention will use borrowed interest devices that either dominate the message or lead the audience off in unintended directions. It was a wise advertising man who once said, "The only time I would ever show a man standing on his head in an ad would be if I were selling pants that had zippers in the pockets."

Another way to risk misindexing (one of equal concern to both left brain and right brain styles) is to look too much like a well-known competitor. There are two dangers to watch for: first, the danger of consciously copying the style of another advertiser, and second, the danger of failing to clearly separate your brand from other brands that may be more firmly established in the consumer's mind. As more and more award-winning,

---

10.   Thomas Whiteside, "The Man from Iron City," *The New Yorker* (September 27, 1969): 60.

talked-about advertising is created, more and more advertising that imitates the style of the award-winning, talked-about advertising is created. And the imitators suddenly find that they have failed to make a unique point or impression about their brand. Imitation of an innovator's style of advertising risks being misindexed as just another message about the innovator's brand. Put an eye patch on the Arrow shirt model and you score an impression for Hathaway. Leaders in various product fields often are those who have been around for years spending millions each year to build their reputations and identities. New entries running up against the likes of a Kellogg's Corn Flakes, Kodak film, Scotch tape, Campbell's soup, or McDonald's have their work cut out for them.

The Problem of Message Distortion

Psychologists tell us that what attracts attention and gets perceived most readily are those things that are familiar to the person being communicated to. "People tend to select out for attention those advertisements which are quickly recognizable as being in accord with interests or beliefs which they already hold; and they are much less likely to pay attention to other advertisements."[11]

This makes the job of reminder advertising relatively easy. In such cases consumers are familiar with the product (they are probably users of the product) and are favorably predisposed toward it. The commercial need only remind them of their favorable attitudes. But most advertising is intended to be persuasive, and persuasion often asks for a change in attitude. People have built-in ways of resisting such messages.

> People see meanings which they *expect* to see. If the message meaning does not "fall into place" with old beliefs, an uncomfortable "imbalance" is created, and feelings of curiosity or doubt are likely to ensue. Such imbalance—often referred to as *cognitive dissonance*—can be resolved in one of two ways: *by changing old beliefs to conform to the message; or through distortion of the meaning of the message so that the message more easily fits in with old beliefs.*[12]

Naturally, the advertiser hopes the result of his persuasive message will be a change in attitude or belief, a swing in favor of the advertised brand. But people resist such change. As a result, the conflicting message is frequently distorted to make it more compatible with already-held beliefs. Two varieties of this distortion are called leveling and sharpening.

Leveling refers to the tendency to overlook that part of a message that does not mesh with old attitudes and beliefs. This can occur when the majority of the information presented is in general accord with what the viewer expects, but when one or more elements are unexpected or in conflict. For example, a commercial may describe a detergent that cleans just as well as other detergents (expected) but works in cold water (unexpected). If the viewer has been brought up to believe that all detergents

---

11.   John C. Maloney, "Is Advertising Believability Really Important?" *Journal of Marketing* (October, 1963): 2.

12.   Maloney, 4.

need hot water to be effective, such a message can create imbalance or dissonance. The viewer must now either:

- reject the message and retain old beliefs;

- accept the message and change beliefs;

- avoid the decision by somehow distorting (misunderstanding) the message to make it compatible.

To accomplish the last, the viewer may level, or overlook, that portion of the message relating to cold water performance and simply accept the commercial's message as a claim that the detergent cleans just as well as other detergents (a less than compelling claim).

To avoid the risk of leveling, the advertiser must make certain that any important copy points that might conflict with viewers' beliefs or expectations are made prominent enough so that overlooking them becomes difficult. This is what pushes advertisers to such aesthetically annoying practices as repetition and supers (titles superimposed over a screen, such as "Works in Cold Water").

Sharpening refers to the viewers' tendency to read into the message additional or unintended meanings in order to make the message conform to their beliefs. If the claim is ambiguous, viewers will interpret it to suit themselves.

Sharpening may work to the advantage of an established leader with a strong, positive brand image. The mere mention of Coca-Cola or Campbell's soup is sufficient to cause viewers to read in all of their pleasant associations with the product. Such is the stuff of reminder advertising.

Sharpening often shows up when an advertiser suddenly departs from a familiar, long-running advertising theme or format. Respondents continued to recall the animated Hamm's bears and the Campbell Kids long after they had disappeared from their brands' TV advertising.

What Makes a Good Left-Brain Commercial

The problem of attention (the problem of proving that viewers remembered the exact message you wanted them to remember) leads the supporters of left-brain advertising (linear, logical, rational, verbal advertising) to design commercials in a way that will make it easier for viewers to comprehend and recall their messages. We have seen that people have built-in perceptual defenses and resistance to persuasive messages that such advertising must confront and overcome. When you have a rational, logical, linear sales message to communciate, you will want a carefully structured left-brain commercial. Such a commercial should have the following characteristics:

Simplicity.   The effective commercial uses a single-minded dramatization of a simple, understandable selling idea. An attempt to cram supplementary sales points into a commercial without sufficient time to develop them only complicates the commercial. At best these other ideas become throwaways; at worst they can actually detract from the communication of the central idea.

Explicit execution of the message.   A commercial should not be afraid to be obvious and spell out its message. It is easy to confuse creativity with the art of being sly and subtle. The average viewer is not interested in trying to figure out the point of a copy line, scene, or entire commercial. Viewers will take their information directly or they may not take it at all.

Correlation between words and pictures.   The video and audio should work together closely and reinforce one another. If the picture shows one thing while the words say another, the viewer's attention will be split between them instead of focused on the central idea. This does not mean that words are constantly needed to explain the picture. A commercial is at its best when it is strongly visual. Words should be used to hold the viewer on the right track and to underscore points made by the picture.

Product message/story line integration.   Comprehension and communication are facilitated if the commercial tracks in a logical, sequential manner. It should have a beginning, a middle, and an end, and the selling message should fit comfortably into the narrative structure. Plot details should not be played back at the expense of sales points.

Simple, explicit, synchronized, structured, familiar—these are the rules for creating the ideal left brain commercial. (The left brain ". . . tends to rely on general rules to reduce experience to concepts that are compatible with its style of cognition."[13]) But advertisers have gone to glory by ignoring such rules. They have created commercials that are unstructured, implicit, visually complex, and unfamiliar. These commercials have been loaded with information that can be processed only by the right side of the brain. Apparently the consumer doth not live by explicit logic alone. There must be other ways in which commercials work.

Challenges from the Right Brain: The Case for Feeling

Much of the recent research into consumer behavior paints a substantially different picture of the way advertising works from that of the classic learning hierarchy (attention→ communication→ attitude→ behavior). In the hierarchical model, cognition (thinking) is the prime mover and affect (feeling) simply the result. New evidence suggests a heightened role for affect. The overall implication is that affect may be a motivator of consumer behavior and not just a by-product of the cognitive process. In other words, it may not be a case of the left brain telling the right brain how to feel. Indeed, the right brain may have much to say about how a commercial works.

Implicit in these newer theories, or models, is a consumer quite different from the one portrayed as spending much of his or her time consciously deliberating over tiny, often imaginary, product differences. If you were to draw up a list of things to worry about in life, it is very likely that deciding which brand of soap or chewing gum to buy will fall near the bottom. You

---

13.   Edwards, *Drawing on the Artist Within,* 11.

may deliberate long and hard over a new car, but most purchase decisions involve much less financial commitment and are not the things around which you organize your life. In many product categories, important, substantive brand differences simply do not exist. So in reality there may be little to deliberate about.

These challenges to traditional learning models do not deny the role of cognition. Obviously there has to be some conscious deliberation in consumer behavior. Consumers are no more likely to get a sudden, irrational feeling about a product and rush out to buy it than they are to leap up and buy after viewing a particularly persuasive commercial. Some form of cognition, albeit rapid or perhaps even unconscious, is bound to occur. The issue between thinking and feeling is really over the role that each plays. Is cognition (thinking) always the dominant force? And does affect (feeling) occur only as a consequence of cognition. Most alternative theories do not reject the classic learning hierarchy, but simply point out additional ways advertising works. For example:

Sometimes Behavior Precedes Attitude Formation

Michael Ray offers a "Three Orders Hierachy" model[14] to explain how advertising works in different circumstances. The first is the traditional learning hierarchy which ". . . typically occurs when the audience is *involved* in the topic of the campaign and when there are *clear differences between alternatives*." An example might be an innovative new product that offers clear advantages over its competitors. "It is under such conditions that audience members first become aware, then develop interest, making evaluations, try, and adopt—the adoption process hierarchy."[15]

The second model Ray calls the dissonance-attribution hierarchy, in which behavior occurs first, then attitude change, and finally learning. "These have typically been situations in which the audience has been *involved* but the *alternatives have been almost indistinguishable*." Consumers may buy a product for one reason (for their children, for example) but still not hold very favorable attitudes toward it (for their own use). Advertising urging consumers to use the product themselves comes into play after they have bought and experienced the product and may eventually get them to consider the product in a new light and thus change their attitudes toward it. The value of advertising, then, is in ". . . reducing dissonance or providing information for attribution or self-perception *after* behavior and attitude change have occurred."[16]

The third model is the low-involvement hierarchy, as put forth by Herbert Krugman in 1965. "He concluded that most television viewers are *not involved* with either the advertising or its topics. This means that there is very little perceptual defense against the messages. Although television ads

---

14. Michael L. Ray, et. al., "Marketing Communication and the Hierarchy-of-Effects," *New Models for Communication Research*, Sage Annual Reviews of Communication Research, vol. 2, 147–173.

15. Ray, 150.

16. Ray, 152.

may not directly change attitude, they might, after overwhelming repetition, make possible a shift in cognitive structure. Consmers may be better able to recall the name or idea of a product. Then the next time they are in a purchasing situation that name comes to mind, they buy, and attitude is subsequently changed as a result of experience with the product."[17]

In assessing the three-orders model, Ray concludes: "The model suggests that the alternative views in the field are not competing; instead, each deals with a different situation. Involvement, differentiation, and communication sources can be analyzed to determine which view is most likely to be operative for each communication situation."[18]

Sometimes Attitudes Are Formed Irrationally

Richard E. Petty and John T. Cacioppo[19] have identified two routes to attitude change. One, called the central route, operates when the viewer is motivated to think about the issue. On this route, the steps of the classic learning hierarchy are followed, with attitude change resulting from careful, conscious deliberation of the arguments presented. However, when the viewer is not motivated to carefully consider the arguments (which holds true for much advertising), a more peripheral route to persuasion may be followed. "Under this second view, attitudes change because the attitude object (product, e.g.) has been associated with either positive or negative cues or the person uses a simple decision rule to evaluate a communication (for example, the more arguments the better)."[20] In other words, attitudes may be formed without a lot of conscious effort.

Petty and Cacioppo do observe that attitudes formed by the central route may last longer and be better predictors of future behavior. This would suggest that the advertiser who has hard information and compelling claims should use them. Attitudes formed in low-involvement (peripheral route) situations tend to be relatively transitory and must be reinforced if they are to be maintained.

Pretend a commercial is a personal salesperson. When he tries to sell you a new personal computer that you are interested in, you listen carefully to what he has to say, you seriously weigh the arguments, and perhaps offer some counterarguments until he has convinced you his brand is superior. If, however, that salesperson were trying to sell you a can of vegetables or something else you were not particularly interested in, you might just nod and smile politely and let your mind wander off into more important thoughts. When he left, you might be favorably predisposed to his line of vegetables simply because of the way he was dressed or the fervor of his arguments, whatever they were. You would, however, be more likely to buy the computer than the vegetables unless the salesperson kept coming back every day to talk vegetables.

---

17.   Ray, 152.

18.   Ray, 172.

19.   Richard E. Petty and John T. Cacioppo, "Central and Peripheral Routes to Persuasion: Application to Advertising," *Advertising and Consumer Psychology*.

20.   Petty, 4.

Petty and Cacioppo also observed, "It is interesting that once the person has tried the product, it may become more personally involving and may make the person more likely to think about the content of future advertisements about the product. In this manner, a peripheral change can lead to a central one."[21]

Sometimes Advertising Preconditions Experience

John Deighton[22] describes a two-step model of how some advertising works. Exposure to the advertising arouses an expectation of the product. This expectation tends to be weak and tentatively held because it comes from a partisan source (Nobody believes advertising.). "In the second step, evidence that bears on the hypothesis (expectation) becomes available—for example, product experience or evidence recalled from memory. The consumer tests the hypothesis, employing heuristics that tend to favor its confirmation, so that confidence in its validity tends to increase."[23]

For example, the consumer sees a commercial for Brand X vegetables that shows a family enjoying the product because, according to the commercial, "Brand X vegetables taste fresher." "It's just a commercial," he thinks, but later, when he has a chance to try Brand X vegetables, the advertising-generated expectation of superior freshness "helps" him like the product and perhaps even perceive it as tasting fresher. The advertising created a positive expectation that cause the experience to be positive. Just the label on an expensive bottle of wine may influence the drinker to discern the excellence of the wine that might not taste as good if sampled blind.

Deighton points out that not all advertising is verbal debate with a resisting consumer. Very often, in fact, the viewer has experienced the product or product category.

The advertiser is not so much adversary as tempter, offering propositions which are both plausible and attractive in the implications. The propositions are often ambiguous ("Coke is It!") or affective ("Oh What a Feeling! Toyota") and rarely contradict existing beliefs directly. The topics are hardly debating forum material. On the contrary, advertising is often used to influence unimportant choices among barely discriminable alternatives.

. . . The reception of advertising is often interwoven with experience. The typical Coke advertising audience has tasted Coke before and expects to do so again. While the classical persuader seeks only to change some pre-behavioral mental state, many advertisers have the opportunity to affect ex post facto interpretations of the consumption experience as much as expectations of what it will offer.[24]

---

21. Petty, 23.

22. John Deighton, "The Interaction of Advertising and Evidence," *Journal of Consumer Research* 11 (December 1984): 763–70.

23. Deighton, 763.

24. Deighton, 763–64.

Advertising may not form or change an attitude, but it may create a favorable predisposition to form an attitude. When harder or more trusted evidence comes along, ". . . advertising induces the inferences that consumers draw from evidence to be more confirmatory than they would have been in the absence of the advertising."[25]

Sometimes Advertising Just Makes the Product Experience Enjoyable

Another advertising researcher, William D. Wells, recognized two roles for advertising—to provide information and to transform the experience of using the product.[26] Informational advertising is just what Rosser Reeves advocated. It requires real and important product advantages. It should attract attention and be clear about what it is saying. Transformational advertising, on the other hand, works by making the experience of using the product (usually an undifferentiated, parity product) more enjoyable. In essence, it connects the brand to the experience, like Coca-Cola has been connected to refreshment.

Under the right circumstances an information advertisement can do its work with a single exposure. But transformation advertising requires enough presence to become part of the consumer's mental life. Frequent exposure is the price of admission.

One corollary of this proposition is that transformation advertising always takes time to become effective. It is necessarily cumulative. And therefore, single exposure copy testing will always underestimate its impact.

Transformation advertising requires consistency. If transformation campaigns are to become part of the consumer's experience of the product, they can not be one thing today and something else tomorrow.[27]

Since transformation advertising is designed to link the product to a positive experience, it will not work for products that are not pleasant to use. "Even the most upbeat advertising can't turn cleaning the oven into a joyous occasion, or scrubbing the kitchen floor, or taking a laxative."[28]

Very similar to the notions of low involvement and transformational advertising is the concept of affect referral, which suggests that consumer choice may simply involve drawing from memory an overall good feeling about the brand. This feeling may be formed from actual brand experience or can simply be a direct transference of feelings from a brand's advertising. The advertising for 501 jeans, for example, makes no claims. It simply shows appealing people enjoying life in 501 jeans. Through repeated expo-

---

25. Deighton, 765.

26. William D. Wells, "How Advertising Works," speech given October 21, 1983.

27. Wells speech.

28. Wells speech.

sure to such advertising, the pleasurable experience of the advertising may be transferred to the product.

Creative adman Keith Reinhard has said:

> In many cases, advertising becomes the *real* difference between competing products. Just as size and shape define the *appearance* of a product, the images and associations created by its advertising define the *experience* of using that product.

> When a customer identifies with the personality of a product, and finds its behavior attractive, he transfers that personality and behavior to himself by buying and using that product. It's like putting on a badge and wearing it proudly.[29]

If talk like this has a ring of déjà vu about it, it may be because it makes much the same case Pierre Martineau was making back in 1957, when he said that advertising should put a psychological label on the product.

"Besides any practical purposes, advertising must help the individual integrate the product with his psychological goals and self-conceptions."[30]

The debate over how advertising does or should work is not a new one. It has been evident in clashes over creative philosophy and in arguments over the role and value of copy testing. But there is growing evidence in the psychological journals that would support the long-held suspicion that not all advertising works along the lines of the classic learning model and that emotional and executional factors may be as important as rational claims.

Linear, left-brain advertising may be very appropriate when the viewer is motivated to learn and when products have important, real, physical differences. But some of these alternative nonlearning models are likely to operate when there is low consumer involvement and when brands are essentially parity products without real differences. Under such circumstances, some of those characteristics of good linear, left-brain commercials (attention hooks, explicit verbal message, logical structure) may be less important than some characteristics that often get written off as production values—casting set details, music, editing—or entertainment values, such as wit, intelligence, and freshness. How people *feel* about the commercial may be as important as what they *remember* about it. Leo Burnett described the likeability aspect of advertising as the "friendliness quotient," and observed the "sheer liking of an ad or a commercial, regardless of the copy points that are played back, is not receiving its deserved place of importance in the advertising scheme of things."[31]

What Makes a Good Right-Brain Commercial

One of the appealing things about left-brain advertising is that it is easier to evaluate than right-brain advertising. It deals in real (physical) product

---

29. Wells speech.

30. Martineau, 52.

31. Leo Burnett, *Communications of an Advertising Man* (Chicago: privately printed, 1961), 72.

information. It relies on words. It has a plot (beginning, middle, end) or logical structure. The viewer tracks the exposition and consciously considers what is presented. If asked, the viewer can generally describe what was said and shown and how he or she reacted to it. But right-brain advertising is something else again. It moves us into the dangerous areas of judgment and intuition. Its basic appeals are emotional and sensual. It deals more with experiences than information. It relies on visual imagery. Its form is often unstructured and episodic. The viewer feels more than considers what is shown. As a result, it is often difficult to verbalize reactions.

Advertising like this tends to make rational, logical businesspeople nervous. "Trust me," they hear, "this will really move the consumer." Or, "No, we don't actually *say* anything about the product, but . . ." No hard claims to spell out and measure. Not only do they hear it cannot be fairly copy tested, they hear it usually requires constant repetition. So it not only costs more, there is no way to guarantee the investment. Because this style of communication defies measurement, because it works without involvement or conscious attention to content, because it depends so much on sheer likeability, does this mean that any thirty seconds a creative team can throw together is effective, as long as it is entertaining? Does this mean that every image commercial is good?

No.

It should be single minded. A commercial should be sharply focused strategically, whether it is emotional or rational. This is obvious in the case of a claim where unrelated sales points can overload the communication and distract or confuse the viewer. Similarly, a brand's image or personality should be focused and consistent. Feeling good is not enough. The viewer should feel a certain kind of good.

It should be believable. The execution must fit the product. William Wells said, "Transformation advertising must be true. Information advertising must be verifiable in a literal sense. But transformation advertising must *ring* true."[32] Again, you cannot create a pleasant experience for products that are not pleasant to experience in real life.

It should be relevant. It should be based on what people believe to be true or what they desire from the product category. It should be important to them. It should communciate with the consumer on his or her terms.

It should pay attention to details. If low-involvement viewers are going to base their attitudes more on minor cues than on literal content, the commercial had better be attentive to such cues as casting, setting, and props.

It should be likeable. Since there is evidence that attitudes toward the advertising and the product experience may interact, it is reasonable to assume that people are more apt to like (prefer?) a product when they like the advertising. The commercial should have some entertainment value or viewer reward. The reward may be as simple as treating the consumer with intelligence, wit, or humanity.

---

32. Wells speech

Whole Brain Advertising:
A Summary

Wise advertising people, with both creative and research leanings, have argued for years that there is more than one way advertising works. They have debated the virtues of hard sell vs. soft sell, USP vs. brand image, thinking ads vs. feeling ads. They have even argued for a creative synthesis of the two. Brand imagists like Pierre Martineau concede a role for copy claims and rational content. Rosser Reeves said that the "best theoretical objective is to *surround the claim with the feeling.*"[33] And Leo Burnett said, ". . . you have to make a friend before you can effectively make him a proposition."[34]

Unrelated to advertising, psychologists studying the human brain have theorized that it is divided into two parts, left and right, which process the world into two distinctly different manners. As you read the descriptions of left-mode and right-mode characteristics it begins to sound exactly like a description of hard-sell and soft-sell advertising. But, we are reminded, these two modes function simultaneously and without conscious distinction.

Finally, advertising researchers have observed that under certain circumstances consumers seem to be processing advertising in ways quite different than models of classic learning theory would suggest. They are picking up impressions without remembering content. They are forming attitudes based on how the advertising *looks* rather than on what it *says*. But, the researchers point out, this tends to occur when consumers are not highly involved in the product and when there are no real differences. Sometimes viewers are interested, do pay attention, do remember. It varies from situation to situation. No one way is always right.

Rarely does a commercial rely entirely on one or the other. Rarely is it all information (left brain) with no executional style or viewer reward. Rarely is it all mood and visual imagery (right brain) with no trace of a rational copy message. Most often, a commercial is a blend of linear and nonlinear elements. The emotional setting helps make the rational message relevant and enjoyable. The copy message gives form and relevance to the imagery. Advertising, to be truly effective, must appeal to both sides of the brain, simultaneously and without conscious distinction. The two should mesh to deliver a single impression.

Some Conclusions:

- There is no one way that all advertising works for all brands under all circumstances.

- There is no one way to measure how all advertising works.

- When viewers are motivated to learn, and when products have important, real, physical differences, one way advertising works is to communicate specific information about a product that differentiates it

---

33.   Reeves, 82–83.
34.   Burnett, 79.

from its competition. Such advertising should be simple, explicit, and logically structured so as to hold the viewer's attention on the product message.

- What the viewer remembers about such a commercial may be very important.

- When viewers are not highly involved and when the products are established brands without material differences from competitors, one way advertising works is to communicate a positive feeling about the brand and its use or experience. Such advertising should be relevant, believable, and likeable and should not rely on a single exposure.

- How the viewer feels about such a commercial may be very important.

- Words and claims are important.

- Visual imagery and production values are important.

- Advertising remains more an art than a science.

Part 2

Strategy to Idea

Chapter 3

Creative Strategy
Asking the Right Questions

The Case for Creative Strategies

Imagine yourself being led onto the stage of a huge auditorium. You know from the murmur of voices that there are thousands of people in the audience, but it is dark and you don't know who they are. Your job is to tell these people (whoever they are) the very thing about a particular brand that will make them want to rush out and buy it.

Don't just stand there. Be creative.

It sounds rather simpleminded to say that before you can do something you have to know what you are trying to do. Before you can communicate information to someone, you have to know who that someone is and what the information is. And when you are dealing with millions of people and millions of dollars, as you are in advertising communciation, decisions such as with whom to communicate and what to say cannot be left to individual whim.

A commercial begins with an objective. An advertiser wants to communicate certain information to a certain group of consumers to motivate them to buy a product. Overall marketing objectives for the product have assigned a particular role to advertising, and advertising objectives have assigned a particular role to television. But before the television commercial comes the creative strategy.

Strategy is not a dirty word, as many creative people think. Nor is it a panacea, as many marketing people think. A good creative strategy simply reminds everybody to whom the commercial is supposed to be talking and what it is supposed to be saying. Strategy keeps you on a steady creative course. It narrows the range of creative decisions and focuses time and energy on the area of greatest potential. It is very easy to start out with your objective in mind only to have it grow fuzzy or shift direction when you happen to hit upon some snappy words or pictures. Strategy helps prevent creative people from being seduced by their own imaginations.

Sometimes so-called strategies are written after the commercials have been conceived. But this kind of ex post facto strategy is just a rationale—a logical-sounding justification for doing what you felt like doing in the first place. Rationales are easier to write than strategies because you know exactly where you want to end up. It is simply a matter of backing up from the already-written advertising and setting the goals already reached. No doubt many successful campaigns have been built on a minimum of strategy and a maximum of gut feeling. No doubt many commercials have been written and sold with eloquent rationales (which everyone called strategies). But just as undoubtedly, many more purely intuitive ads have been dreamed up, vigorously justified, and convincingly explained, only to fall on their creative faces.

This is not to suggest that before copywriters or art directors dare lift a pencil or have a thought they must have a documented strategy at hand. But much wheel spinning can be avoided if there is some understanding and agreement between the marketing and creative people on the direction the advertising should take. Creative strategy gives the creative person something to work to, and it gives the advertiser something with which to evaluate results.

Simply having a creative strategy does not guarantee successful advertising, however. The strategy has to be the *right* strategy. It should originate in the essence of the product and should clearly differentiate your product from competition in a way that makes logical (and emotional) sense to the consumer audience. And then it must be executed with flair and freshness. Creativity will not make a success out of a weak or misdirected strategy, but it can greatly enhance the effectiveness of advertising that is built on a strong strategy.

Any copywriter will tell you, "Creativity is the answer!" But as Gertrude Stein asked, "What is the *question?*"

A good creative strategy asks the right question and leaves the answer to the creative people. It gives them, as William Bernbach put it, "something to be creative about." He continued:

Indeed, if you have not crystallized into a single purpose, a single theme that you want to tell the reader, you CANNOT BE CREATIVE. For merely to let your imagination run riot, to dream unrelated dreams, to indulge in graphic acrobatics and verbal gymnastics is *not* being creative.[1]

---

1. William Bernbach, "Advertising's Greatest Tool," in *Speaking of Advertising,* ed. John S. Wright and Daniel S. Warner (New York: McGraw Hill, 1963), 313.

Three Key Questions:
Who? What? Why?

A creative strategy should specify who the audience of the advertising is, what it should try to communicate, and what effect it should have on the prospect. You have this product (that does certain things, offers certain benefits, has certain advantages) and you have these prospects who seem to be the most likely candidates to buy it. How can you best get the two together? You need to identify how your prospects currently think and feel about your product (and the product category in general). Then you must identify what you could say about your product that would get them to change their beliefs (and ultimately their buying behavior). For example, if your prospects believe your product is just like other brands in the category, they probably have little loyalty to any one brand. You need to convince them that all brands are not alike, that your brand has some advantage over the others, and that they should, therefore, buy your brand over its competitors.

There are many formats that creative strategies can take and the intent here is not to add another. Regardless of format a strategy should answer these three questions for the creative people:

1.   WHO are the prime prospects (target audience)?

2.   WHAT should these prospects feel or believe about your brand?

3.   WHY should they feel or believe that?

Who are the prime prospects for your brand?   The more specifically you can identify your target consumers, the easier it will be to create advertising that speaks their language. "All women" is not a very helpful target. Demographics—age, income, and education—help to some extent, but they hardly bring the audience to life. Demographics are more helpful for media people who must place the commercials on shows that the target audience is likely to be watching. Creative people must understand how the audience thinks and feels. Look for information on how these people use the product. Look for attitudes, beliefs, life-style. It would be more useful for creative people trying to advertise convenience foods to know they were talking to "working women" than simply to "women between eighteen and thirty-five."

What should the prospects feel or believe about your brand?   To answer this question you must first know how they currently feel about your brand and what they are doing as a result. If they hold very positive attitudes toward your brand, chances are they are using it and the goal of the advertising could be simply to remind them of why they like it. More likely, however, advertising is aimed at people who are not using the brand or perhaps not using it enough. This behavior is likely to be the result of some less-than-favorable attitudes toward the product. These attitudes become the target for the advertising. Do they think your brand is of inferior quality? Do they think it is too expensive? Too difficult to use? The goal of advertising may be to stress the fine ingredients that make yours such a high-quality product. Or it may focus on the rewards of using the product that make it a value regardless of price. Or it may demonstrate how simple it is to operate the product. In any case, you are trying to tell them the thing they need to know (feel, believe) to perceive your brand as superior to others in the category. Theoretically, this new attitude or belief should motivate them to change their buying behavior.

Why should they believe or feel that way? What are you promising or proposing? This is the thing that will differentiate your brand from the competition. This is what the creative people will translate into a selling idea. Boil down into one short, simple sentence the primary reason you are asking the consumer to buy your brand instead of another.

For example, consider Arf dog food. Arf is a high-quality, specialty, canned dog food. But dog owners, while they regard it as a good brand, do not think it is worth two cents a can more than Bow-Wow brand, so they use the two brands almost interchangeably when they serve canned dog food. However, dog owners regard their pets as members of the family and want to serve them only the best. If they thought their dog actually preferred Arf, they would consider Arf the better brand and certainly worth the two cents premium. The following creative strategy might be developed:

- Who are the prime prospects?
  Dog owners who use both Arf and Bow-Wow.

- What should these prospects feel or believe about your brand?
  That Arf is better than other canned dog foods.

- Why should they feel or believe that?
  Because Arf has the flavor dogs love.

Most creative strategy formats include a section labeled "support." If the proposition or promise you are making (the reason why people would prefer your brand) is to be convincing and credible, there should be some reason to believe. In the case of Arf, this might come from an execution which shows a dog running home to his bowl of Arf or a demonstration in which a dog passes up Brand X to get to his Arf. Or it may be supported by saying that Arf is made with one hundred percent meat. But if your commercial promises the "flavor dogs love," the support is not the fact that the product comes in a handy, easy-open can.

Brand character is another important element of many creative strategies. This is a short statement that represents the current or desired image of the brand. Every commercial makes an overall impression on a viewer that goes beyond the bare copy message. All of the many ingredients that make up the execution of the idea—style, tone of voice, music, pacing, casting, setting—add up to a whole that is greater than the sum of the parts. Just as every commercial has a personality, so does every brand. All advertising that is created for a brand should be consistent with the character of the brand. A bank whose desired character is secure and serious minded would want to avoid advertising that was slapstick or silly in tone.

Look for a character that is both distinctive and appealing, one that will separate your brand from the field. Fuzzy generalities like *contemporary* or *quality* do not help much. No one wants to be out-of-date or shoddy. Volvo and Cadillac may both talk about quality, but their brand characters, as reflected in their advertising, are quite different. No two brands in the same category can really have the same brand character.

The purpose of a creative strategy, remember, is to guide and inspire the creative work that follows. It is not to stifle and constrict creativity. It should focus attention on the target audience in a way that moves beyond demographics and gets at attitudes and product usage. It recognizes that advertising should influence consumer attitudes and beliefs with the ultimate aim of influencing behavior. To do this, the advertising must bring to the target audience a proposition rooted in the product that will differentiate the product from its competitors.

A strategy should not include multiple promises or claims. If the strategy is ambivalent, you can hardly expect a clearly focused commercial. Nor should a strategy lap over into the creative person's realm. It should not stipulate a particular expression of the selling proposition, nor should it dictate a particular executional format (such as slice-of-life), a specific device (such as a jingle), or a specific production technique (such as animation). However, there may be times when certain executional guidelines are necessary, such as some legal requirements or some campaign element that must maintain consistency from execution to execution. But the goal should be to keep the strategy as simple and unrestrictive as possible.

A good strategy does not mark the end of creativity; it marks the beginning. As William Bernbach said:

> I am absolutely appalled by the suggestion—indeed the policy—of some agencies that once the selling proposition has been determined the job is done, . . . that anyone can take it from there and complete the ad.
>
> It's exactly at this point that we need creativity. It's exactly at this point that we need, not word and picture mechanics, but imaginative, original cratsmen who can take that selling proposition, and through the magic of their artistry, get people to see it, get people to remember it![2]

Where to Look for a Selling Proposition

The goal of strategic thinking is to examine information about your product and prospects in the context of the competitive environment to determine the basic proposition that will differentiate your brand and influence your prospects to purchase it. This proposition (the raison d'être of the copy strategy) is then translated into a selling idea that can be creatively executed in a variety of ways. Figure 3.1 expresses this graphically:

---

2. Bernbach, 313.

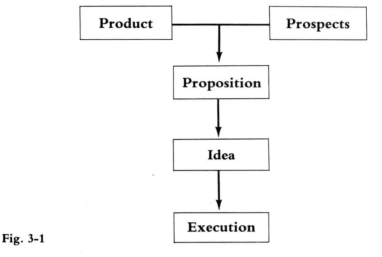

Fig. 3-1

It all looks very orderly and logical. But there is no sure-fire starting point. Almost anything in the product or the consumer can be the springboard for an idea; what follows is intended to be suggestive of the areas in which to dig and is not all-inclusive.

A Close Look at the Product

In examining the product you are interested not just in real product facts (how it is made, how it works), but also in how the product is perceived by your prospective consumers and how your brand stacks up against competition. The goal is to match your product's attributes with what the consumer is looking for and with what is not presently offered or claimed by competitors.

The Product Category

Start with the big picture and see where your brand fits in. How broadly or how narrowly would you define your product category, the arena in which your brand competes? This is the first step toward market segmentation, the breaking down of mass markets into meaningful subgroups. "Beverages" is a sweeping product category. "Beer" starts to narrow it down. But even within the beer category there are differences—light and dark, regular and low calorie, domestic and imported, premium and local. Anheuser-Busch, for example, markets different brands of beer (Budweiser, Bud Light, Michelob, Busch) aimed at different segments of the beer market.

A brand may occupy a particular segment or niche, so you look to discover what appeals to that specific group. Or you might look to the general product category (beverages) to discover its most basic appeal, the primary reason people are drawn to use such products (quench thirst). Even though this is something that every brand in the category could claim, it may be possible to preempt it for your brand.

In the laundry detergent category, for example, Tide's proposition, "Tide's in, dirt's out," is based on a general, all-purpose, gets-clothes-clean strategy. Tide essentially preempted the generic category benefit (cleans clothes) that consumers want from any detergent. Competitors have carved out smaller segments with more specific claims, such as cleans "ring-around-the-collar" (Wisk), and "cleans in all temperatures" (Cheer).

Your Competitive Position

Where does your brand stand compared to its competition? This really involves two things: share of mind and share of market.

In 1972, Jack Trout and Al Ries contended that advertising had entered the "Positioning Era."[3] To reach it we passed through the "Product Era of the 1950s" (epitomized by Rosser Reeves and his USP) and the "Image Era of the 1960s" (David Ogilvy and his Hathaway eyepatch school). Today product proliferation and overcommunication have washed out the effectiveness of campaigns that emphasize product features, consumer benefits, or brand image. There is now so much advertising for so many similar brands that advertising must struggle to position the product in the consumer's mind. Advertising must take into account what other brands are saying. Avis acknowledged Hertz by saying, "We're only number two"; Crosse & Blackwell acknowledged Campbell's soup by calling itself the "Other Soup"; 7-Up found a place in the cola-dominated soft drink market by positioning itself as the "Uncola."

Market share may also influence a brand's creative strategy. Strong category leaders may capitalize upon their positions and adopt leadership strategies (Budweiser's "the king of beers"). It is easier for the leading brand to preempt category benefits. Category followers will find this a more difficult road to follow. As Avis discovered, they have to "try harder." If your brand is a leader in its category, it is more likely to benefit from advertising that promotes the entire category. Kodak can run advertising that simply encourages people to take pictures. If people take more pictures, Kodak will sell more film. But brands of film less well-known have to be more competitive in their advertising to make sure that picture takers buy their brand instead of Kodak.

Your Brand's Stage of Life

Just about every product has a limited life expectancy and tends to follow a predictable course in its sales volume. This is called the product life cycle, and it falls into five stages: 1) *Introduction,* when the product is first put on the market and consumer awareness and acceptance are minimal; 2) *Growth,* when sales increase rapidly because of the cumulative effects of heavy introductory advertising, promotion, distribution, and word of mouth; 3) *Maturity,* when sales growth continues, but at a declining rate because fewer potential customers remain unaware of the product; 4) *Saturation,* when sales reach and remain on a plateau; and 5) *Decline,* when sales begin to diminish as the product is edged out by better ones.

---

3. Jack Trout and Al Ries, "The Positioning Era Cometh," *Advertising Age* (April 24, 1972): 35–38.

There is nothing fixed about the length of either the entire product life cycle or the various stages, but each stage carries distinct marketing implications. During the introductory stage, for example, advertising strategies might emphasize the brand's newness or innovative nature. It might be necessary to promote the product concept itself (the first color TV set manufacturer would highlight the joys of watching programs in living color). During the growth stage, when sales increase and competitors enter the market, product differentiation becomes critical and the advertising has to focus on "our brand of color TV is *better* because . . ." As the product matures and sales begin to level off, advertising may have to seek out new users or point out new, alternate uses for the product. (Cheerios cereal, for example, advertised that it was a perfect finger food for babies.) Finally, during the decline stage, advertising strategies may sever all links with the past and try to totally reposition the brand.

What's New about Your Brand?

Newness is the lifeblood of marketing. While critics holler "planned obsolescence," advertisers continue to search for new products, new features, new packages, new anything that will give them a competitive edge. As the product life cycle suggests, these range from genuinely new concepts that create an entire product category (disposable diapers or personal computers), new models ("Introducing the all new 1989 . . ."), new features (fastening tapes and elastic waistbands on disposable diapers), new forms (liquid soap or soft margarine), new sizes ("now in regular and economical family size . . .") or new packaging (ketchup in squeezable plastic bottles).

The Name of the Product

Sometimes the name of the product may itself suggest a creative or strategic direction. The name may be whimsical, like Screaming Yellow Zonkers, or it may be linked to a character, like Mr. Clean, Rusty Jones, or Green Giant. Many new products have been given names that identify their use or suggest a product advantage: Die Hard (batteries), Face Saver (shave cream), Dry Look (hair spray), Accent (seasoning), Lean Cuisine (low calorie entrées). The name can be the stepping stone to a distinctive personality for the brand. Consider the different personalities of California Cooler and Bartles & Jaymes wine coolers.

The Ingredients

Very often a product story may be based on the premise, "It's what we put in that makes it so good." Many food products boast of real or natural ingredients. Because consumers are more interested in what the product does for them than why it does it, ingredients are more often support for a claim than the claim itself. Ingredient-oriented strategies are most appropriate when the ingredient is commonly understood to be directly linked with the product's performance claim, such as fluoride in a cavity-fighting toothpaste or bleach in a whiteness-claiming detergent. And sometimes the strategy may be built around the absence of an ingredient: no sugar, no salt, no caffeine, no cholesterol.

How the Product Is Made

Maybe what makes your product different and better is the way it is manufactured. Does your wine age in oak casks (instead of stainless steel vats)? Are your cars "engineered for quality" (or do they just roll off the assembly line)? As in the case of ingredients, a how-it-is-made story usually provides the rational support or justification for an emotional claim or appeal. Despite what they may tell you, not all the people who buy flashy sports cars do so because of the quality of the engineering. Nevertheless, how the product is made may be the source of an interesting selling idea. Who would have thought people would buy cookies because they are made by little elves in a hollow tree?

The Company Name and Reputation

Jerry Della Femina borrowed a rejected headline for a Panasonic ad to use as the title of his book: *From Those Wonderful Folks Who Brought You Pearl Harbor*. Although this is a dubious example, there may be times when it helps to remind the consumer of the company behind the product. Products made by companies with strong, positive reputations can use their parentage to leverage themselves. This is particularly true for new, innovative products or categories where the consumer might perceive some risk or uncertainty with trying the product. Knowing the new product was made by a big, reputable company may remove some barriers to trial. "You can be sure if it's Westinghouse."

The Uses and Attributes of the Product

People buy products to use them. Food is for eating, cleansers are for cleaning, razors are for shaving. How well does your product perform? Does it do something better than other brands? The core of the idea may be a demonstration of the product "doing its thing."

Brand Image or Personality

The product's name, package, price, advertising, and reputation all contribute to an intangible but very real personality in the mind of the consumer. One brand of shampoo may be perceived as stylish, another as medicinal. People expect different things from different products. They may want an automobile that swings, but a bank that is conservative and secure; a perfume that is hip, but a cake mix that is old-fashioned. Furthermore, different people may perceive the same brand in different ways. Nonusers can be expected to have a different image of a given brand than that held by loyal users. That is probably why they are nonusers.

Brand images change—sometimes on purpose (through redesign and a change in advertising), and sometimes by accident (through failure to redesign or change advertising). Marlboro is a textbook example of image change. Originally a feminine cigarette, it changed to a bold red and white package and advertising that featured rugged men with tattoos, and later the cowboys of Marlboro Country.

Any evaluation of product facts with an eye toward developing an advertising idea should include an evaluation of the brand's current personality as perceived by the consumer and a determination of what the personality should be in the future. It may be a matter of reinforcing present attitudes or of attempting to create a different image.

A Close Look at the Prospect

Communications experts as far back as Aristotle have warned writers and speakers to know the audience. The better you can define, describe, and understand the motivations of your audience, the better able you will be to develop a selling proposition that will move them. The audience for advertised, mass-marketed products is vast, but there are ways to narrow it down.

Demographics

The traditional way of defining an advertising audience is by demographic variables. Certainly such data is the most readily available and most easily understood. While demographic information can help statistically identify and segment the audience, it does not allow you to truly know and understand your audience as well as some other variables. But it is a place to start.

Age

Age obviously affects what consumers buy and use. Age will define special product needs (baby food, acne medicine, denture cleaner) and will influence tastes and preferences. McDonald's appealed to the older segment of its audience with a commercial in which two senior citizens met over a Big Mac. Meanwhile, in other commercials, Ronald McDonald was appealing to the children in the audience.

Family Life Cycle

Family life passes through various meaningful periods, each of which can produce different needs, expectations, and attitudes that affect product usage. Consider the differences between singles, newlyweds, young marrieds with children, older marrieds with older children living at home, and finally the empty nest, when the children have moved out to start lives of their own.

Sex

Some products are just for women, some just for men. Some products that are used by both sexes can be positioned (designed, formulated, packaged, named) for one or the other, like deodorants, cigarettes, and razors. Women are more willing to accept masculine brands than vice versa. Despite its rugged image, many women smoke Marlboro now. Apparently though, few men smoked the brand before its personality change.

Income

The recent trend toward higher family incomes is expected to continue. There has also been a more equal distribution of income. One reason for the increased affluence of Americans is that more women are working. But the important thing about income is not its level, but how it is likely to be spent. A plumber may earn more than a college professor, but the two will likely vary in their tastes and attitudes and the kinds of products they buy.

Occupation

As just suggested, occupation is usually a more meaningful variable than income. Occupation provides a clue to social roles and life-style. Michelob Light courted the white collar yuppies with their "you can have it all" campaign while Budweiser saluted the blue collar working man with "This Bud's for you."

Education

Another factor interrelated with age, income, and occupation that might suggest the degree of sophistication of the audience is education. But the assumption that the better educated consumer is a smarter buyer, influenced primarily by rational argument instead of emotional appeals, is highly suspect.

Geographic Location

Where you live affects your social customs, dress, recreation, housing, and attitudes. *Sunset* is a very successful magazine editorially dedicated to Western living. It makes a convincing case for regional chauvinism. Furthermore, within a broad region it is important to know if your prospects are city dwellers, suburbanites, or rural residents.

Psychographics/Life-style

Demographics are really more useful to media planners than to creatives. Creatives need to know the prospect as a thinking, feeling person, not just as a set of statistics.

> It's pretty easy to understand why young mothers buy a lot of disposable diapers while elderly singles don't. On the other hand, demographic status certainly doesn't explain everything. Why do some young mothers choose disposable diapers while others still use washable cloth diapers? And why do some of them always buy one brand while others strongly prefer another, and a few use a generic product while still others buy whatever is cheaper or on special sale? Often such differences result from different lifestyle patterns.[4]

---

4. Robert B. Settle and Pamela L. Alreck, *Why They Buy: American Consumers Inside and Out* (New York: John Wiley & Sons, 1986), 270–271

Psychographics are nonmeasurable characteristics of your audience's life-style. They allow you to better know the audience in terms of how they tend to react to different situations and issues. With them you can begin to understand how your product fits into the prospect's life.

What do you know about the personality of your prospects? Are they extroverts or introverts? Leaders or followers? Independent or dependent? Conservative or liberal? Status-conscious or "just folks?" And how do these personality traits relate to your product or product class? Are your consumers willing to pay a high price for a quality product? Are they economy-minded? Unsure of their ability to make a wise buying decision? Likely to be the first of their block to try a new product? How concerned are they about the welfare of their families or the appearance of their homes?

By combining demographics and psychographics, researchers can describe various types of consumers—how they spend their day, how they feel about housekeeping, clubs, entertaining, work, recreation, family. Since the essence of product positioning is to place the product into the life of the consumer, it is important to know all you can about that life.

Product Usage

A person's attitudes toward brands are strongly influenced by the degree to which he or she uses the product. Very often a certain segment of the population will account for a disproportionately large share of the sales of a given product class. Car rentals, beer, hair coloring, prepared dog food, and many other product categories thrive on the repeat business of a small percentage of consumers. This is the very lucrative heavy-user segment advertisers seek to woo.

What is your heavy user like? Which brand is he or she using—yours or your competitor's? How loyal is he or she to this brand? Do your heavy users stick with one brand through thick and thin? Or are they constantly jumping around, always willing to try something new if it sounds interesting? The loyal and the fickle are two very different types of heavy users. Distinguishing between the two can determine whether your advertising is trying to hold on to present users or trying to switch users from another brand. In the first instance the advertising becomes a reminder, reassuring consumers of the wisdom of their choices. In the latter case the advertising must be strongly competitive and offer consumers strong reasons for changing their way of doing things.

Stage of Product Adoption

People do not become loyal users overnight. At any given time there are going to be some people who have never heard of your brand. Others will fall somewhere along a continuum of familiarity. What do you know about your target audience? Are they unaware of the product category (as in the case of a totally new product concept)? Are they aware of the category but unaware of your brand (the second or third brand into the market after a successful introduction by the leader)? Are they aware of your brand (have they seen it in the stores or on TV)? Are they interested? Have they ever tried your brand in the past? Are they satisfied users of your brand? At each stage of this continuum from unawareness to satisfied user, advertising performs a different function. It may need to be especially attention-getting (awareness-building), competitive and explanatory, or reassuring.

Purchase Patterns

How often do consumers buy the product? In what quantity? In what form? Special packs? At what kind of outlet do consumers purchase the product? More than one kind? How loyal are they to these outlets? What role does the outlet play in the buying decision (service, convenience)? What role does promotion play? How much product is bought "on deal?" Is the person who buys the product the same one who uses it? Who influences the purchase decision? Is there any seasonal influence on product purchase (iced tea, antifreeze)?

Buying Motives

What qualities or properties do consumers look for in your product? What is the most important quality they seek? Are they concerned with economy? Convenience? Status? Reliability? Are there any unconscious reasons for buying that may differ from expressed reasons? (Do people really buy a Rolls Royce because it is so well constructed?) The consumer is generally seeking two things from a product—rational, tangible benefits and unconscious, emotional rewards. The rational, tangible benefits are fairly easy to identify and flow directly from the product's performance. The more emotional rewards trace to the consumer's psychological needs and are harder to identify. They include such concepts as security, affection, belongingness, status, self-respect, social approval, self-fulfillment, and self-expression. Successful advertising combines these basic human appeals with some rational support. For instance, Budweiser's "This Bud's for you" campaign appeals to the beer drinker's sense of self-fulfillment (you've earned it) and includes a nugget of rational support for the product's quality with "beechwood aged."

Attitudes toward the Brand and Its Users

This is a matter of looking at brand image from another angle. What are the consumers' experiences with the brand? How do they feel about it? How do they rank it with competing brands? What is their image of the brand and the people who use it? Do their perceptions of the people who use the brand fit with their image of themselves?

Summary: The Chart Grows

The selling proposition is where the attributes of the product mesh with the wants and needs of the consumer. To arrive at it you must know all there is to know about your product. Leo Burnett wrote: "One of the basic concepts in our shop is that there is what we call 'inherent drama' in every product, and that our No. 1 job is to dig for it and capitalize on it."[5]

Furthermore, because improving a brand's business usually requires that consumer attitudes and feelings toward the brand be improved, it is essential to know exactly how your prospects feel about your brand (and how you want them to think about your brand in the future).

To make sure that copywriters and art directors make the most of this valuable product and consumer knowledge is why creative strategies were invented.

A reminder of where to look for this strategic information can be seen in figure 3-2, an expanded version of the simple chart that began this chapter:

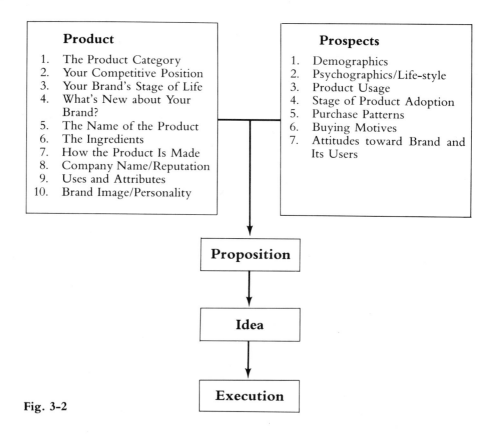

Fig. 3-2

---

5. Leo Burnett, *Communications of an Advertising Man* (Chicago: privately printed, 1961), 21.

Chapter 4

Creativity
How Ideas Are Born

It would seem quite apparent that there is no one creative process, and there may well be as many creative processes as there are creative people.[1]

Defining Creativity: Getting Down to the Real Intangibles

Most writers on the subject of creativity agree that to have a new idea does not mean to conceive of something totally unrelated to anything anyone else has ever thought of before. Rather, creativity seems to involve some kind of rearrangement of the familiar.

An idea is nothing more nor less than a *new combination* of old elements.

James Webb Young, *A Technique for Producing Ideas*

A creative thinker evolves no new ideas. He actually evolves new combinations of ideas that are already in his mind.

Alex Osborn, *Your Creative Powers*

---

1. H. Herbert Fox, "A Critique on Creativity in the Sciences," quoted in *Creativity* by Don Fabun (Kaiser Aluminum and Chemical Corporation, 1968), 54.

[The creative thinking process is] the forming of associative elements into new combinations which either meet specified requirements or are useful in some way.

Wilbert S. Ray, *The Experimental Psychology of Original Thinking*

To think creatively we must be able to look afresh at what we normally take for granted.

George Kneller, *The Art and Science of Creativity*

Creativeness is the basic, scientific ability to see the relationship between apparently unrelated things.

Ernest Dichter, *Handbook of Consumer Motivations*

I have always felt that perhaps the real key to this nebulous thing called "creativity" is the art of establishing new and meaningful relationships between previously unrelated things in a manner that is relevant, believable and in good taste, but which somehow present the product in a fresh new light.

Leo Burnett, *Communications of an Advertising Man*

It sounds so simple. Just take the old and arrange it a new way. An advertisement promoting National Library Week boiled this notion down to its essence. The only illustration on the page consisted of the twenty-six letters of the alphabet. The copy at the bottom of the page said: "Your public library has these arranged in ways that make you cry, giggle, love, hate, wonder, ponder and understand."

A definition of creativity that stresses finding new and meaningful relationships between familiar but previously unrelated elements is especially appropriate for advertising creativity. A creative advertising idea should be new, fresh, surprising. But in advertising, novelty is less important than relevance. The creative advertising idea must be understood by the consumer to be about the product, and the message it conveys must be meaningful.

"*Our* job," said William Bernbach, "is to sell our clients' merchandise, not ourselves. Our job is to kill the clevernesses that make us shine instead of the product. Dullness may not sell a product, but neither will irrelevant brilliance."[2]

Communication research suggests that people are more receptive to messages that are familiar to them and compatible with the attitudes and beliefs they already hold. Other messages run the risk of being selectively screened out, misindexed, or distorted. But advertising that is too familiar risks being seen as dull and old hat. The creative advertising idea must

---

2. William Bernbach, "Bill Bernbach Defines the Four Disciplines of Creativity," *Advertising Age* (July 5, 1971): 22.

contain enough surprise to break through and enough familiarity to tell the consumers this is for them.

As advertising researcher Clark Leavitt stated:

> Familiar objects have less claim on our attention. The more familiar, the quicker the casual reader (viewer) can index an ad as "old stuff," as something he's seen before. Yet the secret of the good ad is not a simple matter of reversing this logic. It is plain that what we consider good ads by any criterion are not merely bizarre, exotic or strange. The problem is not how to get people to look at the pretty pictures, but to get people to progress through the ad-as-a-whole until they have a substantial message of some sort. This is what I have called intrigue—the quality of a stimulus that encourages investigation, exploration and resolution.[3]

What Leavitt calls "intrigue," Stephen Baker calls "congruous incongruity." It is the art of combining the familiar in an unfamiliar way that makes sense and relates to the message you are trying to get across. This is the essence of a creative advertising execution—it attracts attention through surprise and by arousing curiosity; it holds attention through intrigue, which compels the viewer/reader to stick it out and resolve the apparent incongruity; and it permits correct interpretation and communication of the message by using familiar parts to lead to a logical conclusion.

For example, consider the surprise of an illustration showing a hand with a thumb and six fingers. We have all seen hands and fingers (familiar) but never in this combination (surprising and unfamiliar). Our attention is attracted by the incongruity. Intrigued, we read further and discover the ad is for a photographic retouching company. The incongruity is suddenly congruous. The six-fingered hand is now a dramatic demonstration of what can be achieved with skillful retouching. The ad is different (new), but for a reason (meaningful). The reason is to communicate something about the product or service being advertised.

How to Be Creative

How does this new, meaningful combination of previously unrelated elements come about? How do creative people come up with those ideas of theirs? Betty Edwards provided this basic description of the creative process:

> The creative individual, whose mind is stored with impressions, is caught up with an idea or a problem that defies solution despite prolonged study. A period of uneasiness or distress often ensues. Suddenly, without conscious volition, the mind is focused and a

---

3. Clark Leavitt, "Intrigue in Advertising—The Motivating Effects of Visual Organization," *Proceedings of the Seventh Annual Conference of the Advertising Research Foundation* (New York, 1961), 23.

moment of insight occurs, often reported to be a profoundly moving experience. The individual is subsequently thrown into a period of concentrated thought (or work) during which the insight is fixed into some tangible form, unfolding, as it were, into the form it was intended to possess from the moment of conception.[4]

Just another day in the agency creative department.

The last place you would expect (or should hope) to find a formula, procedure, or set of rules would be in a discussion of creativity. But it would be wrong also to conclude from the fact that many copywriters and art directors wear blue jeans to the office that creativity is without discipline. "Creative work, at least at the conscious level, involves a far more orderly set of procedures than many artistic people like to think."[5] What follows are the five basic stages of the creative process.

Raw Materials: The Sine Qua Non

To begin at the beginning, you need a head full of basic ingredients. Alex Osborn wrote in *Applied Imagination,* "To develop creativeness the mind needs not only to be exercised, but to be filled with material out of which ideas can best be formed."[6] Gathering facts (raw materials) is at the top of everyone's list of steps to follow to have an idea. The advertising idea is certainly no exception. Notice the similar approach to the different creative problems of painter Julian Levi and advertising man William Bernbach:

> In painting a sea coast I have tried to acquire as much objective knowledge of the subject as I possibly could. I know the people of those regions and I have become reasonably familiar with their activities. I have studied their fishing gear, their boats and assorted paraphernalia.[7]

> Let me tell you about the Volkswagen campaign. When we were awarded the account the first thing we did was to spend much time in the factory in Wolksburg, Germany. We spent days talking to engineers, production men, executives, workers on the assembly line. We marched side by side with the molten metal that hardened into the engine, and kept going until every part was finally in its place. We watched finally as a man climbed behind the steering wheel, pumped the first life into the new-born bug and drove it off the line. We were immersed in the making of a Volkswagen.[8]

4.   Betty Edwards, *Drawing on the Artist Within* (New York: Simon and Schuster, 1986), 2–3.

5.   Morton Hunt, "How The Mind Works," *The New York Times Magazine* (January 24, 1982): 64.

6.   Alex Osborn, *Applied Imagination* (New York: Charles Scribner's Sons, 1963), 70.

7.   Brewster Ghiselin, *The Creative Process* (Berkeley: University of California Press, 1952), 57.

8.   William Bernbach, "Advertising's Greatest Tool," in *Speaking of Advertising,* ed. John S. Wright and Daniel S. Warner (New York: McGraw-Hill, 1963), 316.

There are two kinds of raw materials necessary for creating the advertising idea. The first consists of specifics that relate directly to the product and the audience (see chapter 3). This information is the kind you dig out of research summaries and verbatims, personal interviews and discussions with experts and consumers, and first-hand experience with the product. This is the homework every good creative advertising person does before sitting down to dream up an ad or commercial.

The homework involved in gathering the second kind of raw materials never stops. It includes watching and listening to people, reading, traveling, and seeing movies and plays—even watching television. It is maintaining a general awareness of the world around you, what's "in" and "out."

> Every really good creative person in advertising whom I have ever known has always had two noticeable characteristics. First, there was no subject under the sun in which he could not easily get interested— from say Egyptian burial customs to modern Art. Every facet of life had fascination for him. Second, he was an extensive browser in all sorts of fields of information. For it is with the advertising man as with the cow: no browsing, no milk.[9]

Creative advertising usually reaches into sources outside of advertising for the words, images, sounds, or techniques that give a selling message a spark of life and freshness and a sense of timeliness. Think of all the commercials you have seen that have drawn inspiration from current movies, pop music, fashion trends, or a popular expression or fad. Writing in *Adweek* of how advertising reflects and capsulizes its times, Barbara Lippert observed, "We were aware people wore yellow ties and red suspenders before BBDO's spot for Apple's Macintosh, but we hadn't had a chance to study their folkways. The more I see these spots, the more I see everything we need to know about corporate morality in the '80s."[10]

Creative people do not live by facts alone. They must know what their audience talks about, worries over, listens to, watches, and enjoys. They must know their music, their jargon, their dreams, their hang-ups. Only then can they establish contact.

Hard Thinking: Somebody Has to Do It

Ideas start to happen when you take all the specific facts relevant to the problem, along with all the general information, impressions, and feelings you have stored away, and begin to look for that meaningful new combination. James Webb Young calls this step "mastication" or "mental digestion," and he describes it as follows:

> What you do is to take the different bits of material which you have gathered and feel them all over, as it were, with the tentacles of the mind. You take one fact, turn it this way and that, look at it in different lights, and feel for the meaning of it. You bring two facts

---

9. James Webb Young, *A Technique for Producing Ideas,* 4th ed. (Chicago: Advertising Publications, 1960), 35–36.

10. Barbara Lippert, "Adweek Critique," *Adweek* (July 20, 1987): 19.

together and see how they fit. What you are seeking now is the relationship, a synthesis where everything will come together in a neat combination, like a jig-saw puzzle.[11]

Don Fabun calls it "manipulation" and describes it this way:

Now, with all this material before him—in his mind, on the work-bench, or in piles of notes on slips of paper—the creative person begins to try to find some new pattern. He pokes at the material, shuffles it around, turns it upside down, looks at it sideways. He may seek metaphors, just as in literature poets seek them. ("She walks in beauty like the night.") Or, in invention, one may conceive that the flow of electricity outside a conductor is *like* the flow of water inside a pipe. The manipulative process is an attempt at synthesis, the putting together of hitherto unrelated concepts, and what it hopes to do is "to make the familiar strange."[12]

This hard thinking about the problem is hard work. It is at this stage in the creative process that you begin to notice that your pencils need to be sharpened, your plants need to be watered, your office needs to be tidied up. Every distraction is an opportunity to escape from that terrifying blank sheet of paper. You can feel your brain slow down and your muscles tighten.

One thing that helps is to dirty the paper with thoughts. Veteran adman John Caples advised, "Write down every idea that comes into your head—every selling phrase, every key word. Write down the good ideas and the wild ideas. Don't try to edit your ideas at the start. Don't put a brake on your imagination."[13]

Often it is not a question of "braking" your imagination, but trying to get it into gear. So just write something down. Draw. Doodle. Call it what you like, but loosen the log jam in your head. With luck (creativity), one thought will lead to another, then off in yet another direction, eventually arriving at something that begins to make some sense. This is nothing more than a form of free association.

From some starting point the mind recalls one experience, image, symbol or bit of information—and this leads to the recall of another experience, image, symbol or bit of information—*etc., ad lib., ad infinitum.* It is a process in which the mind "hauls" one recollection after another before the consciousness for "inspiration," as it were—in halting, stop-and-go fashion—with no apparent directional intent or conscious volition or guidance—until, in effect, the mind "recognizes" or takes cognizance of something; or comes alert/awake; or forms a sort of "Hey!" response/awareness; or simply, something "registers."[14]

---

11. Young, 42–43.

12. Fabun, 54.

13. John Caples, "A Dozen Ways to Develop Advertising Ideas," *Advertising Age* (November 14, 1983): M-5.

14. Jack Taylor, *How to Create New Ideas* (Englewood Cliffs, N.J.: Prentice-Hall, 1961), 76.

As you get more deeply into the problem you will probably do more weeding out in your head. You may put less on paper, but you will have a higher percentage of "keepers." In the beginning, however, don't be afraid to put everything down on paper. Don't worry about being wrong or silly—not yet. At this stage of the process it is important not to bog down by prematurely massaging the first half-decent thought that comes along.

Ideas, especially advertising ideas, are not always the product of a single mind. Very often they are the result of two people working together—a writer and an art director. A team. Traditionally, the writer comes up with words, and the art director makes them come alive visually. Or the art director has a visual that cries out for copy. In the case of great teams, it often works either way. Their two minds work along the same lines, but differently enough to bring variety to the partnership. The thoughts of one spark the other. Writer Carol Leonard and art director Mike Venezia describe the chemistry of teamwork this way:

"Lots of times when I'm writing and he's sketching, I'll think of something and laugh," says Leonard. "Mike says 'Out with it,' and off we go."

"Sometimes we find ideas by accident," adds Venezia. "We get so involved with our own thoughts, we don't hear the other person talk. Every now and then it'll occur to me that Carol has said something, and I'll have to ask, 'Did you just say . . . whatever?' She says 'No, but that's a funny idea.' We do that to each other a lot."

Creative teamwork is the distillation of the notion of brainstorming advocated by Alex Osborn.

> There are several reasons why group brainstorming can be highly productive of ideas. For one thing, the power of association is a two-way current. When a panel member spouts an idea he almost automatically stirs his own imagination toward another idea. At the same time, *his* ideas stimulate the associative power of all the others.[15]

Brainstorming and other group-think techniques of "running it up the flagpole" associated with life in an advertising agency are useful primarily in oiling the gears of individual creative minds. It can be very stimulating if kept on track. But there are more successful creative teams than think tanks. The temptation to wander off into unproductive (though often entertaining) directions is great and increases as you add participants. Leo Burnett, for one, advocated the lonely man approach to creative problem solving, but conceded:

> It is not necessarily true that five people in a room are five times as stupid as any one of them, but the only creative conference worth a damn, in my opinion, is one in which everybody in the room starts from the same base of fact, a consuming appetite for ideas, no matter how wild they may first appear, and a humble respect for them.[16]

---

15. Osborn, *Applied Imagination,* 154.

16. Leo Burnett, *Communications of an Advertising Man* (Chicago: privately printed, 1961), 75.

Incubation: The Case for Going Home

Nine times out of ten, in spite of all your good intentions and hard thinking, the pieces do not fall into place immediately. After all the fact-finding and sorting out, after all the doodling and bouncing off thoughts, you come to a dead end. It is time to back off for a while, to take your problem and sleep on it. This stage has been called incubation. It is the period during which you allow your subconscious to work on the problem.

Einstein once stated that when he had a problem to solve he applied himself to it earnestly with all the power of his conscious mind, then relaxed and left the responsibility to his subconscious mind. Later the solution might come quite suddenly while taking a walk or doing something else quite unrelated to the subject at hand.[17]

Advertising Age once asked a variety of top creative advertising people how they came up with their ideas. The recurring theme of their answers suggests that you should not feel guilty about going home after a day in the office.

Sometimes they come in the middle of the night. . . . Sometimes they come, willy nilly, when I'm doing the dishes, or cooking—alone times.

Paula Green

I find ideas can happen anywhere, at any time—most often while doing something else, or while thinking about something other than the particular creative job I have to do.

Don Tennant

My best ideas often occur when I'm away from the office and, most often, at home when I'm relaxed and allowing my imagination to wander.

Phil Dusenberry, *"The Sources of Invention"*

The point is that the creative mind is at work even when the creative person is not. You often need some conscious time off before the rewarding next stage occurs.

Illumination: The Light at the End of the Tunnel

E. H. Land once defined creativity as the sudden cessation of stupidity. And so it seems. The solution appears in front of you like the proverbial nose on your face. It may come the next day when you again sit down at the typewriter or drawing table; it may come some night when you slide down into a tub of bath water, as the idea of specific gravity came to Archimedes, causing him to exclaim, "Eureka!" (the name often given to this stage). The

---

17. Stanwood Cobb, *Importance of Creativity* (Metuchen, N.J.: Scarecrow Press, 1967), 85.

inspiration that comes out of the subconscious (after a long bout of conscious thought) is a far cry from a bolt of sudden insight hurled down from the gods. This kind of inspiration happens on purpose and (you hope) before the deadline.

When the solution does come you will see why it is said that a good creative idea combines the unexpected with the inevitable. When the idea finally emerges, it appears as the *only* way to do it. There is an inevitable rightness about it. You are surprised, perhaps, but the more you think about it you cannot imagine any other solution. And you kick yourself for having taken so long to arrive at it.

Verification: The Emperor's New Clothes

If you have ever had a "brilliant idea" right before you went to sleep at night, jumped up and scribbled it down on a notepad beside your bed, then looked at it in the morning and wondered who snuck into your room and wrote all that gibberish, you will appreciate the value of this final stage of the creative process. This is when you test your idea to see if it is as good as you thought. James Webb Young called this stage "the cold, grey dawn of the morning after."

> In this stage you have to take your little newborn idea out into the world of reality. And when you do you usually find that it is not quite the marvelous child it seemed when you first gave birth to it.

> It requires a deal of patient working over to make most ideas fit the exact conditions, or the practical exigencies, under which they must work. And here is where many good ideas are lost. The idea man, like the inventor, is often not patient enough or practical enough to go through with this adapting part of the process. But it has to be done if you are to put ideas to work in a work-a-day world.[18]

When the idea in question is for a television commercial, the test is very often the storyboard. Put the idea down on paper and take a hard look at it. Show it to someone who is not as close to the problem as you are and see if it makes sense to him or her. Apply some practical considerations, like can it be accomplished in thirty seconds, or can it be produced within the available budget? Creative people may not like to bother themselves with such details, but they are all important matters to consider.

In summary, here are the five steps to follow to make an idea happen:

Gather grist for the mill. Accumulate the specific information (about the product and consumer) you need. This should complement your long-range accumulation of general information and impressions of life.

Grind it all up. Mentally sift and sort, mix and match, what you have learned with what you already know and feel. You are looking for that key relationship.

18.   Young, 52–53.

Sleep on it. Give your subconscious a chance to tackle the problem by deliberately getting away from it for awhile. This is when the trees group themselves into a clearly defined forest.

Eureka! The solution comes to you, disguised as a flash of inspiration.

Look again. Reexamine your idea in the harsh light of day. If some of the luster has worn off, polish it, refine it, then test it again. If it works, you have yourself an idea.

If five steps are too many to remember, Leo Burnett offered a shorter formula: "Steep yourself in your subject, work like hell, and love, honor and obey your hunches."[19]

How Not to Be Creative

So much for the steps to success. Here are a few tips on how to avoid the hard work and honest creative effort required to have a good, original advertising idea.

Be Different for the Sake of Being Different

The first "creative" impulse is to throw out the rule book (without bothering to read it first). For example, if cat food commercials all show cats eating the advertised brand, set out intentinally to create the first cat food commercial in which no cats eat anything. Another breakthrough! But before you break a rule, make sure you understand why it was written and calculate your risks accordingly. For example, if it turns out that all cat owners are worried about whether or not their cats will eat a particular brand, and if showing a cat eating in the commercial helps reassure them that their cats will like your brand, then maybe leaving out the obligatory eating shot is not such a great idea after all. The trick is not to be different; the trick is to be better. Set out to find a way to show cats enjoying your brand, that is fresher, more surprising, more unique.

Settle for the First Thing that Comes Along

Deadlines have a way of clouding judgment. When time is running out, you tend to welcome any idea that shows up. But great ideas rarely come easily or quickly. Conversely, do not massage a good idea to death. Someone once said it takes two people to create a painting—one person to paint it and another to pull the painter away when he or she is finished.

Avoid the Obvious

If the idea is too simple, it cannot be creative. Anybody could do that. But people do not buy products very often for complicated reasons. Sometimes

---

19. Burnett, 84.

plain talk and straightforward visuals can make a compelling sale. A solution may seem obvious because it communicates so rapidly and directly. The interest and drama should rest deep in the product itself—and it may be so basic that no one ever noticed it before. It is easy to reject a possible approach because you fear it has been done. Chances are it has been done, in one or two of the hundreds of possible ways.

Borrow a Technique

Art directors' clubs and other groups publish annuals of award-winning ads and commercials. These are terrific source books—not for swiping ideas, mind you, just for inspiration. Sure enough, there on page 47 of the latest collection is a gold medal winner, a truly brilliant commercial that used a nifty computer animation technique. Why not use computer animation for your commercial?

Most award winners that are really worth their medals cannot be easily taken apart, modified, or converted to fit another problem. They represent the best solutions to their own specific problems. And it is rare that one ingredient—such as a computer animation technique—is the reason for their success. What counts is the way the technique is used to enhance the message. If you borrow a gimmick or technique and it seems to fit your product just as well as some other brand, chances are it is just that, a gimmick.

Use an All-Purpose Commercial

In addition to the volumes of ready-made, already-done solutions that never quite fit your problem of the moment, there occasionally appears a ready-made idea that seems to fit almost any problem. It may be a script that was written another time, rejected, then filed away with other almost-greats where it lay, gone but not forgotten, until the present crisis arose. Now it gets pulled out, dusted off, and its creator discovers that with a few minor niggles, the old commercial works for the new product. In fact, on closer examination, it works for almost any product. Just insert brand name here.

But each solution should grow out of its own problem. The form the commercial takes should be relevant and ideally unique to your particular brand. If you can drop any product into a plot or format you probably have a weak idea, a weak execution, or both.

Conduct Your Own Research

A *New Yorker* cartoon once showed an advertising copy chief explaining his new campaign idea to a scowling old agency president: "All right, you think it's crummy and I think it's crummy, but are *we* 'Young Marrieds?'"

The final judge of whether a commercial is "crummy" or effective is the audience for whom it is intended. And it is sometimes difficult for the creative person to put him or herself into those shoes. It is not always enough to be able to look the client squarely in the eye and say, "Well, this would sure sell me." And it is no less objective to cite the opinion of a handy typical consumer, such as, "My wife buys corn flakes and she thinks this is a great idea."

Advertising research has enough problems of its own without being equated with off-the-cuff surveys taken among family and friends. The ad that cracks up the folks at the agency may very well be a dud to those who are expected to respond to its message. Television is the most "mass" of our mass media. Commercials are watched by ordinary people who work in shops, drive trucks, and keep house. When David Ogilvy said, "The consumer is no moron. She is your wife," he did not mean that every campaign should be based on whar *your* wife (or husband) happens to think is appropriate. The audience may have a different frame of reference, different tastes, different likes and dislikes. It may not know much about art, but it knows what it likes.

This does not mean that every commercial should be aimed at the lowest common denominator (although this often seems to be the prevalent philosophy). Nor does it mean that the creative person should not listen to his or her own instincts and sense of what is right. It simply means that the person who is making the commercial often has to pause, back off a few paces, and apply a little cold objectivity. Does the commercial speak the language of the audience or the jargon of the trade? Is its mood, atmosphere, and tone of voice in keeping with the consumer's image of him or herself? Is the selling idea important to the people who use the product, or is it merely cute or clever?

Blame Your Strategy (or Other Extenuating Circumstances)

Advertising Age used to run a little feature called "The Creative Man's Corner," devoted to praising or attacking (usually the latter) some current campaign. On the heels of some of the critiques would come angry letters defending the wronged and challenging the credentials of the anonymous "Creative Man." The defenders complained that the critic was in no position to judge the merits of the ad without understanding the particular underlying strategy or the severe restrictions under which the creators had labored.

But neither are consumers. They know nothing about long-range marketing objectives, copy strategies, client biases, last-minute changes, product deadlines, legal restrictions, or any of the other crises that are a part of daily life in advertising. All they know is what they see on their home TV screens. And they do not bother to write critiques. They just click off their minds, and another "strategically sound" commercial has died. A strong rationale can be built for the weakest ideas. An ad may be presented to the client prefaced by some this-is-what-we-are-trying-to-do remarks, so that when the ad is unveiled it seems to be the perfect solution to what, moments ago, seemed an impossible problem. It may be just what you were trying to do. But were you trying to do the right thing?

It is not enough to have a strategy. You have to have the *right* strategy. And the right strategy has to be executed in a dramatic, appealing style.

Consumers respond to commercials, not strategies. The viewer should not have had to read the book to enjoy the movie.

Keep a Closed Mind

Personal preferences or biases can narrow your creative potential. They may close your mind to an appropriate solution. The person who hates rock music will have trouble communicating with today's youth. The person who is a nut on harpsichord music and insists on it in a commercial sound track may discover many people do not share this appreciation. The advertising creative person cannot afford to cater to personal tastes at the expense of the audience. Aesthetics do not always count in the marketplace. Something inside you may die when you discover that a charging white knight can sell laundry detergent, but from the advertiser's point of view, if it works it's beautiful.

Part 3

Idea to Execution

Chapter 5

How Ideas Take Shape
Execution I

Ideas and Executions: Which Is Which?

The purpose of creative strategies is to make sure the advertising is right, that it is setting out to say the right thing to the right people. However, there are two comments that can spell doom for any proposed TV commercial. The first is *off strategy*. This means that the advertising solved the wrong problem, is misdirected, or carries an inappropriate message. Such advertising is not worthy of further consideration. The second comment is *on strategy*. To a creative person, this describes copy so hopelessly uninspired that its only redeeming social value is its adherence to the strategy. "There's practically nothing that is not capable of boring us" said William Bernbach. ". . . You won't be interesting unless you say things freshly, originally, imaginatively."[1]

The purpose of creativity is to make sure the advertising is wonderful, that it grabs its audience and registers the selling message. It is the job of copywriters and art directors to translate the selling proposition/basic promise/focus of sale of the creative strategy into an advertising idea. And that idea needs a form of expression—an execution.

We assume that every commercial has—or is—an execution. Yet we suspect that not every commercial has an idea. At least not a great one. Sometimes you hear the criticism that the execution overpowered the idea. This implies that the idea and execution are separate, freestanding entities, the latter simply a carrier for the former. In other words, if you have a great

---

1. William Bernbach, *Advertising Age* (July 5, 1971): 22.

idea you can execute it in any of a variety of ways and the only real danger is that the style of execution is so creative that the great idea gets obscured.

This is a dangerous way to think about advertising. When it appears that the execution overpowers the idea, it is more likely that there is no idea. The very best advertising is that in which the idea and execution blend in such an inevitable way that you can scarcely separate one from the other. The execution becomes the idea, and vice versa. "I think there is a tendency to try and pry apart the concept and execution," says one creative director. "Often when you conceive of something, the idea comes to you as a specific vision; the idea and execution are intertwined."[2]

Perhaps because we talk about advertising there is a tendency to think of the idea as the words. The idea is what you say. (The execution is how you say it.) But even if the idea were just the copy, how do you separate *what* is said from *how* it is said?

Just as we often think of the idea of a print ad to be the headline, so do we often think of the slogan or end line of a commercial to be its idea. The execution draws you in and leads you through to a set of words that crystallizes the idea and memorably expresses the selling proposition laid out in the strategy. A classic example: Clairol hair color promised women natural-looking color. The idea: "Does she or doesn't she? Only her hairdresser knows for sure."

To be sure, there are many times when the magic of an idea is captured in a line of copy. Pampers diapers told mothers "Even when they're wet they're dry." Tide detergent summarized its cleaning positioning with the memorable copy, "Tide's in, dirt's out." Cheer capsulated its cleans-in-all-temperatures claim into "All tempa-Cheer." AT&T touched a responsive chord for its long distance service with "Reach out and touch someone." American Express reminded travelers, "Don't leave home without it." But words are only part of the equation. If the visual did not contribute to the power of a TV commercial, advertisers could just as well stick with radio. As important as copy is, it does not work alone.

Here is just the copy from an award-winning TV campaign:

> Hello there. With all the wine coolers out on the market we are always being asked which one we think is of the highest quality and tastes the best. Well, to be sure of being completely honest and unbiased, Ed and I have placed each of our answers separately in an envelope. Ed's answer is the Bartles & Jaymes Wine Cooler. That is funny, so is mine. Well, you cannot argue with research. Thank you very much for your support.

From the copy alone you can understand what the commercial is about. The advertiser's name is mentioned. There is a superiority (preference) claim. But if the copy (notice there is no tag line that summarizes the message or themes the campaign) were the idea, then the execution could utilize any presenter, right? But not many advertisers would feel that the copy alone represented a very persuasive case for buying Bartles & Jaymes wine coolers. There must be some other execution elements that make the commercial (campaign) a good idea.

---

2. *Adweek* (October 19, 1987): p.C, p.8.

The strength and appeal of the Bartles & Jaymes campaign comes not only from the droll copy, but from the characters Frank and Ed and the offbeat personality (considering the market for wine coolers) created for the brand. What they say is less important than how they say it. It is the deftness of casting and performance that makes the copy work.

Here is the copy from another commercial:

> I love you, little Jenny-Catherine. I've got something very, very important to tell you. Daddy got a raise. Are you listening? I got a raise. That means, it means I can buy you a sandbox, a playhouse, it means I can buy you a sliding board, or a bicycle, a diamond ring. It means I can buy you a mink coat. Maybe we could buy . . . Or maybe we should put some of it away. What do you think about that? What do you know about the stock market? I love you, little Jenny-Catherine, very, very much. Guess what, daddy got a raise.

No claim, no message, no mention of the advertiser's name. What is missing of course is the video portion. So to be fair to the copywriter, let's expand the definition of copy to include the words we see as well as those we hear. Here are the words you see in the commercial:

Bill Heater

Age.... 30
Married, two children
Income.... $35,000

Estimated Expenses

Income tax	$8,500
Rent	8,500
Food, clothing, insurance	11,500
Misc	1,500
	$30,000

Needs

Long term security for his family
To build investments

Answer

John Hancock Variable Life -Insurance with five investment options:
    Stocks
    Aggressive Stocks
    Bonds
    Money Market
    Total Return

John Hancock advertising reprinted with the permission of John Hancock.

Those frames are intercut throughout with scenes of a young father whispering to his baby daughter as he paces back and forth with her nestled to his shoulder. The power of the commercial comes from the real-life honesty of the father's emotion and from the juxtaposition of this warm emotion with the jarring harshness of the father's financial needs and the real answers offered by John Hancock. The idea comes not just from the copy, but from what we often write off as execution or production values—casting, performance, directing, editing.

A commercial truly works when the idea and execution perfectly mesh. As in the case of these two examples, the "what you say" is "how you say it." It is copy, it is pictures, it is all the subtleties of production. It can originate with any of these—as a line of copy, a visual image, a production technique—but when it is all finished, no single aspect should call unnecessary attention to itself. All the ingredients work as a chorus line, in perfect harmony and coordination, to deliver a single impression. "Great idea!" everyone exclaims. But is it a great idea or a great execution or a great strategy?

Yes!

The Ingredients of a TV Commercial Execution

A copywriter [or art director] entering the world of television is like a child turned loose in a candy store. He has a surfeit of goodies. Sight, sound, motion, and . . . color. Animation, stop motion, freeze frames, and skip frames. The use of opticals, like wipes and dissolves, with which he can signal, without words, the passage of space and time. Sound effects and music, with which he can turn on moods and memories. Personalities, pacing, lighting, and intonation—he has an inexhaustible well of wizardry.[3]

The first thing to strike creative people facing their first television assignment is the complexity of the medium. Everything you need to make a print advertisement fits within a rectangle drawn on a layout pad. Illustrations, typography—that's about it. The rest is simply a matter of arranging them into a design. But there are three basic differences in television:

1. *Both print and television have pictures, but only television has motion pictures.* A commercial is not limited to a split second in the life of a product or its user. The model is able to demonstrate the product rather than just pose with it. A single photograph can *suggest* a story. It can freeze an expression or emotion, leaving the viewer to fill in the drama that surrounds it. Television's motion pictures *tell* a story. Motion pictures can show the viewer exactly what leads up to the instant that the photograph freezes—and what happens afterwards. Very often there is more drama in the single photograph. The point is not that one medium is better, but that they are different.

---

3. Hanley Norins, *The Compleat Copywriter* (New York: McGraw-Hill, 1966): 149.

2. *Television communicates through an additional sense—the ear.* Television reaches the viewer through both sight and sound. The sound of the right voice can add emotion or credibility to copy. The printed page and the tone of voice of different typefaces carry their own kind of authority, but they cannot capture the deadpan charm of Frank Bartles or the smarmy insincerity of Joe Isuzu. And sound means more than voices. It includes the moods created with natural or artificial sound effects and, of course, music.

3. *Print ads tell their story at a glance; television commercials develop their story moment by moment.* A print ad is structured in *space*. Headline, illustration, and copy are arranged to direct the reader through each element, but the total impression is made immediately. The reader knows instantly whether or not he or she wants to read on. A commercial is structured in *time*. A commercial doles out its information and impressions bit by bit. It progresses from beginning to middle to end. It is only at the end of thirty or sixty seconds that viewers have their total impression.

Motion pictures, sound, sequential structure, and continuity—television does present unique creative challenges. Add to these the mind-boggling array of visual special effects and production techniques available today, and you can see why the best single piece of advice is to keep it simple.

There are three basic dimensions to every commercial execution that bear closer examination: basic approach/style/tone of voice; dramatic format; and production technique. These elements combine in seemingly endless combinations to produce the wide variety of commercial executions consumers have come to know and love. Here is how it all looks in chart form, building on the chart from chapter 3:

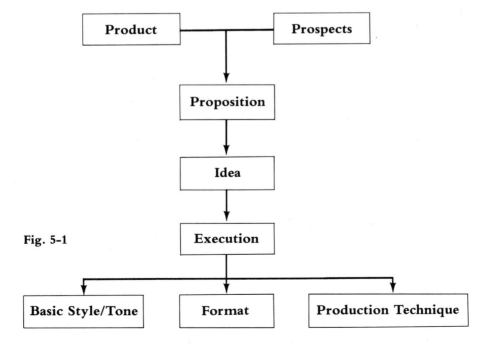

Fig. 5-1

The next two chapters will examine format (structure or method of presentation, such as testimonial, slice-of-life, vignettes) and production techniques (such as animation and special effects). Let us consider first the overall style or tone of voice of the execution.

Words, Images, and Symbols

Advertisements and products are loaded with symbolic meanings. People will read symbolic meanings into your communication whether you want them to or not. Communication consists of creating images in the mind of the reader, listener, or viewer. Various devices are used to recall certain experiences, impressions, and associations to bring them from the subconscious memory into the front of the mind. When people say, "I see what you mean," they mean they have a mental picture of what they think you are talking about. The job of the creative advertising person is to supply the ingredients, mixed and blended in just the right proportions, that will enable the consumer to construct (or reconstruct) a favorable visual image of the product. These ingredients are called symbols.

A symbol is something that stands for something else. H_2O stands for water. The word *water* stands for the thing water. What any given symbol stands for must be learned. Two human beings who wish to communicate with each other can, by agreement, make anything stand for anything. This symbolic process (by means of which we can arbitrarily attach a certain meaning to a certain thing) touches almost every aspect of our lives. As S.I. Hayakawa observed:

> Warriors, medicine men, policemen, doormen, telegraph boys, cardinals, and kings wear costumes that symbolize their occupations. Savages collect scalps, college students collect membership keys in honorary societies, to symbolize victories in their respective fields. There are few things that men do or want to do, possess or want to possess, that have not, in addition to their own mechanical or biological value, a symbolic value.[4]

Symbols become a kind of shorthand into which we condense our accumulated experiences. A symbol, be it visual or verbal, can stand for more than one thing. Its meaning depends largely on the context in which it appears. For example, when a red light appears at a street corner, it stands for (means) stop. A red light over an exit in a movie theater points the way to safety. And a red light takes on still another meaning when it appears over a doorway in the bawdy part of town. While the same symbol (the red light) can mean many different things, clearly each of these meanings must be learned. To someone from another culture that red light may mean nothing, regardless of its context.

The same is true of our verbal symbols—words. Words have no meaning in themselves. They only stand for something; they are not the thing

---

4. S.I. Hayakawa, *Language in Thought and Action* (New York: Harcourt, Brace, 1949): 25.

itself. To use the semanticist's classic analogy, a map is not the territory it represents. Words serve only to call to mind the things they symbolize. The word *cow* creates a mental image, but that image can be quite different for people in Wisconsin, Texas, and India. There are dairy cows and beef cows and sacred cows. There are cows of all sizes, shapes, and colors. But there is no "cow." Without getting further bogged down in semantics, remember this: Words are only symbols that stand for something else. The same word can mean different things to different people. And the meaning of words, like the meaning of red lights, can be changed by changing the context. When and how a word is used can affect the way a person interprets and responds to it. In conversation, the meaning or the context of words can be manipulated by an inflection or tone of voice. Sarcasm is a good example of how we can say one thing and mean something else.

In an advertisement, the spoken words of a salesperson are replaced by the printed words of a copywriter. The context changes. Much of the persuasiveness, feeling, sincerity, and urgency that can be conveyed by voice, gestures, and facial expressions is lost. Graphic design and a variety of type styles and sizes provide people with a visual context to help them understand the intended meaning of words.

When an announcer speaks a copywriter's words on the radio, the listener picks up clues from his voice and pacing and forms a visual image of the person talking. Music and sound effects contribute their own symbolism to provide a context. The sound of the words contributes to their meaning and to their ability to create a vivid visual image in the mind of the listener.

In the case of a television commercial, the power of visual communication is apparent. The props, the talent, and the setting all supply symbolic clues that help the viewer get the message. Everything in an advertisement carries symbolic meanings. And this symbolism has attracted a lot of attention, as this item from the *Wall Street Journal* suggests:

> In just a few years, Lever Brothers Co. built a $300 million fabric softener brand through the charms of a huggable teddy bear named Snuggle. Most marketers only dream of creating such a powerful advertising symbol, and Lever didn't want to do anything to jeopardize this little gold mine. It felt it needed to know more about why Snuggle was so successful and how the bear should be used in ads. So Snuggle got psychoanalyzed.
>
> Carol Moog, a psychologist turned advertising consultant, did an analysis of Snuggle that went way beyond cuddliness. "The bear is an ancient symbol of aggression, but when you create a teddy bear, you provide a softer, nurturant side to that aggression," she says. "As a symbol of tamed aggression, the teddy bear is the perfect image for a fabric softener that tames the rough texture of clothing."[5]

Not only the messages and the characters, but the products themselves are loaded with symbolic meaning. People view a particular product in

---

5. Ronald Alsop, "Agencies Scrutinize Their Ads for Psychological Symbolism," *The Wall Street Journal,* June 11, 1987.

terms of how it fits, meshes with, adds to, or reinforces the way in which they think of themselves (their visual image of themselves). Sidney J. Levy says:

> Modern goods are recognized as psychological things, as symbolic of personal attributes and goals, as symbolic of social patterns and strivings. In this sense, all commercial objects have a symbolic character, and making a purchase involves an assessment—implicit or explicit—of this symbolism, to decide whether or not it fits.[6]

Advertising history is rich with tales of the symbolic content of brands and the successes built upon them. None is more famous than Marlboro cigarettes, which changed its image from vaguely feminine to clearly masculine by changes in packaging graphics and advertising. Early Marlboro man ads featured men with tattoos, long associated with sailors and virility and mysterious pasts. Afterwards, the advertising settled on one personification of masculinity, the cowboy. A more urbane but no less mysterious use of masculine imagery was created by David Ogilvy for Hathaway shirts. The model with the eye patch identified, without words, the image of the man in the Hathaway shirt. A far different kind of symbolic imagery is packed into the Jolly Green Giant, a character that embodies the good earth, care, trust, and a bountiful harvest. Symbolism continues to play a role today.

> The J. Walter Thompson ad agency recently put a group of psychologists, sociologists and literary scholars to work studying symbols, or what it calls "icons." One result of the "iconology" is a Shick razor commercial that shows a bare-chested man shaving and a woman lovingly stroking his face and singing the Pointer Sisters' hit "Slow Hand."

> It may seem like just another sexy ad. But the images and music were carefully chosen after a study of ads for rival brands of razors. Gillette Co.'s razor ads use images of men as "lone wolves" in rugged, outdoor situations, says Nancy Posternak, a sociologist and senior vice president at J. Walter Thompson. "We wanted a different positioning and created an ad for Shick in which the underlying message is to be touched and loved and to be a lover."[7]

Brands and advertisements are composites of symbols, each of which may contribute some part to the total impression. By paying careful attention to the symbolic connotations of various objects, colors, and words, the art director and copywriter can give the viewer clues (or cues, as the psychologists prefer to call them) as to whether or not the ad or brand is for him or her.

For the art director, symbolic connotations influence the choice of sets, props, and staging. An automobile, for example, is supposedly neuter. Yet

---

6. Sidney J. Levy, "Symbols by Which We Buy," in *Dimensions of Consumer Behavior,* ed. James V. McNeal (New York: Appleton-Century-Crofts, 1965): 59.

7. *The Wall Street Journal,* June 11, 1987.

if it is pictured actively racing over rough terrain or climbing a steep mountain road, it takes on strong masculine connotations. If it is shown passively, parked in a meadow beside a quiet pond, it becomes more appealing to women. Open the doors in such a setting and it can suggest romance, by implying that the male and female passengers have parked and gone for a walk. A car pictured with a toy poodle or a Siamese cat on the front seat becomes a woman's car. A car shown with a boxer dog or a cougar becomes a man's car.

The people and settings pictured in ads and commercials inevitably suggest some social-class status. An ad for Cutty Sark whisky with the headline "Cutty and denim" and the tag line "Cutty Sark. You earned it," showed only the legs and hands of the male model. In an article about semiotics (signs and symbols), Jay C. Houghton observed:

> This Cutty Sark ad is particularly rich because of the symbols: denim, Rolex, argyle socks, the starched shirt, sweater, manicured nails and a collie. The way the glass is held, the way the dog is nuzzled, the way the legs are being crossed (masculine not feminine). These are all pieces of a symptotic jigsaw puzzle leading to the net impression of the user (and, therefore, the product) as one that is successful, confident, individualistic, if not eclectic (the argyle socks). [But, he reminds us, it all relies on the viewer recognizing and understanding the symbols.] The Cutty Sark ad won't communicate a thing unless the prospect knows that Rolex watches are prestigious and argyle socks are back in style.[8]

The prevailing assumption in advertising is that everyone aspires upward. So ads tend to favor people and settings that reflect a class level somewhat higher than that occupied by the average person. But the way a product is portrayed must be compatible with the life-style of the people who use it and with the way they use it. If you are advertising frozen macaroni and cheese, you would not show a woman from the country-club set serving it to guests at a fancy dinner party. Contemporary soft drink advertising has realistically glamorized a life-style within the reach of most young people (assuming they are healthy, attractive, and irrepressibly active).

Symbolic communication is a tantalizing notion. Communication operates on both a verbal and nonverbal level, both by design and by accident.

> "It's mind boggling to try to control all the non-verbal symbols in our creative work," says Elissa Moses, a research executive at the BBDO ad agency. "But if advertisers aren't aware of subtleties, they may inadvertently communicate the wrong message." Consider an ad for Grey Flannel cologne. The marketer was startled to learn from a psychologist that the ad showing only a man's back could be perceived as "rudely giving the consumer the cold shoulder."[9]

---

8. Jay C. Houghton, "Semiotics on the Assembly Line," *Advertising Age* (March 16, 1987): 18.

9. *The Wall Street Journal,* June 11, 1987.

Both the words you use and the pictures that accompany them contribute to the formation of an image in the mind of the person with whom you are communicating. Everything about the product contributes to its image—its name, its package, its price, its quality, its advertising. These images or consumer perceptions can change with time and with changes in the competitive environment. Yesterday's progressive leader may be today's old-fashioned has-been. Everything that goes into a commercial for product is also going to contribute to this image or personality. You cannot simply say, "I don't care about image, I just want to sell the thing," because the commercial that just tries to sell also creates an image, whether it wants to or not.

A Variety of Styles

What should be the style of your commercial? Should it be hard sell or soft sell? (Remember the Rosser Reeves-Pierre Martineau debate from chapter 2?) Should it be rational or emotional? Serious or humorous? Realistic or exaggerated? The answer is an unequivocable "it all depends." It all depends upon your product and your audience. It all depends upon the nature of the message you are trying to communicate. It all depends upon the kind of brand character or personality you wish to project. No particular style is always right or always wrong. Nor is one necessarily exclusive of the others. You can be very serious, rational, and very emotional in the same commercial. (In a commercial for Fleischmann's margarine, for example, a thirty-year-old man talks calmly to camera about how his recent heart attack changed his eating habits.) You can provide rational information in an emotional situation. Humor can make a serious point. But whatever the style or tonality is, it makes an important contribution to the execution. Sometimes, as in the case of products that fill emotional needs, emotion becomes more than a tone or style, it becomes the reason to purchase. Let's consider some options.

Rational

Consumers want information from commercials. Just ask them, that is what they will tell you. And isn't that the basic function that advertising serves in our economy—to provide information about products so that rational consumers can make informed buying decisions based on real product differences? True, but . . . Sometimes there is not much real information about the product. Sometimes the products are pretty much the same. And sometimes consumers are not all that rational.

> One does not have to read the advertising trade literature very long to find that consumers are characterized as rational at one time, impulsive at another; individualist and then again conformist and status-conscious; skeptical about advertising—and then relatively gullible;

seekers of novelty and also followers of tradition; interested in cost and then again willing to overlook cost for status or quality.[10]

Despite the fact that consumers are not always rational and not always interested in getting as much information as they say they always want, there may be times when the best creative approach is straightforward and informative. If nothing else, it may be a way to separate your brand from the competition. To separate from the jokes, music, barrooms, and parties of beer advertising, Coors chose to put Mark Harmon in quiet outdoor settings talking about the reasons why "Coors is the one." In one commercial he said, "It's the product people love. . . . Not the hoopla. You think about it. . . . How many products can you say that about?" (How many indeed?)

A logical, matter-of-fact presentation of what your product does or why the consumer should buy it may be very disarming or impactive. Such a presentation assumes, however, that the message you deliver so sincerely is interesting, relevant, newsworthy, or important. If it is, you do not always need a lot of "hoopla." Leo Burnett quoted Ralph Waldo Emerson: "Nothing astonishes men as much as common sense and plain dealing."

Unfortunately, there seems to be an inverse relationship between inherent drama of the product message and the whipped-up drama of the execution. The less important the message, the wilder the approach. The less truly newsworthy the product, the louder the commercial screams, "New!" The hope is that with all the razzle-dazzle no one will notice that the promise is a little threadbare.

The more interesting the message, the more direct can be the approach. The more functional the product, the more rational can be the argument to buy it. Consumers want to know more about how a dishwasher works than how a soft drink is made. (Not a lot more, but some.)

One danger of striving for an informational style is that you may confuse quantity of information with quality of information. This often results in loading down the commercial with secondary and tertiary support points. No matter what consumers may tell you in focus groups or interviews about their thirst for product information and reasons-why for every promise or claim, there is a limit to the amount of information they can absorb from any single commercial. It is far better to dramatize one important piece of information than to try to cram in two or three little bits and hope that it all adds up to something.

Straightforward, rational advertising should not be taken as a license to be dull. If anything, simple, direct presentations require more careful writing, casting, and direction than do all-singing, all-dancing commercials. The idea has no place to hide. The presenter must be sincere, convincing, and appropriate. (The choice of Mark Harmon and the choice of the settings say as much to potential Coors drinkers as the copy.) The demonstration must be simple and compelling. (A commercial for Corning's heat-resistant Vision saucepans, for example, made its selling point by putting a

---

10. Michael Schudson, *Advertising, The Uneasy Persuasion* (New York: Basic Books, 1986): 64–65.

conventional saucepan into the Vision pan and cooking it until the conventional pan melted out of shape and could be poured from the undamaged Vision pan.)

Emotional

> MAN IN AN ENGLISH PUB: If I was in charge of the advertising for Watneys, I'd tell everyone that Watneys Pale was cool, crisp ale, and if you drank it, lovely ladies in diaphanous nighties would come into your room and dance about. Why, I bet men would flock to Watneys. And if you asked them why they drank it, they'd say, "because Watneys Pale is cool, crisp ale." But that wouldn't be the reason at all.

That humorous British commercial for Watneys Pale Ale (paraphrased from distant memory) recognizes that advertising operates on more than one level, that a brand decision may be based on both rational and emotional reasons, and that the reasons people say they buy a product may not be the real or only reasons.

Rational, informational advertising is fine if you have real (relevant) product information that the consumer will process rationally and logically and conclude, "This product is for me." But consumers react as often (more often?) from feelings and emotions as from logic. Very often you are dealing with everyday, low-risk, undifferentiated products where information is less important than the feelings and emotions that surround the brand. This calls for an emotional style of advertising.

In its review of the best commercials of 1986, *Advertising Age* noticed an increasing use of emotional appeals.

> In the forefront of those spots appealing to emotion was E. & J. Gallo Winery's "The Wedding," evoking warmth and nostalgia with various shots of weddings drenched in sunshine and sentiment. Music by Vangelis added to the mood.

> Chevrolet's "Heartbeat of America" stirred pride and good feelings with a staccato beat and quick-cut views of Americans at work and play across the land, sometimes with a Chevy in view, as the heartbeat tempo blended with the music.

> Burger King's "Town Anthem" offered similar appeal with a succession of views of small-town America, equating the flavor of backyard barbecues with Burger King.[11]

Carol Foley, a research director at Leo Burnett has taken a close look at the role emotions play in people's brand decisions and her conclusions form the basis of the discussion that follows.

We generally think about products as being useful to fulfill various needs and to provide various benefits. Some of those needs and benefits are

---

11. Merle Kingman, "Emotion Imbues TV's Best Spots," *Advertising Age* (March 22, 1987): 35.

thought of as primarily functional, rational, or utilitarian; some are emotional. On the functional side, for example, you brush your teeth in order to prevent tooth decay. You eat cereal in order to have enough fiber in your diet. You purchase homeowner's insurance in order to protect yourself against disasters. (Of course, there are also emotional needs and benefits attached to the use of these products. By brushing your teeth you freshen your breath. This makes you feel more appealing to others. By eating cereal you contribute to your own sense of being healthy. This makes you feel energetic and good about yourself. Having homeowner's insurance may make you feel like a responsible person who watches out for your family's best interests. However, the emotional benefits are less focal than the more compelling functional reasons for using these products.)

In other cases, the needs and benefits associated with product consumption may be primarily emotional. For example, some women wear perfume in order to feel attractive and alluring. Some people eat ice cream in order to feel comforted. Some play their stereos in order to feel "high."

Functional and emotional benefits in product categories are not mutually exclusive. Cars are a good example. On the one hand, they are exceptionally functional. You use them to get from point A to point B. For many people, a car would be very difficult, if not impossible, to live without. But getting there is half the fun. The experience of driving can also be highly emotionally charged. (Saab recognized this when they ran a two-page spread with long copy and explanatory diagrams on one page and a full-color photo of a red Saab splashing through water on the other. The headline: "21 logical reasons to buy a Saab. One emotional reason.")

Thus you have some products whose benefits are primarily functional, some primarily emotional, and some both.

The reasons for using perfume are overwhelmingly emotional. As a result, users will be more responsive to advertising that recognizes this. Conversely, if consumers see little beyond the immediate functionality in the use of their toaster oven, they may not respond to a strategy that ignores these functional motives. This is not to say that advertising for functional products should be devoid of emotion—just that emotion may play a different role in such cases.

When the primary reasons for using products are to attain emotional gratification, the kinds of emotions experienced are by definition positive ones. They frequently have to do with feeling good about yourself or with feeling that you look good in the eyes of others.

As the reason for using products becomes increasingly functional, the emotions associated with usage are not only less present, they are frequently less positive. (You have different feelings when you eat ice cream than you do when you eat spinach.)

Finally, there are a number of highly functional categories in which the emotions associated with product usage are negative. Cleaning products, for example, are frequently used in the context of unpleasant situations. Even more potent are the negative emotions associated with life insurance and air travel.

Not every functionally oriented product experience has negative emotions associated with it. Using antifreeze probably does not generate much feeling one way or the other. Neither do products such as batteries or toaster ovens. (Still, GE's emotion-laden campaign, "We bring good things to life," added an important element to emotionally empty products like hair dryers and coffee makers.)

What this all adds up to is that people strive to experience pleasant emotions and to minimize unpleasant ones. Extending this concept to product use suggests that consumers, when confronted with potentially emotionless or negatively charged product experiences, will be responsive to things that can improve them. Advertising, which through its emotional content can make the product experience "feel better," is likely to have a strong leg up.

The consumption of products whose principal benefits are emotional has been referred to as hedonic consumption. Its advocates suggest that just as we seek positive emotional experiences from life in general, so too do we seek positive emotional experiences from using products. Consumers look to products not only to fulfill functional needs, but also to enhance their emotional well-being. In certain product categories emotional desires dominate utilitarian motives, but in all categories there is at least some emotional component. In other words, there is always a desire for the product experience to be as emotionally positive as possible.

This emotional fulfillment is not just viewed as a nice extra or side benefit of product use. Rather, the favorable emotional aspects of product use are thought to be vital to emotional well-being.

When consumers use products to fulfill emotional needs, products take on symbolic meanings, and the product usage experience itself takes on imaginary or fantasy dimensions. The greater the degree of hedonism, the greater the role that symbolic and fantasy elements play in the purchase decision. There was little but symbolic meaning in this recent commercial for Chanel No. 5:

> A pool, large and magical. The shadow of a plane skims across its surface. A woman in a bathing suit reclines at its edge, waiting. The thin figure of a man appears on the other side. He dives in, materializing near her. We do not see her reaction. They never touch. There is a suspension of time. Music tingles like wind chimes from another world. A man's voice softly asks us to "Share the fantasy."[12]

Rosser Reeves, where are you?

You would expect emotional advertising for products whose reason for being is emotional (such as perfume). But there are also implications for other product categories. Few of the advertised brands in functional categories have important substantive advantages over competing brands. But hedonic consumption implies that given functional parity, the brand that manages to associate itself with a more positive consumption experience will be perceived as superior. A brand might accomplish this in a number of ways:

- by dramatizing functional differences in ways that make them seem more compelling;

- by developing a favorable, category-appropriate brand image;

---

12.   Theodore Halaki, "Reflections on a New Wave," *Advertising Age* (March 8, 1982): M-27.

- by making the brand likeable;
- by portraying the emotional benefits of using the product;
- by idealizing the product experience;
- by alleviating negative emotions associated with using the brand;
- by creating advertising that is involving, entertaining, and likeable.

If you think about it, when we watch television we are involved in the consumption of a hedonic category. We generally view TV for the purpose of seeking emotional reward. We do not watch television to be irritated or bored. We hope to be enlightened or entertained. Commercials happen to appear in the context of this hedonically oriented viewing situation. As a result, you could hypothesize several things:

- Ads that are hedonically rewarding will be better attended to, better received, and better remembered.

- Conversely, ads that are unengaging, overly informational, or hard to follow will be screened out because they lack emotional reward.

- Ads that are hedonically rewarding may potentially affect a transfer of this feeling to the brand itself. The ad itself functions as a symbol for the product. If it is emotionally rewarding, then perhaps so will be the consumption of the brand.

The role of emotion in advertising is obviously bigger than just style or tone or voice. At its roots are some basic questions about how advertising works and what causes people to choose one brand over another. It plays a part in any commercial, whether its tone be rational, serious, humorous, exaggerated, or determinedly emotional. Even if you cannot buy into such concepts as hedonic consumption, it is hard to imagine you would be making a mistake by creating advertising that stirred positive feelings and rewarded the viewer for watching.

Serious

Advertising, to an advertiser, is serious business. There is a lot at stake. The last thing proud manufacturers would want to suggest to consumers is that their products should be taken lightly. This seems to be especially true when the products involved are those which solve "serious" consumer problems, such as headache pills, diarrhea medicine, floor wax, or denture cleaners.

A serious solution to a serious problem deserves a serious tonality. If you have a product that cures the common cold, eliminates tooth decay, or represents a breakthrough in the prevention of cancer, people would be surprised if you came on the air and joked about it. Lifestyles condoms won a Bronze Lion at Cannes in 1987 with a simple, tight-framed, one-take commercial of a young woman talking to camera. "I never thought having an intimate relationship would make me afraid." Her subject is AIDS. She says the surgeon general has recommended the use of condoms and the ones she uses are Lifestyles. "I'd do a lot for love," she says, "but I'm not ready to die for it."

But before your advertising turns too deadly serious, ask yourself two questions: How serious is the problem, really? And how significant is your solution? If the problem falls into the category of "ring-around-the-collar," you may come off silly by trying to treat it too seriously. Consumers are always glad to hear about new and improved products, but a somber presenter talking in grave tones about a razor that gives you a closer shave may not bring the audience to the edge of its chairs.

There are many serious problems, from cancer to gum disease, to which products can make positive contributions. But unless your brand is a wonder drug, its solution likely falls in the category of "it couldn't hurt." There have been a lot of commercials lately looking very serious and concerned about our health and nutrition. They offer products high in fiber or low in calories or cholesterol, products made with natural or pure ingredients and free of salt or sugar or preservatives. This is all a step in the right direction (toward the way things used to be before people started adding the bad stuff). But switching to one of these products will not save or prolong your life. And advertising that seriously suggests it may well elicit a negative "Oh, come on. . . . !" reaction. ("Oh, come on. . . . Eating bran flakes will prevent cancer?") There is certainly nothing wrong with proudly promoting the health benefits of your product. But the tone should be in line with the benefits.

Probably no category of advertising has been so consistently serious as public service advertising. And rightly so, for it deals with serious issues and problems. Stopping drugs. Saving lives. Curing diseases. Preventing accidents. This can be strong stuff. (The power of the antismoking commercials probably hastened the exit of cigarette advertising from television.) Certainly the sobering images of starving children or tortured drug users or battered accident victims can grab people and impress upon them the seriousness of these problems. But people do not like to be reminded of unpleasantness, especially between episodes of "The Cosby Show" and "Family Ties." (They are hedonic consumers, remember?) So if you get too serious, too scary, too unpleasant, the viewer may tune you out. (Recent seat belt advertising using a couple of funny crash dummies suggests there is another way to make a serious point.)

Humorous

Over the years, such advertising giants as David Ogilvy, Fairfax Cone, and Rosser Reeves have cautioned against the use of humor in advertising. It was Rosser Reeves who said, "*Nobody* ever bought anything from a clown. . . . Salesmanship is a form of teaching. I do not believe that the great salesmen sing, dance, and play golden flutes."[13] And Fairfax Cone took issue with the widely admired "Disadvantages" campaign for Benson & Hedges when he said, "When it is suggested that I should opt for a cigaret that is uncomfortably long, so long, indeed, that it is caricatured as being snipped off by closing elevator doors, or snuffed out by a falling pizza, I

---

13.   "The Man from Iron City," *The New Yorker* (September 27, 1969): 92.

think the alternative is even less than desirable. In fact, I think it is damned foolishness. By the only possible inference it makes a joke of advertising."[14]

Viewers, on the other hand, like humorous commercials. Video Storyboard Tests, which runs a popularity poll on commercials, finds that many funny, entertaining commercials stick in people's minds. "If a commercial is funny or clever, I always watch, no matter what I'm doing," says one man polled by VST. "Laughing makes me feel good."[15] The success of campaigns like Federal Express, Miller Lite, and Bartles & Jaymes testifies to the potential of humor.

Not even the detractors of humor would rule it out entirely. (Fairfax Cone: "I should make it clear that I am not advocating that advertising be devoid of humor. Far from it.")[16] They are usually saying, and rightly so, that advertisers should not misuse humor. There is nothing funny about a commercial that entertains the viewer but fails to move the product.

Humor is being misused if it is used to gloss over a weak selling idea. Many copywriters apparently subscribe to a theory that if their tongue is in their cheek no one will notice that it is forked. If a product claim is too puffy to be palatable, the easy way out is to poke a little fun at it, chuckle along with the viewer, then try to salvage the sale with an "all kidding aside. . . ."

There are three ways that humor can turn around and bite the hands that feed it: by making fun of the product, by making fun of the consumer, or by making fun of advertising in general. Satirist Stan Freberg observed, "I never make fun of the product. I have fun with the product."[17] Used properly, humor can convey a sense of self-confidence for the advertiser. Freberg again: "If a company does a funny spot, it's obviously not taking itself too seriously, right? It must have a good product or else it couldn't afford to kid around."[18] The advertising for Volkswagen's Beetle, beginning with the famous "Lemon" ad, is a classic example of having fun with the product while making very strong sales points. Just as you would not want to ridicule your product, neither should you make your consumer appear stupid or foolish. The famous "Where's the Beef?" commercial for Wendy's treads a delicate line. "While the ad intended only to poke fun at the size of the burgers served by other fast-food chains," noted the *Wall Street Journal,* "senior citizen groups complained that the portrayal of the older woman is demeaning because it makes her seem senile and infirm."[19] Finally, there are humorous commercials that spoof the techniques of advertising (a very tempting target). Barry Day, vice-chairman of McCann-Erickson Worldwide, was unsettled by one of the funniest of the genre.

---

14. Fairfax Cone, "Advertising Is No Joke. . . ," *Advertising Age* (December 15, 1969): 49.

15. Kim Foltz, "Entertainment: That's What People Want," *Adweek,* April 7, 1986.

16. *Advertising Age* (December 15, 1969): 49.

17. Cary Bayer, "A Laugh a Minute," *Madison Avenue* (January 1984): 104.

18. Bayer, 104.

19. John Koten, "After Serious '70s, Advertisers Are Going for Laughs Again," *The Wall Street Journal,* February 23, 1984.

One of the most talked-about campaigns running right now is for Isuzu cars. In it, a quintessentially oleaginous presenter expounds the virtues of the import: "It gets 94 miles per gallon in the city, 112 on the highway . . . top speed is 300 mph. If you come in tomorrow, you'll get a free house. You have my word on it." Captions contradict him: ("He's lying. . . .") and give the facts, which are impressive enough in all conscience. It's very funny. It takes every bad Presenter commercial you've ever seen and pushes it over the edge, which is where it belongs. . . .

But isn't it also just a little worrying? We may be laughing *with* the commercial, but aren't we laughing *at* the process of commercial making, lumping the good in with the bad and the ugly?[20]

There is nothing wrong with humor. It is just a little dangerous and must be handled carefully. The humor must grow out of the product and must contribute to the communication of the selling idea, not simply to the memorability of the commercial. The humor must be relevant. Humor is part of life and humor that reflects the human condition will add to the emotional reward of the advertising.

The humor must be understood. The audience has to be in on the joke. Copywriters must write for the audience and not for themselves.

Finally, humor has to be funny. Everybody has suffered through a good joke poorly told. It is not much fun. If it is in bad taste, too, it can become downright embarrassing. Because humor is so subjective, the margin for error is great. Needless to say, the humorous commercial must be carefully written, cast, and directed.

So if the joke fits, wear it. Consumers enjoy a little laugh, as long as it is not at themselves. Most of the products and propositions put to viewers in television commercials are not extremely serious. Most will stand up well under some gentle, relevant humor. But copywriters should not set out to make a funny commercial. They should set out to tell the viewers something about the product that will move them to try it. If it comes out funny, fine. Leo Burnett wrote in a memorandum to his agency in 1969: "As I see it, humor, properly used, in advertising certain products, provides what a friend of mine once called 'amicable acceptance.'" A consumer put it this way: "If an ad makes me feel good, then I feel good about the product and I want to use it."

Realistic

Most advertisers would tell you they would like their commercials to ring true and realistically portray the product and its users. But advertising has tended to be more flattering and idealized than realistic. The 1980s, however, has seen realism take on the look of a whole new genre. Gone is phony slice-of-life dialogue and the stiff, stilted camera work of the past. Instead we have seen commercials with a gritty, documentary look—"real life/real answers" for John Hancock; the slick, trendy corporate world of Apple

---

20. Barry Day, "Split-Level Communications," *Advertising Age* (March 23, 1987): 18.

computers; the "nervous camera," cinema vérité look for Miller Draft beer, Maxwell House ("It's coffee made our way"), and AT&T small business systems; the patriotic life-style vignettes of Chevy's "Heartbeat of America"; and the laid-back documentary look of urban youth in Levi's 501 Blues.

> Although there's some jerky camera work here (Levi's 501), it isn't extreme. Mostly, he's (director Leslie Dektor) exploring the visual limits of scenes in which very little is happening. That makes for an underlying restlessness, a truth about youth that's compelling. . . . The music is great and always unexpected, never shrunk-to-fit to the images.[21]

Even though the images of this new school of reality advertising tend to be carefully preplanned and staged, they convey the feeling that the viewer is eavesdropping (visually) on real people just being themselves. Some of the surface mannerisms will likely fade from favor, but it is difficult to imagine that advertising will ever turn its back on realism. Commercials will always seek to make contact with its audience-of-the-moment. They will always seek to create empathy, to recognize and portray people the way they really are (or would like to be) so that consumers can see themselves in the advertising using the product.

Realism is not just a matter of *look* (although the casting of real, believable, imperfect people instead of plastic perfect models is a must). It has to *sound* real. The music has to be appropriate. The dialogue has to be natural and believable—the way people really talk. Reactions to the pleasures of the product have to be reasonable. (People taking a bite of food do not usually react by looking at the food and smiling with rapture.) "The woman who cried out in torment of equal intensity over the loss of a suitor, her inability to make a decent cup of coffee, or the unpleasantness of bathroom odors, has become a fixture in the folklore of television advertising."[22]

Even if you do not set out to create a documentary style of realism around the entire commercial, you should still be sensitive to the little grace notes of realism that can contribute to the overall believability of the spot—an appropriate phrase, expression, or behavior; accurate details in wardrobe, sets, and props.

Exaggerated

If you have trouble recalling commercials that you would characterize as realistic, you should have no problem coming up with commercials that resort to exaggeration. From exaggerated claims ("The best. . . ," "Whiter than white") to exaggerated visuals (from the Ajax White Knight riding through neighborhoods zapping clothes clean with his lance, to the image of Manhattan Island landing in England for British Airways), advertising and exaggeration have marched through time hand in hand.

---

21. Barbara Lyppert, "Adweek Critique," *Adweek* (August 10, 1987): 21.

22. *Advertising Age* (December 15, 1969): 49.

Exaggeration in commercials is the stepchild of advertising's historic tendency to hyperbole and modern pressure for memorability. As it became harder and harder to attract and hold the attention of the viewing public, the creators of advertising responded by trying harder and harder. This quest to startle and to produce breakthroughs was aided and abetted by the growing capability of film technicians to create any spectacular special effect that ad people could dream up (and afford). Some of the results of this collaboration have been sensational, some have been silly. The success of exaggeration depends largely on how real the unreality is.

A *Time* essay on exaggeration in political rhetoric observed:

> Sometimes the artful exaggeration is a way of evoking, of discovering, an essential truth lying below the prosaic surface of things.[23]

For example, an essential truth about going to a bank (as many consumers perceive it) is that banks have become overly automated and impersonal. The U.K.'s Barclays Bank created a futuristic exaggeration of this truth in a megabudget commercial directed by Ridley Scott. In it, a consumer comes into a space-age bank to ask about a business loan. He gets the computerized runaround. Frisked by Darth Vader look-alikes, barked at by hyper robots, the customer finally reaches a human manager—or so he thinks. But when the manager swivels in his chair, he reveals an electric plug in his head. The customer screams in frustration, "I just want to talk to someone," and rips out the plug. Smoke clears to show the customer in an uncluttered bank office where he is greeted by a friendly (human) loan officer. He is at Barclays this time. The exaggeration is based on real feelings of frustration, and the point is made that the customer will not feel that way at Barclays.

The important thing to remember about exaggeration is that the approach need not be literally believable *so long as the claim itself is believable*. The Ajax White Knight was not a believable character, but the claim, "Stronger than dirt," was believable.

Exaggeration can take many forms in commercials. You can exaggerate the negative results of not using the product or of using a competitor's product (the Federal Express commercials in which the packages never arrive on time, causing disgrace and embarrassment for whoever shipped them incorrectly). You can use exaggerated characters (the lying presenter for Isuzu or the computer-generated Max Headroom for Coke). You can exaggerate the situation in which the product is used (Pepsi's *Top Gun* spoof in which a hot-dogging jet fighter pilot flies upside down in order to pour his Diet Pepsi). You can exaggerate the performance of the product. (A British commercial for Vauxhall Nova showed how the car "makes light of heavy traffic" by having it drive on top of the hoods and trunks of gridlocked traffic.) You can exaggerate the emotional experiences associated with using the product (the fantasies of Chanel No. 5). You can exaggerate the lengths people will go to use the product. (Michael J. Fox goes down his apartment fire escape in the rain to get a Diet Pepsi for the beautiful blonde next door.)

Whatever is exaggerated, however, should dramatize the idea of the commercial. It should make the claim important and memorable. Like

---

23. "A World of Exaggeration," *Time* (December 14, 1981): 102.

humor, exaggeration can be easily misused. If it insults or offends the viewers' taste of intelligence, the long-term negative effects may outweigh any short-term gains in memorability. If it calls attention only to itself and not to the product message, it will not even have any short-term benefits.

Summary: The Chart Grows

In good commercials, the idea and the execution are difficult to isolate. What you say and how you say it become so interwoven that the result is greater than the sum of its parts. The idea/execution is more than just words, more than just pictures, more than just format, more than just production techniques, more than just style. It is all the things you say and show explicitly and all the things you suggest symbolically.

One ingredient is the basic style or tone of voice, several options of which can now be added to the chart of what goes into a commercial:

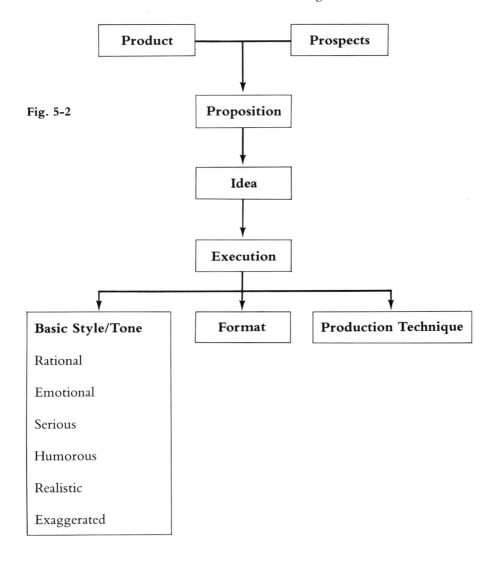

Fig. 5-2

Chapter 6

A Catalog of Formats
Execution II

An Introduction to Formats:
Cliché or Clio?

A commercial for a brand of color television sets begins with a close-up of a girl's face that splits in half vertically. One half of the screen remains clear while the Brand X half breaks up into common types of interference. A Volkswagen commercial begins with a shot of two suburban houses. The owner of one house pulls up in his brand new $3,000 car (it is a very old commercial). Then he looks on while a series of deliverymen wheel major appliances into his neighbor's house. The neighbor then drives up in his brand new Volkswagen, bought with the money left over from his $3,000 after buying all the appliances. In a third commercial, two men in business suits splash on competing brands of after-shave lotion, then set out on a walk across the desert to demonstrate which is the more refreshing and longer-lasting. The man with Brand X lotion collapses into the sand while the winner walks on, cool and unruffled.

These three commercials differ in their basic approach (from serious to humorous to exaggerated) but are similar in their format. Each uses a form of side-by-side comparison demonstration. So after the selling idea has been determined (eliminates TV interference, costs less than a typical car, keeps you refreshed longer), and with a basic style or tonality in mind, the next step is to come up with a method of visualizing and presenting the idea. Next you need a *format*.

The notion of a format is an anathema to the creative person because it suggests the tried and true method of the past. If there have been so many commercials made a certain way that it constitutes a category or format, how can any commercial that follows such a pattern be truly creative? "I'm not going to do slice-of-life. It's been done." But it is not the format you use but how you use it that makes the execution creative. Well-written dialogue believably acted by appropriately cast talent can lift a cliché format into award-winning advertising. Nobody seemed to mind that the John Hancock "real life/real answers" campaign that won the gold at Cannes was rooted in good ol' slice-of-life. The creative challenge is not to find ways to avoid using the structures and formats of the past. The challenge is to seek out ways to use them freshly and relevantly. There is nothing inherently dull about a format. But because the patterns tend to be familiar, the burden will be on what you say and how you say it to keep any format from sinking into boredom.

Commercial formats are limitless in variation, but most could be squeezed into the following general categories.

Product Presentation

Harry McMahan labeled this category "product as hero." The commercials rely on the inherent drama of the product and allow it to take center stage.

By focusing on the product, a commercial can communicate how the product works and exactly what it does with a minimum of distraction. Such a commercial makes the product, instead of the format, an interesting and exciting thing to watch and remember. Since such executions assume that the product story will be interesting to viewers without embellishment, it is necessary that what is shown translates into a consumer benefit and is not just a manufacturer rhapsodizing about a product. The idea that the product illustrates, the problem it solves, is critical; it must relate to the reason consumers buy the product and to the way they use it. Since the visual of such a presentation tends to be open-ended, the copy can complete the story and tell the viewer the significance of what is being shown. For example, a commercial for Crayola crayons simply showed children's hands coloring and making pictures with the product. The copy supplied the impact: "Crayola crayons: they work on brains, not batteries."

In a commercial for the Honda Accord the camera visually caresses the car while the announcer quotes automotive magazines praising its performance. The little touch that lifts it from the ordinary is when the announcer says it's all enough to make one blush—and the tail lights glow red.

Many food products demonstrate their appetite appeal by simply focusing on how good they look. The sight of chocolate sauce dripping down ice cream, fruit bubbling in a hot pie, or lobster dipping into melted butter can make for powerful TV. Let the visual trigger the taste buds.

This "close-up-look-at-the-product" style of commercial, especially for food products, is often referred to as *tabletop*. (And for good reason, since the products are filmed set up on top of a table.) Many tabletop commercials also qualify for the next category of commercial formats—demonstrations.

Demonstration

Demonstration and television—the two were made for each other. Seeing is believing, as the old saying goes. And a good demonstration of meaningful selling points imparts believability to a commercial. If the product has a competitive difference, and if this difference is a benefit to the consumer, then the commercial should strive to visually demonstrate this.

Memorex demonstrated its tape cassettes' recording fidelity by showing a singer shattering a glass with a high note and then, by playing back the tape recording of her voice, breaking another glass. The idea: "Memorex—reproduction so true it can shatter glass" ("Is it live or is it Memorex?"). Vision saucepans demonstrated how heat resistant their product was by "cooking" a competitor's pan in theirs. Sears demonstrated the starting ability of its power mowers by having an announcer start them on live television. They proved it was live by airing the commercials during breaks in a basketball game and having the announcer repeat the score of the game at that moment. (And the spots gained further believability when the mower failed to start once on the first try.)

Hank Seiden listed the following criteria for good demonstration:

1. It must be interesting, exciting, or dramatic.

2. It must be relevant to the point you want to make.

3. It must prove the point conclusively.

4. It must be uncontrived in staging.

5. It must be simple to follow and understand.

6. It should be preemptive.

7. Most important, it must be believable beyond a shadow of a doubt.[1]

What are the characteristics of a bad demonstration? First, irrelevance. It does nobody any good to dramatically demonstrate something about the product that makes no difference to the consumer or does not really prove superiority. Second, deceptiveness—a demonstration should be everything it appears to be and should prove the point it is making. Advertisers have often run afoul of the government watchdogs in the gray area of demonstrations.

The FTC cited a commercial which showed that one brand of deodorant sprayed on an eyeglass lens was clear while the other spray was white and thick. The FTC held that this did not constitute evidence of being a superior antiperspirant. Thanks in part to the legal documentation required, cases of out-and-out deceptive demonstrations are rare these days. Still, the viewer remains skeptical. No amount of substantiating documentation will be of much solace to advertisers who fail to make their demonstrations convincing and believable. Here are some of the basic varieties of demonstrations.

---

1. *Madison Avenue* (November 1971): 26.

Explanatory (Product in Use)

This is what the product does and this is how it works. Remember the Veg-o-matic? ("It slices, it dices . . .") and the introductory commercials for Polaroid camera and Xerox copiers? This format is similar in spirit to product presentation but often has the added dimension of a real in-use situation. But most often this format is characterized by its simplicity. A brand of paper towels demonstrated its absorbency by pouring liquids into a roll of towels. A Black & Decker Air Station is shown filling (pun intended) a variety of needs from soccer balls to bicycle tires. And to demonstrate how well Cheer detergent cleans in cold water a man puts a dirty napkin into a cocktail shaker with some Cheer and ice and it comes out clean.

Side-by-Side (Comparative)

This format shows how the product performs compared to competition. As the examples cited earlier indicate, it can utilize a variety of approaches, from serious to silly. Teflon treated half a skillet, then showed how the Teflon side was easier to clean after cooking. Duracell batteries pitted battery-powered toys, one with Brand X, one with Duracell, against either other to demonstrate how the Duracell toy outlasted the other. ScotTissue once showed a race in which two rolls unfurled along the track of a stadium. The crowd roared as Brand X ran out, demonstrating that ScotTissue

Courtesy of Duracell U.S.A., Bethel, CT ©Duracell Inc.

had more sheets per roll. And no one who ever saw them will ever forget those little B's racing A's to the headache.

Before-After

"See this dirty stain? Watch while we add our product. . . . There, the stain is gone!" This format demonstrates the happy results of using the product. It is a favorite of beauty products. Grecian Formula has demonstrated how much younger men look after they use the product to get rid of their gray hair. Diet pills and programs delight in showing their users before and after weight loss.

Torture Test

Subjecting the product to an exaggerated demonstration of strength or performance has long been a favorite. In the early days of TV, John Cameron Swayze watched as a diver plunged from the cliffs of Acapulco to prove that his Timex watch would "take a licking and come up ticking." A Bic pen was attached to the heel of an ice skater, dragged around the rink, then stuck into an open flame, and still "writes first time every time." Samsonite subjected its soft-sided luggage to rigorous testing by a seemingly mild-mannered shopper who winds up rolling the suitcase through the store's plate glass window.

A torture test need not be torture. Sometimes you need to demonstrate gentleness, not strength. A Canadian commercial for Q-Tips cotton swabs showed a Q-Tip wiping dust off a single red rose, petal by petal.

If the product can live up to it, a torture test demonstration can make its point very memorable. But what is being demonstrated must be relevant to the viewer. When all the exaggeration is stripped away, what does the demonstration say about how the product will fit into the consumer's life and better solve everyday problems. And remember that viewers are skeptical. If the test is too torturous it can come off as phony, even though it is real.

Demonstrator faith

One variation of the torture test is to demonstrate how much faith the presenter puts in the product. In a British commercial for bulletproof glass, a businessman stands in a limbo set talking to camera while cutaways show a second man assembling a high-powered rifle. The camera looks through the rifle sights at the presenter. Cut back as a glass screen shatters inches from the presenter's head. He winces, then smiles. Point made. He trusts that bullet-resistant glass. In a commercial from Brazil, four demonstrators show their faith that the Volkswagen Passat cars have eliminated the problem of bad starting. Four cars are parked, engines off, on railroad tracks. As an express train comes barreling into view, the men get into the cars. We see four keys turning. Four engines spark first time. The cars drive off the tracks before the train thunders past. A recent U.S. Volkswagen commercial showed confident German engineers lined up in a circle while the car drove in circles. With each lap they stepped closer, tightening the circle to demonstrate the tight turning radius of the Volkswagen.

Samsonite Corporation, Denver CO

Problems and Solutions

It has been charged that some commercials for headache pills are so loud and obnoxious that they cause the pains they promise to cure. Commercials may not cause problems, but they can identify and dramatize them. Copywriters seek to express the problem in a distinct, memorable way so that only their product will be associated with the solution. In doing so, they come up with new names for old problems. There was bad breath before there was "halitosis" or "medicine breath"; there were dirty collars before there was "ring-around-the-collar"; upset stomachs before "the blahs"; whiskers before "five o'clock shadow" or "the nubs."

One problem with "problems" is that they may be more memorable than the solutions. The challenge is not only to make the problem unique, but to hook up your product so that it is *the* solution. Gillette made its Dry Look hair spray the solution for "problem" slicked-down hairstyles labeled "wet heads."

Here are some variations of formats that focus on problems and solutions:

Show the Problem/Need

A commercial can present the problem in many ways. It can highlight some of the things that cause the problem (Era liquid detergent showed dramatic food spills that cause stains that Era gets out.); it can dramatize the unfortunate results of not using or not having the product (General Telephone showed the need for a kitchen extension phone by showing a woman burn the egg she is frying when she is called away to answer the phone.); it can focus on the emotional effect on the person who has the problem (Bank of Baltimore showed an exasperated woman leaving her bank while an audio flashback recreates her frustrating interview with the bank officer.).

Show the Problem with Others

In a commercial for Oral-B toothbrushes the announcer informs us of the evils of a hard-bristled toothbrush while we watch one scratch the shiny enamel off an automobile. This treats the problem of the other guy seriously. Another school of this approach prefers to make fun of the competition. Its headmaster is director Joe Sedelmaier. His famous "Where's the Beef?" commercial for Wendy's suggested in no uncertain terms that other fast food hamburgers were smaller than the Wendy's burger. His humorous Federal Express commercials showed what happened to the poor saps who dared use another air express company. And he took on banks and their automatic tellers in a commercial for GMAC financing in which the frustrated customer ends up with nothing but a calendar from the bank guard. The danger of having too much fun at the expense of the competition is that you forget to make a positive point for your own brand.

Show Ridiculous Alternatives

A Sedelmaier commercial for Alaska Airlines showed vignettes of people going to absurd lengths to put a little summer into their winter. A man barbecues hamburgers in a snowstorm, three ladies turn on a spit in a tanning salon. A more reasonable alternative—a low-cost Alaska Airlines vacation. To promote its seven o'clock newscast, KRLD-TV (Dallas) showed a stern-faced businesswoman leave her office after a hard day's work. She then dons a leather helmet and climbs into a cannon which catapults her above the city in order to reach home for the conventional six o'clock news. And a French commercial for Lactel milk made the point that you do not need to keep a cow to have fresh milk every day by showing a city where everyone had his or her own personal cow.

In commercials of this style what gets the dramatic attention is the problem and unacceptable alternatives. There is typically a clear division drawn between the problem or the other guy and the solution—the product. The trick (as stated before) is not to lose sight of the solution. The most familiar problem/solution format tries to meet this challenge by integrating the two into a single story.

Slice-of-Life

This format dramatizes a real-life situation in which the product rescues people from their real-life problems. Does this sound familiar?

"Big date tonight, but my breath . . ."

"Relax, Charlie. Gargle with this. . . ."

(LATER, AT THE PROM)

"Thanks for the tip, pal. Suzie even said she'd go steady."

Does this stuff really work? Ask Procter & Gamble. Despite the fact that the technique is derided as "phony, contrived story-telling," Harry McMahan wrote, "The 'slice-of-life' remains the single most successful vehicle for communication and persuasion that this business has come up with in its first 23 years of success and failure."[2]

The structure is quite simple: 1) The hero/heroine has a problem. (Not by accident, it is a problem experienced many times by the viewer under similar circumstances.) 2) Someone happens along with some good advice. It may be a neighbor, the grocer, or a continuing character who is an established expert on the subject (such as Rosie for Bounty paper towels). Whoever they are, they have tried the product and it worked for them. 3) The hero/heroine tries the product and it works. Along with solving his or her problem comes the reward—a compliment or a kiss or whatever. This format can easily become a parody of itself.

The structure is so familiar, the opportunities for triteness are unlimited. It is up to the copywriter—now a dialogue writer—to avoid the predictable, the unbelievable. The format requires real people speaking real

2. *Advertising Age* (July 15, 1970): 84.

dialogue, not cardboard cutouts mouthing the words of the copy strategy. Remember that it is "life" you are slicing. Try to capture life. Here are some tips for keeping slice-of-life alive:

- The problem must be real and relevant to the viewer. And the actors should react to it in a believable manner. The discovery of "ring around the collar" brought out such exaggerated agony in one commercial we wonder how the husband and wife would cope with important problems. There should be a sense of reality—real situation, real characters—in the way in which the problem is presented. If it is being exaggerated for the sake of humor ("ring around the collar?"), this should be made clear to the viewers so they do not take the commercial seriously.

- The product (solution) should be introduced in a believable manner. Neighbors do not just happen to be carrying gallon jugs of floor cleanser the moment the heroine notices that her floor is dirty. Again, if you are playing it for laughs or blatant exaggeration, make sure it is funny and blatant.

- People should talk the way people talk. Crisp, believable dialogue is essential. Since people do not usually "sell" each other, it may be advisable to cut away to a voice-over announer for the hard, technical product copy.

- Include a demonstration. Somebody still has to show the viewer how the product works and prove that it does everything the characters say it does.

- Close with a reward. This is the benefit for solving the problem. When a woman has been struggling all commercial long to achieve pretty hair, the emotional payoff is to have her husband or boyfriend notice it. The payoff for a food commercial need not be a phony, "Great dinner, Mom!" In a commercial for Shake & Bake, Mom got her reward when her teenage daughter was so intent on enjoying the product that she did not respond when the telephone rang. High praise indeed!

- Humor—honest, human-interest-type humor—can help. On a continuum of problems including death and taxes, washday worries fall near the bottom, so try to avoid sounding ponderous.

- Make the characters personalities, not cutouts. Keep their attitudes and reactions consistent with their roles and the situation. Good casting and direction are as critical as good writing.

- The character who speaks for the product should have credentials. This format is dramatized word-of-mouth advertising, so the person handing out the advice should know what he or she is talking about. The mailman cannot convincingly pass along tips about detergent, but Madge the manicurist is in a position to know about soft hands.

- The message is contained in the dialogue, but you still have to make the viewer notice, watch, hear, and care. One thing that helps is the situation, where the little drama takes place. It does not have to occur in the kitchen or supermarket aisle. A conversation for Citicorp Travelers Checks took place in a Japanese bath house with the husband and wife up to their necks in a huge tub. When the husband suddenly remembers he has left his traveler's checks in his suit, a Japanese gentleman (their bath neighbor) assures him there is no need to worry if the checks are Citicorp. Relieved, the man introduces his wife to the Japanese gentleman who starts to stand in the tub. The embarrassed wife says, "That's all right, don't get up."

- A little conflict can help. The poor women who endure snide remarks from their husbands about their rotten coffee will welcome the rescue of Mrs. Olson. Some issue value will help involve the viewer, but the issue has to be pertinent and the product must be central to it.

Presenters

There is probably no strategy that could not be executed with a stand-up spokesman, eyeball to camera, talking about the product. It could be any actor or actress, neither known by the viewer nor identified in the commercial, who is simply the voice of the advertiser. It could be some recognized authority or well-known personality or celebrity. At the very least, a presenter should be able to deliver the sales message accurately, clearly, and in an easy-to-follow manner.

But will the viewer want to follow? The chances get slimmer the closer the words, settings, casting, and acting come to the clichés of the category. If the copy is just a dull recital of sales points or if the spokesperson is too pushy, too bland, or just plain unlikeable, why should anyone want to listen to, much less believe, your commercial? A presenter commercial must be fresh, likeable, and deserve attention. Handled creatively, this mundane format can break through the ordinary, as evidenced by the successful Bartles & Jaymes campaign and Isuzu's liar.

Here are some of the basic variations on stand-up presenter format.

The Salesperson-Spokesperson

This is the company's representative talking to the viewer. It might be an unidentified actor or actress who tells the product story in a pleasant, sincere, authoritative manner. It might be a character, such as the aforementioned Frank Bartles and Ed Jaymes or Joe Isuzu. It might be the actual president of the company who appears in person to impress viewers with the company's sincerity and dedication, such as Lee Iacocca for Chrysler assuring America that "the pride is back" or Victor Kiam of Remington electric shavers telling us he liked the product so much he bought the company.

The Authority-Spokesperson

This format shows some recognized expert in the field whose opinion on the brand's performance carries extra weight or credibility. In the old days it was the doctor talking about pain killers. These days it might be a pediatric nurse talking about disposable diapers, a mother of small children talking about stain-removing detergents, or an Italian chef talking about spaghetti sauce. A dishwashing liquid played it tongue-in-cheek by having a professional dishwasher as a spokesperson.

The Satisfied User-Spokesperson

This is the prospect personified. The spokesperson presents the product story from personal experience, often in the form of a dramatized testimonial. The approach is human and straightforward and the aim is to create empathy with the viewer/prospect. Fleischmann's margarine used a thirty-year-old man who had had a heart attack to talk about the virtues of a low-fat diet. In a simple commercial for Jell-O cheesecake mix a man happily devoured cheesecake in the background while his wife talked about how good and how easy it was to make.

The Celebrity-Spokesperson

These show famous people the viewer already knows. They can range from superstars, like Michael Jackson appearing for Pepsi-Cola, to people whose names are more familiar than their faces, like the ex-jocks for Miller Lite or the anonymous celebrities who wouldn't leave home without their American Express cards. It is difficult to watch television without seeing celebrities in commercials. There have been Cybil Shepherd for the beef industry, Bruce Willis for Seagram wine coolers, Michael J. Fox for Pepsi, Charlton Heston for Contel, James Garner for Mazda, Bill Cosby for Jell-O, and on and on.

What makes this such a popular format? Instant recognition. Advertisers want to take advantage of the popularity of the presenter to make their product stand out. Celebrities can provide stopping power. But to be convincing they must fit the products they represent. John Houseman was convincing for Smith Barney, but less convincing selling cooking oil and hamburgers. "In the 1970s, Bristol Meyers thought it had a pot of gold when it snared John Wayne. The company and its agency stuffed the Duke into a tuxedo to extol the virtues of Datril. The ad bombed. Why would a man who survived ten Indian massacres, a botched cavalry charge, Iwo Jima, and the Alamo (well, almost survived) need to worry about an aspirin substitute? Great Western Savings and Loan had a better idea. Setting Wayne on horseback in his familiar cowboy duds . . ."[3]

As a useful check, ask if the message you want the presenter to deliver is interesting enough to get noticed regardless of who presents it. After that, ask what added dimension can the presenter bring. Attention? Credibility? Humor? Personality?

3. *Madison Avenue* (April 1984): 58.

What the move to celebrities suggests is that the message alone is seldom enough. You must bring some other interest or reward to the commercial to make the viewer want to watch and listen—and it should be something that is relevant to the product message. A relevant, credible celebrity is one way, but there are others. One creative agency (Hal Riley & Partners) chose some "unbelievable" spokespersons (one was psychic Clarisa Bernhardt) for an "unbelievable product" (Breyer's low-fat Grand Light ice cream).

A presenter commercial for Braniff Airlines showed a man traveling in a crate as baggage to demonstrate the speed and care Braniff exhibits when handling luggage. He is eventually unloaded onto the baggage claim revolving belt where he must wait for the person who is supposed to pick him up.

In a U.K. commercial for Xerox, a stand-up presenter talks to us about the Xerox 10 Series photocopier. What is unusual is that his talking image then appears on a piece of paper as it is sent through the copier. He continues to describe product advantages as his image illustrates them: it copies front and back (a copy is picked up and turned over and we see the back of his head), it enlarges and reduces (and his image changes sizes accordingly).

In other words, a stand-up presenter can do more than stand up and present.

Continuing Characters

A continuing character is a character or personality created for the product (as opposed to being borrowed, as celebrities are). The character may function as a spokesperson (like the old-fashioned New Englander for Pepperidge Farms or the cuddly bear for Snuggle fabric softener), but more often continuing characters perform in real-life dramas. Ideally, such characters combine the advantages of a celebrity-spokesperson (recognizable and memorable) and authority-spokesperson (credibility and knowledge about the product) with the involvement of a slice-of-life story format. Continuing characters can be real or fantasy.

The continuing characters who manage to really continue are those that are connected logically, believably, and imaginatively to the product and its selling idea. Maytag's Lonely Repairman dramatizes the dependability of Maytag products by having nothing to repair. Morris the cat epitomizes the finicky cat every cat owner imagines his or hers to be and holds out for 9-Lives cat food. Ronald McDonald personifies for children the fun experience of going out to eat at McDonald's. The Pink Panther was created for a movie, but was cleverly appropriated for Owens Corning's pink insulation. Frank Bartles and Ed Jaymes are more continuing characters than presenters in the droll personality they project for Bartles & Jaymes wine coolers.

Continuing characters can come complete with their own world or dramatic situation. Rosie (for Bounty paper towels) works behind a luncheon counter so she has ample opportunity to wipe up spills. Madge the

BARTLES & JAYMES
WINE COOLER
"TRUCK"

:30 Commercial

FRANK: We thought you folks should
know your enthusiasm for our new
Bartles and Jaymes wine cooler has
made us very proud.

To be honest, it's made us some money,
too, which is good because our
marketing director had to get a bigger
truck.

The sign painter has a good start on it,
and says he'll finish it up . . .

as soon as he gets done with a Trans-Am
he promised somebody he'd stripe.

Anyway, we wanted you to know we're
doing all we can to keep our cooler
coming.

Thank you again for your purchases.

©BARTLES & JAYMES CO.
MODESTO, CA

©Bartles & Jaymes Co. 1986

manicurist likewise finds it easy to guide conversations to the subject of soft hands, the selling strategy behind Palmolive dishwashing liquid. In the world of fantasy, the Jolly Green Giant has his own valley where he grows his vegetables. The Keebler Elves make their cookies and crackers in a hollow tree.

A key ingredient of success for a character is believability. Even fantasy characters should seem real within the limits of their own clearly defined worlds. In some ways, a fantasy character can be more believable than a so-called real character. You can accept a kid talking to Tony the Tiger even though Tony is a cartoon. But you wonder about the supposedly real people who operated and dined at Betty's Breakfasts, a quaint but questionable inn that appeared some years ago in a cereal campaign, where the featured item on the menu was packaged raisin bran.

Testimonials

The essence of the testimonial format is to try to translate the power of word-of-mouth to a television commercial. Real, unscripted people report on their personal reactions to the product. If they are believable, they can capture and hold attention and be very convincing. Their words have to be real—not what the copywriter puts into their mouths—and the people have to be real.

Testimonials may take a variety of forms. It may be a presenter or spokesperson commercial in which someone relates his or her experiences with the product. It may be a "letters" commercial in which the words come from actual consumer mail even though the visuals may be a dramatization. It may take the form of an interview, either "man-on-the-street" or "hidden camera," in which the testifier does not know that he or she is being filmed. (The latter is a favorite for taste tests, in which surprised consumers discover that they like your brand better than their usual.) Testimonials can take a leaf from the vignettes book and feature a succession of speakers, sometimes sprinkled through a product demonstration.

If a testimonial commercial is not believable these days, it is not likely to be because it is untrue. Testimonials come under close scrutiny by those whose job it is to verify truth in advertising. People who do not use a product cannot be passed off as users. Opinions that come out in a hidden camera interview cannot be aired just because the person expressed them; the claim has to be substantiated. If a woman says, for example, she likes a candy bar because it is real chocolate, that testimonial cannot be aired unless the candy bar is, in fact, real chocolate. Comments cannot be taken out of order or out of context (something one might suspect about edited testimonials). Any testimonial must be authentic, supportable by facts, and based on the actual experience of a real person.

You can still use the format creatively. White Cloud bathroom tissue showed real people responding to questions that appeared to be asked by an animated cloud. And you can be sure that those ex-pro athletes in the Miller Lite beer commercials are not giving testimonials in their own words. But whether it is a dramatized testimonial or an actual testimonial from a real person, the people should come off as real people and be relevant to the product and message. The viewer should want to listen and believe.

Vignettes

Instead of one long look at one person's experience with the product, the vignettes format uses a series of short looks at many different people having similar experiences. Vignettes became popular in the mid-sixties with Alka-Seltzer's "stomachs" commercial and the campaign for Benson & Hedges 100's. (The latter broke the oft-stated rule that you show the consumer enjoying the product by instead showing the plights of people unaccustomed to the "disadvantages" of a 100-mm cigarette. It was impossible to watch these commercials and not get the idea that these were longer cigarettes.)

The advantage of this format is that it shows variety—different people, different occasions. But this is also the risk. Because it is a series of quick scenes, the situations must be instantly recognizable and related to the selling idea.

Repetition is the operative word in vignettes commercials. Hit upon a single visual idea—a visual moment, a second or two of action—that encapsulates the reason-to-buy. Then repeat it, repeat it, repeat it, just changing the people and the scenes. The secret, however, is not just repetition, but how well the thing you are repeating captures the drama and emotion of your product. Sure antiperspirant captured the confidence that comes with underarm dryness by urging people in a lively song to "Raise your hand if you're sure." Vignettes showed athletes, students, dancers, fishermen, an astronaut, and the Statue of Liberty with upraised hands. Kodak Disc cameras showed a series of cute little boys and girls at play while their parents catch each adorable moment, mid-action, with the Kodak Disc camera. The line: "I'm gonna getcha with the Kodak Disc."

Given the basic discipline of one strong visual idea, repeated, the vignettes format can accommodate a whole range of advertising ideas. As well as showing a benefit, like dry armpits, vignettes can show the need for the product. (Subaru, for example, showed vignettes of people unintentionally abusing their cars to the tune of "You Always Hurt the One You Love" to dramatize the need for a sturdy car that is "inexpensive and built to stay that way.") Vignettes can satirize the plight with competitors. (AT&T, for example, showed a succession of folks chatting on the phone until thwarted by some unexpected disaster. Phones fall apart in users' hands, mouthpieces fall off, a cord breaks while we hear a variation of the song, "Second Hand Rose." The announcer explains that a lot of people are reporting complaints about phones that are not made by AT&T and reminds us that "you get what you pay for.") And vignettes can emphathize with the prospect by portraying the lifestyle of the product user. (Levi's 501 jeans reflects the urban youth who wear blue jeans, California Cooler commercials capture the surfer world credited with inventing wine coolers,

Commercial segments courtesy of Subaru of America, Inc.

McDonald's commercials have long captured the healthy, happy, all-American lifestyle that includes a visit to McDonald's, and Chevrolet's "Heartbeat of America" surrounds each of its car models with contemporary life-style images.)

The vignettes format can work for you only if you can find a single visual encapsulation of the selling idea that is relevant, dramatic, and convincing—and that reads quickly. Without this you will end up with a montage of impressions that will not add up to a single, compelling message.

Story

Vignettes provide variety; story commercials involve the viewer in a single episode that proceeds from beginning to middle to end. They work like a little movie, drawing the viewer into a story that unfolds visually, helped along by copy (when needed) and (often) music.

One such classic story began on a gray, snowy morning as a man opened his garage, drove his small car through the deep, freshly-fallen snow to another garage, disappeared inside, and then emerged driving a snowplow. The copy paid it off: "Did you ever wonder how the man who

Levi's 501 Blues Courtesy of Levi Strauss & Co.

drives the snow plow drives *to* the snow plow? This one drives a Volkswagen"

Storytelling is television advertising at its emotional best. Recall some of the sentimental McDonald's stories, like the old gentleman getting up the nerve to sit next to the old woman in the almost empty McDonald's, or the little boy battling sibling rivalry when his new baby sister comes home for the first time, or the retiree off to his first day on his new job, crew kid at the local McDonald's.

Besides being sentimental, the story can be romantic. In a DeBeers diamonds commercial, an elegantly dressed couple arrive at a hotel after an evening out. While walking to their room, they flirt with each other and say they should not be doing this because they are happily married—to each other it turns out when he takes out a diamond ring and wishes her happy anniversary (with "the gift that says you would marry her all over again").

Or the story can be humorous, such as this commercial for Henry Weinhard Beer: Cowboys are heading for the chuck wagon as the sun is going down. One asks another where he had to send to get his saddle. "New Mexico," is the answer. The cook, new to the outfit, hands out bottles of beer to the weary cowhands. "Where'd they have to send to to get that beer?" "Oregon," is the answer. (Its Oregon origin is the selling point behind the brand.) The cook then announces some additions to the beef on the menu—"Lawn buffalo in a light cream sauce. Roast antelope

LEO BURNETT COMPANY, INC.

AS FILMED AND RECORDED (2/87) "New Kid Rev." :60

McDONALD'S CORP.

MCGT1956

THE NEW KID

1. SING: FIRST DAY OF WORK...
BILL: Well, wish me luck.

2. WIFE: Oh, you'll do fine.
SING: WANNA BE ON TIME...

3. FISHERMAN: Hey Bill, wanna go fishin'?

4. BILL: Nope, I'm goin' to work.
SING: WANNA MAKE A GOOD IMPRESSION.

5. CREW GIRL #1: I heard there's a new kid startin' today.
CREW GIRL #2: Oh, I hope he's cute.

6. (SFX: KNOCK)
CREW GIRL #1: We're open in a few minutes, sir.

7. SING: WHAT IF THEY THINK IT'S A LITTLE LATE...

8. TO START A NEW PROFESSION.

9. YOU'VE GOT WHAT IT TAKES.

10. YOU KNOW IT'S TRUE.

11. BET YOU'LL SHOW THEM A TRICK OR TWO.

12. BILL: Let's see, that's three Bacon, Egg, and Cheese Biscuits, one Egg McMuffin, two Sausage McMuffin with Egg and one large O.J..

13. CREW GIRL: You sure you never did this before?
BILL: Thank you, come again.

14. WIFE: How'd it go?
BILL: I don't know how they ever got along without me.

15. WIFE: Oh, I could've told them that.

with peach brandy glaze. Braised jack rabbit en croute." "Where'd they have to send to get that cook?" one cowboy asks skeptically. "Los Angeles."

Story commercials should be simple and easy to follow. They demand the best in dramatic writing, cinematography, and editing. And they must be built around a selling idea. Try this simple test: Can you tell the story of the commercial without mentioning the product? If so, you are suffering from what copy researchers call insufficient product narrative integration. For all its drama and emotion, a story commercial is only as good as the product message it communicates.

People/Narration

As a format, this comes close to being *all others*. (Few commercials would fail to qualify.) The focus is on people. The people are not talking to camera about the product, as in presenter and testimonial commercials. And there is not a full-fledged story with dialogue and problem/solution, as in slice-of-life. The camera just shows us a person or persons. It can show him, her, or them using the product, enjoying the benefits, or experiencing a need for the product. The visuals are usually accompanied by voice-over narration which comments on the action and relates the people to the product. The narration may be of a detached "announcer"; it may be an internal monologue, as though we are hearing the thoughts of the person we see; it may be a song; or it may be a combination.

In a commercial for Apple computers we see a young boy at the computer while his father tries to lure him away with a skateboard, then a basketball, finally his own Apple. The voice-over explains: "Using an Apple II is very easy. The only hard part is getting your kid away from it."

A commercial for Visa takes the viewer to an "in" Boston restaurant called Rosalie's and dazzles us visually with the ambiance and appetizing food. The voice-over concludes, ". . . Bring your appetite and your Visa card. Because at Rosalie's they don't take no for an answer, and they don't take American Express."

In a commercial from an engaging campaign for Michelin tires we see the simple but appealing visual of a cute baby playing on and around a tire. The voice-over dialogue questions whether it is worth the extra money to buy Michelin, but then remembers the child and concludes it is. "Because so much is riding on your tires."

Budweiser produced a moving documentary-style people commercial to salute the Summer Olympics. Two farmers pause in their pre-dawn labors to watch a police car with flashing lights escorting a runner carrying the Olympic torch. As the runner passes them, the farmers are moved to respectful applause. The narrator points out that winning is secondary to "discovering the best in all of us."

This is a format with great structural flexibility (if it is a format at all). It relies on the inherent appeal of the human condition. People can be loving, lovable, caring, vulnerable, sentimental, funny, naughty, wistful, exuberant, and many other things that can touch an emotion in the viewer. People

commercials demand sharp, sparse copy. And they must guard against being just verbal ideas illustrated with pretty pictures.

Satire

There is probably a little satire in every commercial, intentionally or accidentally, but in its pure form, a satirical commercial parodies a person, event, or genre familiar to the viewer. Satires usually come in clusters soon after a big news event or very popular movie. You may remember secret agent commercials on the heels of the James Bond movies, disco commercials after *Saturday Night Fever,* swashbuckling adventure stories after *Raiders of the Lost Ark,* spaceships and aliens after *Close Encounters* and *E. T.* Diet Pepsi recently borrowed from *Top Gun* in a commercial in which a hotshot jet pilot opened a compartment containing his Diet Pepsi but found the bottle stuck. His rival chides from a nearby jet, "Trouble with your refreshment system?" He solves the problem by flying his jet upside down so the Pepsi can pour out. (Diet Pepsi has the taste that's "turning the world upside down.")

Besides topical movies there are always the classics. Transamerican Insurance updated *King Kong* by showing the giant ape climbing up their building. The heroine scolds, "Ya big ape, who's going to pay for this mess?" ("With Transamerican Insurance, any mess can be paid for, even a king-sized mess.")

And Miller Lite paid homage to the western movie. The leader of the cavalry bravely drops his weapons and advances to negotiate with the chief Indian. They can't decide between "tastes great" and "less filling," so the battle resumes (to be carried on in later years by countless ex-pro athletes).

Satire is always tempting but not always easy to bring off. It has to be broad enough to be recognized as parody by the viewer. If people do not realize it is a spoof, it may just look like a silly, irrelevant commercial. If the subject is topical, timing is critical. The third parody of *Star Wars* was less fresh than the first. And if the commercial satirizes something that the viewers hold dear, they may hold this breach of good taste against the advertiser.

Pepsi–Cola Company

No matter how funny the commercial is, it cannot be justified unless the humor comes out of the product and selling idea. Volkswagen made its point about the built-in obsolescence of the competition when it did a spoof of the "1949 Auto Show," in which singers, dancers, and pitchmen praised the newest Packard, Hudson, Studebaker, and DeSoto while the humble (but enduring) VW Beetle sat unnoticed in the corner.

Musical

Music has long been an integral part of the commercial scene. Its importance and its evolution can be encapsulated in the advertising for Pepsi-Cola, from the inane but unforgettable radio jingle, "Pepsi-Cola hits the spot," to the megamusical productions of the eighties starring Michael Jackson and Lionel Ritchie.

In the early 1960s, music in advertising began to reflect the pop music of the times. Soft drinks and other image-oriented products started building commercials around music. Some commercials' songs were even released as records (Alka-Seltzer's "No Matter What Shape Your Stomach Is In," Diet Pepsi's "Girl Watcher's Theme," and Coca-Cola's "I'd Like to Teach the World.")

There are many reasons for using music. Music can reinforce the personality of the brand or commercial. The musical treatment in many of Joe

Sedelmaier's humorous spots (Wendy's, Federal Express, Alaska Airlines) is as comedic as the pictures. Music can heighten the emotional or dramatic impact of the commercial, just as motion picture scores contribute to the mood of the film. The stirring Vangelis music in the Gallo wine commercials elevates the image of the brand. Chevrolet's pulsating "Heartbeat of America" music contributes energy to the commercial's visuals. And the "Magnificent Seven" music from Marlboro Country lingers in many memories even though cigarette advertising has passed from the TV screen. Music can also help position a brand to a particular market segment. The music in soft drink commercials leaves little doubt that these products are appealing to a young, contemporary audience. Many advertisers in the 1980s began to revive the musical sounds of the late fifties and early sixties to appeal to the baby boom generation. Buick adapted the Buddy Holly song "Oh Boy" ("Oh Buick") and Liquid Drano turned to "Splish Splash." Musical variations in a theme can help an advertiser with broad appeal target different segments, as Chevrolet does with its "Heartbeat" music. "A tinkly piano ballad or New Age synthetic-swoosh targeted an upper-class white audience; doo-wop or jazzy/bluesy sax goes after upwardly mobile blacks, while an acoustic guitar goes after rural or student consumers."[4]

Finally, music can give birth to, or be an integral part of, the idea itself. Chevy trucks borrowed "Lean on Me" to underscore vignettes of working people leaning (depending) on their trucks. Subaru used the song "You Always Hurt the One You Love" to help demonstrate the love/hate relationship people have with their durable Subarus. A bank in Brazil used the old song "Night and Day" to communicate their twenty-four-hour automatic teller. And Heinz ketchup used Carly Simon's "Anticipation" as hungry people waited for the thicker ketchup to pour from the bottle.

If an existing song fits, fine. It may carry some built-in associations and instant memorability. But a better solution is often an original musical expression of your original idea. These songs have a way of sticking in the mind, too, and have the further advantage of being unique. Many brands have built personalities—and selling ideas—with original music, like Oscar Meyer's singing testimonials, "My Bologna Has a First Name," Cherry 7 Up's "Isn't It Cool in Pink," Budweiser's "This Bud's for You," and Wheaties's "What the Big Boys Eat."

Personification

According to the dictionary, *personification* means the attribution of personal nature or character to inanimate objects or abstract notions. Commercials can personify the product benefit, the problem, or the selling idea. Snuggle fabric softener personified softness in a cuddly teddy bear character; Mobil created Mr. Dirt to personify all the bad, dirty things that can foul a car's engine. Charlie the Tuna personified the tuna that Star Kist rejects. (He lacked "good taste.") Parkay margarine personified the selling

---

4. *Adweek* (September 14, 1987): F.F. 21.

LEO BURNETT COMPANY, INC.
AS FILMED AND RECORDED   (2/87)   "Diner"   :30

THE SEVEN-UP CO.

SLCH1993

1. (MUSIC INTRO)

2. SING: ISN'T IT COOL IN PINK.

3. ISN'T IT CRUEL...

4. ...

5. TO THINK...

6. WHAT THE OTHERS MISS...

7. WHEN IT COMES TO THIS...

8. CHERRY...

9. 7UP.

10. CAN'T GET ENOUGH...

11. LOOKIN' YOUR CHERRY BEST. FEELIN' SO REFRESHED.

12. ISN'T IT COOL IN PINK.

13. NEW CHERRY 7UP.

14. ISN'T IT SO COOL...

15. IN PINK.

idea of buttery taste in a talking package that literally said "butter." And Alka-Seltzer created a classic spot in which a man's animated stomach argued with him because he kept overstuffing it and giving it spicy foods. ("Alka-Seltzer. When you and your stomach disagree.")

By visualizing and giving literal form to an abstract idea, personification can help a brand preempt a concept or attribute that many brands could claim.

Symbolism/Analogy

A symbol is something that stands for something else. Many commercials are built around visual symbols that make a point more memorable than would the things they represent. In Bud Light commercials people in bars ask for a light (any light beer) and receive lights ranging from torches to lasers to flaming hoops through which trained dogs leap. They finally wise up and specify "Bud Light." To visualize and symbolize how many people fly British Airways across the Atlantic each year (more than the population of Manhattan) British Airways showed a replica of Manhattan Island landing in England like a huge spaceship.

Analogy is a form of symbolism that makes its point through comparison. Ajax cleanser promised it "cleans like a white tornado"—not literally, of course, but supposedly with analogous strength. Nike Air Jordan basketball shoes likened the leaping ability of basketball star Michael Jordan to an airplane. Jordan is shown soaring in slow motion toward the basket accompanied by a sound track of a jet taking off. Great Western Savings drew a parallel between the solid security of their institution and the solidity of Yosemite's El Capitan mountain, not unlike Prudential's "strength of Gibraltar." To illustrate the value of their team of financial experts, Paine Webber showed an average guy playing tennis against Jimmy Connors. ("Investing in today's highly competitive market is like playing against Jimmy Connors.") But our average guy is backed up on the court by an office full of Paine Webber people who return Jimmy's best stuff and eventually fire off a winner. Wendy's drew a humorous analogy between the lack of menu choice in other fast food restaurants and a Russian fashion show in which sturdy peasant women model the same drab housedress. Nestea iced tea created a memorable refreshment analogy when they showed people drink refreshing Nestea and then fall back into a swimming pool. The refreshment of 7 Up soft drinks was likened to a summer rain that "feels so good comin' down."

Analogy and symbolism spots can be memorable and highly communicative if they are simple, familiar, and readily understandable. If they stretch too far, they can come off as silly or confusing.

Summary: The Chart Grows

A truly complete list of possible commercial formats would have to list every commercial. There are many twists and variations on each. A commercial may use more than one of the formats described here. A slice-of-life commercial may include a side-by-side demonstration. There can be vignettes of testimonials and musical presenters. You can probably think of many commercials that do not fit neatly into any of these categories.

The choice of format, like that of style or tone of voice, grows out of the creative strategy. The format should be judged on its relative ability to dramatize and communicate the intended selling message. There is nothing inherently dull or magical about any format; it all depends upon how creatively you use it. Before turning to another important element of commercial execution—how it is produced—let's add formats to the chart that has been building:

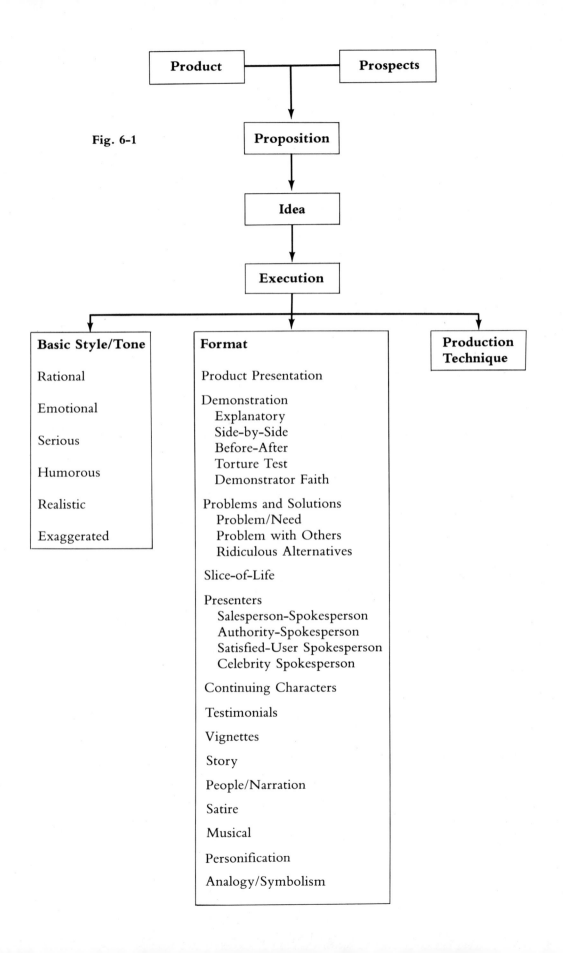

Fig. 6-1

Product | Prospects

Proposition

Idea

Execution

Basic Style/Tone

Rational

Emotional

Serious

Humorous

Realistic

Exaggerated

Format

Product Presentation

Demonstration
  Explanatory
  Side-by-Side
  Before-After
  Torture Test
  Demonstrator Faith

Problems and Solutions
  Problem/Need
  Problem with Others
  Ridiculous Alternatives

Slice-of-Life

Presenters
  Salesperson-Spokesperson
  Authority-Spokesperson
  Satisfied-User Spokesperson
  Celebrity Spokesperson

Continuing Characters

Testimonials

Vignettes

Story

People/Narration

Satire

Musical

Personification

Analogy/Symbolism

Production Technique

Chapter 7

Production Techniques
Execution III

Production Costs vs. Production Value

On October 26, 1987, the advertising community was shocked by this headline in *Advertising Age:*

"Spot Production Costs Drop 4%"

Escalating commercial production costs had been as certain as death and taxes. But the American Association of Advertising Agencies' "Survey of Television Production Costs 1984–1986" found that the average commercial cost $113,940 in 1986, compared to $117,962 in 1985.[1] This was the first sign of a drop in living memory. If it was true, it came not a moment too soon. Cost concerns have been haunting advertisers and agencies alike. Cost consultants have opened up shop to try to help advertisers cut "fat" out of their production estimates. Several agencies have turned to in-house production to try to save clients some money. Regular-size advertisers were beginning to wonder if they could afford to be on television anymore.

One factor driving up costs has been the quest for greater production values, which in turn have resulted from the need to break through the clutter. It takes visual impact to make a commercial arresting. For the agency creatives this often means the latest computerized graphic, the wildest special effect, the hottest director. These things cost money. And

---

1. *Advertising Age* (October 26, 1987): 46.

when money collides with art, as it does so often in commercial production, each side eyes the other suspiciously. The cost-conscious (bill-paying) advertiser suspects that so-called production value is so much wasteful self-indulgence inflicted by irresponsible creatives who are more concerned with awards than sales. The creatives, on the other hand, view fiscal responsibility as narrow-minded penny pinching designed to clip the wings off a brilliant idea.

As usual, truth lies somewhere between the two extremes. It costs more than it rightfully should to produce a television commercial. But good production is often the difference between brilliance and mediocrity. Chapter 6's discussion of formats should serve as a reminder of how easily commercials can look like each other. What will make one slice-of-life a standout and another a cliché are very often the production values—casting, direction, cinematography, editing, music. The careful attention to detail will make one commercial ring true and another look phony. Style is no substitute for content. A weak idea will not suddenly become strong just because it is filmed in the current vogue of shaky-camera realism. But the right direction can bring added believability to dialogue, added appetite appeal to table-top food photography, added energy or realism to vignettes or documentary-style commercials. The right style of animation can add humor or personality or simplify an abstract idea. A particular special effect can add surprise, drama, or visual interest. Quality ideas deserve quality production.

Time and Money

Every copywriter dreams of beginning a script with words like, "Open on a beach in Hawaii. . . ." But exotic production trips to a tropical island are rare. The real world is one of budgets and deadlines, each one tighter than the other. It is not enough to have a brilliant idea. It must be a brilliant idea that can be produced on time and for the money that has been allocated.

Time and money are inevitably interrelated in commercial production. Try to save the former and it will cost you the latter. Rushing to make an air date (advertising's one genuine deadline) usually requires compromise in some phase of production. It may result in inadequate preplanning (with surprise costs coming up later), overtime, or the inability to make desired revisions.

The air date is when the commercial goes on the air. The time has been contracted for and the finished commercial must be delivered to the network or station by that date. The ideal production schedule works backward from the air date so that materials will be ready on time. Some things cannot be rushed. Other things can be rushed, but for a premium. Because commercials vary so in complexity, it is difficult to generalize about how long it takes to produce them. But here is a rough rule-of-thumb production timetable for different types of commercials, based on the number of weeks that should be allowed between approved-for bids and answer print (finished commercial).

Video Tape	1 to 3 weeks
Simple Filmed Live Action	5 to 6 weeks
(*i.e.,* inserts, voice-over, food, simple opticals)	
Live Action	8 to 10 weeks
(*i.e.,* slice-of-life, location shooting, on-camera dialogue, simple opticals)	
Animation, Stop Motion	14 weeks
Combinations	16 weeks
(live action plus animation, live with stop motion, animation with stop action, complex opticals)	

Ideally, any schedule includes enough time to accommodate delays due to revisions and unexpected problems. Obviously, some commercials will take longer than others. For example, one that calls for location shooting may require a week or more for the search and selection of the right location and also carries the added risk of weather delays.

Accelerating these schedules by ten to fifteen percent (because of a late start and a tight air date) may get you into an overtime situation or the unpleasant choice between doing it right and doing it fast. Overtime adds to the cost of production. It may mean longer working days to complete the job (and the various unions look after members who are asked to work longer than prescribed hours). Or it may mean adding additional personnel to complete the work on time. But what is more alarming is that this additional money is committed with no guarantee that it will result in a satisfactory product. If work is rushed through incorrectly, there is no chance to send it back for revisions or refinements. Interestingly, if the end result is unacceptable, some responsible person will say, "Stop! Forget the money, do it the way it should be," which prompted a wise but slightly cynical adman to say, "There's never time to do it right but always time to do it over." Plan enough time to do it right.

How Much Does It All Cost?

It is difficult to generalize about the cost of commercial production. Costs can vary as widely as ideas. But it is safe to say that an advertiser paying the bills for major commercial production is shelling out a big hunk of change.

Here is some idea of where all the money goes (prices are from 1987):

- **Sets and locations.** The average studio for a shooting day rental is about $850 to $1,000. Normal location fees run around $1,200 to $2,000. But added to the location fees are the costs to transport crew and equipment, as well as per diem (hotel and meals) for the crew.

- **Crew costs.** The average-size crew for a day of shooting in New York is fifteen to twenty; for Los Angeles the average is twenty to twenty-five. Here is a sample of standard hourly rates:

	New York	Los Angeles
Assistant Director	$500–600	$500–600
Assistant Camera Operator	$250–350	$250–350
Sound Team (of two)	$600 per day	$600 per day
Electrician	$300–350	$325–350
Grip	$250–350	$325–350
Makeup	$350–400	$350–400
Stylist	$400–450	$400–450

- **Sound recording.** An hour of voice-over recording at a small studio costs about $150 to $180. Recording voice-over to picture or mixing at a large studio averages $225 per hour.

- **Directors.** Director's fees cover a wide range, but figure on average $5,000 per day. Star directors are getting $10,000 to $12,000 per day.

- **Animation.** Animation costs have increased dramatically and now average about $2,000 per foot. (A sixty-second commercial on 35-mm film would contain ninety feet.)

- **Film stock.** The standard budget rate for raw film stock is about ninety cents per foot. And much more stock is shot, developed, and printed than is actually used in the finished spot. A typical thirty-second commercial uses between three thousand and four thousand feet, depending upon the director.

How do all these costs add up? Quickly.

Here is an estimate for the production of a relatively simple thirty-second live action commercial (one twelve-hour day in Chicago):

Studio	$41,495.00
Editing/post production	4,500.00
Music (original)	10,000.00
Talent (five on-camera principals and twelve extras)	9,350.00
Recording	300.00
Artwork	1,000.00
VTR-transfers	2,500.00
Total (net)	$69,145.00

Remember that net cost is before the addition of the agency commission, travel, shipping, and other miscellaneous costs. And because it was a location shoot, there was also a $15,286 contingency for a weather day (which includes crew, director's fee, location fees, props).

Here is another example, a thirty-second animated commercial:

Studio	$110,942.00
Editing/postproduction	20,648.00
Music	15,000.00
Talent (three voices)	2,500.00
Recording	1,000.00
Artwork/color-corrected packages	6,000.00
VTR-transfers/cassettes	1,000.00
Total (net)	$157,090.00

Finally, here is an example of a vignetttes-style commercial. These estimated costs are for two thirty-second commercials involving four days of shooting in New York:

Studio	$267,540.00
Editing/postproduction	9,000.00
Music	15,000.00
Talent (sixteen on-camera principals and fifty extras)	45,000.00
Recording	100.00
Artwork/color-corrected packages	5,600.00
VTR-transfers and finishing	10,000.00
Total (net)	$352,240.00

These random examples of commercial costs are intended to make two points. First, production is expensive business. Everything possible should be done to make sure all that money is well spent. Second, there is no such thing as an average commercial when it comes to cost. A person should be very careful about quoting ballpark figures until a storyboard has been thoroughly analyzed and estimated. Spending over $400,000 for a couple of thirty-second commercials is bad enough. It is an even more bitter pill to swallow if you had been led to believe by some off-the-cuff "guesstimate" that it would be about $300,000.

Production Techniques in Perspective

Commercial history is rich with lavish commercials only the rich could afford: Apple's $800,000 (?) "1984" launch for its Macintosh computer; British Airways's Manhattan landing in England; Chanel No. 5's elegant fantasy, Pepsi's Michael Jackson spectaculars. Many elaborate and expensive commercials even have ideas worth the money. But advertising can also be stunning because of its simplicity. Consider some of the factors that can make an advertising idea and production elaborate, complicated, and expensive (as well as extra-special, if the idea is a good one):

- Large cast
- Exotic locations
- Expensive sets
- Special props and wardrobe
- Complicated action (changes of scene)
- Special effects
- Complex opticals and editing

For every brilliant cast-of-thousands commercial you can find a compelling commercial with no on-camera principals at all. (Remember, the typical TV screen is small and intimate compared to the movie theater screen.)

Sometimes you have to take a crew of twenty people to the Grand Canyon to make a point, but when the idea focuses on human dimensions, an everyday location may underscore it better. Before you build and decorate a lavish set, ask yourself if you would rather have the viewer pay attention to the idea than its surroundings. Sometimes a limbo set can make it even sharper. You can opt for costly props. But is it any more dramatic to see a glue commercial in which two eleven-ton dump trucks are stuck together than to see a nail glued back together and then hammered into a board?

First comes the idea, then comes the production technique. This is a safe way to think about their relationship. Techniques are there to enhance and express the idea. But as stated before, the best commercials are those in which idea and execution are difficult to isolate. Sometimes the technique becomes such an integral part of the execution that it becomes part of the idea. The selection of techniques that follows is far from complete and is intended only to suggest how production techniques can be idea starters.

Live Action and Animation

The first basic production distinction between categories of commercials is between live action and animation. On the surface it looks like a simple distinction between real and cartoon. But live action can convey fantasy, and animation can convey a sense of reality. Let's look at some of the virtues and dimensions of each.

Live Action

Live action is the bread-and-butter technique of television commercial production. It is to television what photography is to print. It covers everything from a one-take, stand-up presenter to an elaborate cast-of-thousands location shoot. It can make food look appetizing and demonstrations believable. Live action can be natural and realistic (John Hancock, Apple computers); it can be stylized and surrealistic (Chanel No. 5); it can be sexy (Jovan) or sentimental (McDonald's). It can be anything movies can be.

The question of how to use live action to enhance the idea or execution often comes down to finding the right visual style or look. Perhaps you want to create a live look or sense of immediacy, like live television. The truly live commercial is a rarity these days, but videotape can capture the look and feel of live TV (without the risk of unplanned goofs). Perhaps you want to create a documentary look. Many advertisers have turned to black-and-white, with a home-movie cinema vérité style. Sometimes the black-and-white footage is intercut with color scenes. Sometimes just the product is in color. Perhaps you want to create a futuristic or historical look, such as Apple's "1984" commercial or a recent Bud Light commercial in which a caveman returns with fire (light) to his disappointed friends who wanted a (light) beer. Perhaps you want a fantasy storybook look, such as the colorful, youth-appealing McDonaldland sets for Ronald McDonald commercials. Perhaps you want something completely different.

As you think of the look you want for your commercial, make sure it grows out of the product and not simply out of admiration for a style you saw in somebody else's commercial. Every time there is a breakthrough look, whether it is appropriate or not, there is a rush to jump on the bandwagon. Eventually, everybody has the same new look. As one production executive observed, "Once everybody catches up with you, then it's not standing above the clutter anymore—it becomes part of it, and will no longer be breakthrough."[2]

Animation

Animation is defined as the art of giving the appearance of life (movement) to inanimate objects. Stop motion and claymation are types of three-dimensional animation; for all practical purposes, animation refers to drawn objects—cartoons.

Animation achieves its illusion of movement in the same way as the live-action motion picture—through the rapid projection of a series of still pictures that appear (because of our persistence of vision) to move continuously. But the method of photographing is different. Animation requires a frame-by-frame exposure. Each drawing is photographed separately. (See appendix I for more on animation production.)

Those who care to can trace the beginnings of animation to the early cave drawings, Egyptian wall decorations, Greek vases, and Japanese scrolls. But it was the motion picture, of course, that provided the first practical way to make drawings move. The first animated film has been generally credited to the American J. Stewart Blackton (*Humorous Phases of Funny Faces,* 1906) or the Frenchman Emile Cohl (*Phantasmagorie,* 1908). In 1928, Walt Disney created *Steamboat Willie* and began a series of artistic and technical advancements that culminated in the production of *Fantasia.* A

2. *Advertising Age,* October 5, 1987.

change from the fluid Disney style came in the late 1940s and early 1950s with UPA's (United Productions of America) *Gerald McBoing Boing* and *Mr. Magoo*. The animation was simple, flat, and more stylized. The animated Beatles film *Yellow Submarine* in the 1960s was another visual mind-opener for animation fans raised on a steady diet of Disney.

Although economic pressures have made animated films for theaters a rarity, the technique is alive and well and working in television. Animation was king in the early days of commercials but faded in the late 1950s in favor of the realism of live action. Today, animated commercials are no longer regarded as just cartoons for children. They have become much more sophisticated in both concept and execution. The variety of styles is limited only by the artist's imagination. The look of popular illustrators and cartoonists has been adapted to animation (Charles Schultz, R. O. Blechman, Robert Osborn, Rowland Wilson, and Gary Larson, to name a few). Rotoscoping (tracing from live-action film) creates a look that dramatically bridges live and cartoon. And computer-generated animation has opened up new dimensions of graphic design.

Why the popularity of animation in commercials? One reason is entertainment value: People like to watch cartoons. So animated commercials have a better-than-average chance of attracting, holding, and befriending an audience.

Second, animation can create a unique identity for an advertiser. This may be a character who personifies or speaks for the brand (the Jolly Green Giant, Tony the Tiger), or simply an animated logo or signature that can visually tie together a variety of commercials, like the powerful weave logo used by Burlington Industries.

Third, animation can simplify. Its popularity in educational films is due to its ability to reduce a complicated thought to a simple, easy-to-remember expression. Viewers of a Trac-II razor commercial, aided by an animated demo, could grasp how a little whisker is cut off by the second blade before it can pop back up after the first blade.

Fourth, animation can give form to an abstract idea. This might be as simple (or simple-minded) as a detergent "eating stains" or as complex as showing how a communications network is put together.

Fifth, animation can create a world of fantasy that makes puffery palatable. Cartoons can get away with doing and saying things that real (live) people cannot. People tend to suspend literal belief and enter into the spirit of things in the animated world. An animated character symbolizes a real person, and viewers tend to react to it on both levels, symbolic and real. When a cartoon little old lady says the Green Giant cooks a better dish than she does, the viewer accepts this claim as meaning the product is better than average. If a real little old lady held up a package and said, "This Green Giant dish is better than my own homemade," her claim very likely would be rejected. There are, however, real limits even in the world of fantasy. A claim can be so contrary to what the viewer believes that even playful fantasy will not make it convincing.

Furthermore, the characters must behave in a way that is consistent with their world or what they represent. Otherwise they will be rejected. "C'mon, talking plants can't fly!"

Animation is no panacea. It has its disadvantages, too. It works marvelously on a symbolic level, but on a personal level it lacks the human emotion and involvement of live action. To the viewer, the cartoon character is someone else; it is not the viewer. This lack of identification with a character can result in some loss of empathy and believability. The same thing that makes exaggeration acceptable may make conviction more difficult.

Animation is also a costly and time-consuming technique. Although costs are often easier to anticipate and control than in live action (and there are no on-camera performers to whom residuals must be paid), animation does not come cheaply. And figure on ten to fourteen weeks to produce a typical thirty-second animated spot.

The secret of a successful animated commercial is really no secret. It is the same as it is with any commercial. There has to be a solid selling idea, and the technique has to fit the idea. Even though animation can do anything, it will do some things better than others. Its forte is humor, fantasy, action, and exaggeration. It would be simple enough to make an animated slice-of-life commercial, but there would be no appearent reason to. On the other hand, live-action Keebler elves could stretch credibility too far.

Animation in advertising takes many different forms to serve many different needs.

Cartoon Story Animation

This is the animated equivalent of slice-of-life. Animated characters act out a little story that revolves around the product and its selling idea. These are stories in that they have a beginning, middle, and end—a narrative structure. The characters strive for a real personality, and so they demand real animation. This is full animation. Characters are painted on transparent cels and photographed on rendered backgrounds. This type of animation requires a separate pose for every one or two frames of film and produces a very fluid movement.

Interpretative

Animation can be used to visualize a narration or to dramatize an idea. A commercial for Prudential insurance opened with the line, "If you can dream it, you can do it"—a good jumping-off point for a series of images related to a family's financial dreams. Xerox used animated "word people" and "number people" to dramatize the merging of data and word processing. Herbal Essence shampoo used stylized animation of a long-haired girl in an Eden-like environment to interpret the experience of using its shampoo. Interpretative animation can be very representational or very abstract and symbolic.

Diagrammatic

Animation is often used to simplify a complicated idea or to describe a process that would be invisible otherwise, such as the circulation of blood or the operation of an automobile engine. Rarely would such animation constitute an entire commercial, but it is often used as a short demonstration or to depict a reason why in a commercial (for example, how a disposable diaper stops leaks by absorbing and redistributing moisture).

Typographic

To add variety or impact to a logo or title, the words or logo can be animated to pop on, write on, move around, or change shape.

Moving Stills

Called filmograph, this animation technique brings movement to still photographs or artwork through optical effects, zooms, and pans. It can be used effectively with documentary photos or to visually punctuate a musical score. Visual squeeze is a variation that flashes a succession of stills as fast as the mind can accept them.

Three-Dimensional Animation

Stop motion, or stop action, refers to that category of animation in which 3-D objects (miniature models and puppets) are photographed frame by frame to create the illusion of movement. An early advertising application of this technique was the durable Speedy Alka-Seltzer. Another successful stop-motion character is Poppin' Fresh, the Pillsbury Doughboy. Two recent favorites, using a variation called claymation, are the animated clay raisins for the California Raisin Advisory Board and the mischievous Noid for Domino's pizza.

A typical production involves the design and construction of a miniature set in which the props are firmly anchored so they will not move during the action. The characters and models are then positioned in the set, a frame of film is exposed, the characters are adjusted, and so on until the scene has been completed. It takes twenty-four exposures to accomplish one second of action. Bodies of the characters may be adjustable, using wire with rubber coating for the joints, so that a single model can be used, its position changed fractionally for each frame of shooting. Or it may be necessary to make a completely different model for each action. In the Pillsbury commercials, as many as twenty plaster doughboys are required to complete one bit of screen action—a finger poking into Poppin' Fresh's stomach. Obviously, such tedious and intricate work requires an exact predetermination of what the action is to be (and an exact record of what action has been completed). There is little margin for error.

Combinations

It is possible to combine live, animation, and stop motion into a single commercial. A cartoon story may begin the commercial and then give way to live-action product inserts. Or the techniques may be combined within the same scene, so that live-action people can appear to interact with an animated character, a technique that reached its state-of-the-art in the feature film "Who Framed Roger Rabbit?" Or cartoon characters can be combined with 3-D backgrounds and stop-motion props.

Combinations are achieved through rotoscoping, matting, and other optical devices. Rotoscoping refers to a method of projecting and then tracing significant parts and elements of a frame of film (live action) so that animation units can be planned to work with it. For example, the image of a real car is projected and the animator carefully traces onto paper where the driver's seat ends and where the steering wheel is so that a cartoon driver can be positioned and then matted into the scene.

Computer animation has opened up a whole new look in 3-D graphics. In a recent commercial for Bud Light, little 3-D animated spaceships escape from a video game and fly around a crowded bar while the player shoots at them with lasers from his fingertips. The following description of the production from *Computer Pictures* magazine provides a glimpse at the complexity and the jargon of this exciting new field:

> . . . Optimus art director Troy Hayes and animator Rich Bobo began creating the spaceships, using a Bosch FGS 4000. Location shooting was done on 35mm film. . . . The live action required tricky lighting effects to give the impression that the glowing spaceships were illuminating the faces of the bar people as the spaceships zipped around their heads. Of course the actors had to imagine that the spaceships were there and react appropriately.
>
> The 35mm film was transferred to 1-inch video tape and boundary box representations of the spaceships were generated on the Bosch to determine their interplay with the live action. Then, a "video test story board" was created with selected frames fully rendered to determine the final coloring of the ships. When that was approved by the client, the whole sequence was generated and then composited with the live action.
>
> Finally, scene by scene the composited footage was input into an Abekas A62 digital disk system, from which frames were captured and sent to a Quantel Paint Box for enhancement. Artist Ann Smeltzer painted in the spaceship contrails, fingertip laser beams, explosions and more. Smeltzer had also guided the live action in the "bar" toward dovetailing with the computer work.[3]

Mickey Mouse has come a long way.

A Short Catalog of Special Effects

It would be impossible to list all the tricks and effects that are possible with film, videotape, and computer technology. Almost anything is possible—for a price. Just make sure that technique does not become an end in itself. It is easy to get so caught up in the how-to of production that you lose sight of the why. Just because the human mind is able to grasp multiple images or

---

3. *Computer Pictures* (July/August 1987): 108–109.

subliminal cuts does not mean these tricks will enhance the idea of the commercial.

With that warning, here are some of the possible special effects that might trigger an idea or enhance an execution.

Optical Illusions

These can be achieved by a variety of technical tricks ranging from simulating backgrounds (by back projection or miniatures), to combining scenes (by matting), to different kinds of distortions (by photographing in different planes or using altered or unusual lenses). The techniques are actually quite simple, but the effects can be complex and visually interesting.

Back projection is the familiar studio technique (used more in features than in commercials) in which actors, sets, and props are filmed in front of a background that consists of a translucent screen on which a picture (moving or still) is projected from behind. This is a cheap way to simulate exotic locations. A common example is a shot of people in a car, presumably driving, with the scenery zipping by behind them.

Matting is an optical process whereby two different scenes can be combined into one. Animation can be combined with live action, or vice versa. Live sequences can be combined to create unusual juxtapositions such as the famous Hertz man flying through the air and into the seat of his rental car. ("Let Hertz put you in the driver's seat.") In videotape production, matting effects are achieved through a process called chroma key, in which complementary colors are used to mask areas of one picture and insert matted areas of another.

Perspective distortion can be used to create optical illusions without mattes. Through the use of models and changes in perspective, tremendous variations in scale can be achieved. A boy stretched out in one visual plane can appear to lie across the entire top of a school bus that is actually filmed in another distant place and matched in the camera to the foreground object. This is an excellent technique for filming giants, be they green and jolly or Paul Bunyan types handing down chain saws to normal-sized men.

Miniature scale models can recreate larger structures, objects, or scenes. Ships being tossed in a violent sea, flood waters surging through the streets of New York City, and other effects can be achieved with models much more practically than could the real thing. The original Jolly Green Giant was actually a normal-sized man standing over a miniature scale model valley.

Lens Distortion

By photographing the image through filters or gauze it is possible to create a diffused or soft-focus effect. This is often used for romantic or sentimental moods. A fish-eye lens covers 180 degrees and gives the effect of looking at an image stretched over the surface of a ball. (This distorted effect was used in a deodorant commercial to create a mood of nervous tension. The camera represented the point of view of a person entering a room filled with people who leaned and leered toward the lens.) Ripple effects and other distortions result from special lenses or glasses inserted between the lens and the subject and can simulate eerie or supernatural effects.

Film Speeds and Directions

Perhaps the most familiar kinds of special effects are achieved by slowing down or speeding up the film, resulting in fast motion or slow motion. Time-lapse and high-speed photography carry these more or less commonplace techniques to their technological extremes. In addition, frames can be either skipped or repeated to create still other effects. And film can be run backwards, either at normal speed and in actual sequence or in combination with any of the alterations mentioned above.

Slow Motion (Overcranking).   If the motion of the film through the camera is faster (overcranked) than the standard rate, the action will appear slower when it is projected at the standard rate. Slow motion may be used to suggest mood or to slow down action that would otherwise happen too quickly to see. An example of the former is the couple running romantically toward each other in the Clairol commercial ("The closer he gets, the better you look"). An example of the latter is any of countless tire commercials that show blowouts occurring (or being prevented) as a tire passes over a spike in the road. Slow motion is also used for appetite appeal in table top food commercials.

Fast Motion (Undercranking).   If the motion of the film through the camera is slower (undercranked), the action will appear faster when it is projected at the normal rate. The effect that results is often humorous, reminiscent of the old silent comedies. It might be used to demonstrate with comic exaggeration how fast a product works or how busy a housewife is during the day.

Skip-Framing.   The same kind of sped-up, jittery action can be created by an optional process in which frames of the original scene are periodically skipped (left out) in printing.

Time Lapse.   Time-lapse photography permits the filming of actions that happen so slowly they would otherwise be imperceptible, such as the blooming of a flower. A frame is exposed at widely separated intervals so that when it is finally completed and projected the action is greatly compressed. In commercials, time lapse has been used to show the sun rise and set over a city, an electric oven clean itself, and biscuits rise in the oven.

High Speed.   This is just the opposite of time lapse. For example, you can photograph a bullet passing through a light bulb. This is possible through the use of a high-speed strobe light (flashing at 1/20,000 of a second) or with special high-speed cameras capable of shooting at 1,200 frames per second (instead of the normal twenty-four frames per second).

Reverse Action.   Anyone familiar with home movies knows the effect of running the picture through the projector backwards. But this technique can be planned in advance for dramatic effects that seem to defy the laws of gravity. A famous Chevrolet commercial once showed a car assemble itself out of scraps. To achieve this, the car was blown up and the explosion was printed in reverse.

Freeze Frame.   A shot can be lengthened or motion suspended by printing a single frame in the film over and over again. This is used to freeze some especially dramatic or poignant moment for the viewer's lengthy consideration. A very dramatic antismoking commercial showed a bride and groom making their vows, then leaving the church and getting into their car while the voice-over narration continued to recite the vows. The groom casually took out a pack of cigarettes, and just as he started to take one out, the action was frozen and the narration stopped with " 'till death . . ."

Opticals and Images

Split Screen/Multiple Image.   This is a montage effect that shows different portions of the screen blocked off to reveal two or more separate pictures. It may be a two-way split (for phone conversations or side-by-side demonstrations), or the screen may be split up into many segments to show multiple images. The same image may be repeated on the screen simultaneously, or the screen can be sectioned off to create a montage of different images, for example, shots of a soft drink pouring over ice, people drinking, the hot sun. Unfortunately, the small-size screen of television makes multiple images less dramatic than the big-screen features that inspired them.

Kaleidoscope.   Named after the toy tube that creates color designs, this is a multiple-image effect resulting from the use of mirrors. The number of images produced varies with the angle of the mirrors.

Spin.   This effect consists of spinning a scene, product, or title around on its own axis. It is strictly an attention-getter and can be accomplished on an optical printer or an animation stand.

Double Exposure.   Another artistic or moody effect can be achieved by the successive exposure of two scenes so that two superimposed images are visible.

Overlapping Dissolves.   Another shorter double image results when two scenes are cross dissolved over each other so that in the middle of the transition from scene to scene both images are visible simultaneously. The effect is to make the transition very deliberate and conscious and may serve to heighten mood (if the images are similar) or contrast (if the images are conflicting).

Solarization.   This is a "reversal effect produced by exposing a photographic image to intense light for a comparatively long period of time. The sun, for example, would appear black in a photograph exposed under these conditions instead of white."[4] It can be a very dramatic, almost weird, effect. It has found commercial use in spots for Dial, Coke, and others.

Editing

Many special effects are also possible through creative editing. Quick cuts can be strung together to a musical beat. Still photographs can appear to move when cut together in rapid succession. Objects and people can appear to jump around, vanish, and reappear. Jarring, unexpected cuts combined with a shaky hand-held camera can give a commercial the realistic look of home movies.

---

4.   Eli L. Levitan, *An Alphabetical Guide to Motion Picture, Television and Videotape Production* (New York: McGraw-Hill, 1970), 636.

Chapter 8

Putting It All Together
Execution IV

The Chart As Summary

Chapters 5, 6, and 7 discussed some of the ingredients that go into the execution of the idea of a television commercial. The idea and execution are the creative expression of the selling proposition that grows out of a careful analysis of the product and the prospects. Your advertising has to be on strategy (promise the right benefit to the right prospects). But it takes a big leap to get from even the best strategy to the best advertising. It takes creativity to express the desires of your strategy in advertising that is interrupting, daring, fresh, engaging, human, and believable. In truly creative advertising, the idea—what you say—and the execution—how you say it—are so tightly interwoven that it becomes impossible to have one without the other. The expression of the idea involves a basic approach, style, or tone of voice; a format, or structure; and finally, a technique of production. It embraces all of these and more. It is writing, casting, acting, music, editing—all the subtle values of production. These relationships are summarized in the following chart.

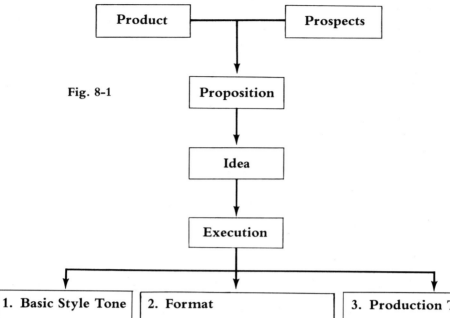

Fig. 8-1

1. Basic Style Tone

Rational

Emotional

Serious

Humorous

Realistic

Exaggerated

2. Format

Product Presentation

Demonstration
  Explanatory
  Side-by-Side
  Before-After
  Torture Test
  Demonstrator Faith

Problems and Solutions
  Problem/Need
  Problem with Others
  Ridiculous Alternatives

Slice-of-Life

Presenters
  Salesperson-Spokesperson
  Authority-Spokesperson
  Satisfied-User Spokesperson
  Celebrity Spokesperson

Continuing Characters

Testimonials

Vignettes

Story

People/Narration

Satire

Musical

Personification

Analogy/Symbolism

3. Production Technique

Live Action
  Live Look
  Documentary Look
  Futuristic/Historical
  Fantasy

Animation
  Cartoon Story
  Interpretative
  Diagram
  Typographic
  Moving Stills
  Three-Dimensional
  Combinations

Special Effects
  Optical Illusions
  Lens Distortions
  Film Speeds and
    Directions
  Opticals and Images
  Editing

The Chart As Starting Point

This chart is both a summary of an idealized creative process that begins with an examination of the product and prospects for a strategic selling proposition, and a thought-starter for creative people. What follows is an example of the latter.

Assume that you have a new product to advertise—plastic clamps used to fasten diapers instead of old-fashioned safety pins. (Forget about disposable diapers for the moment and pretend this simple product represents a breakthrough in diapering.) The benefits of these diaper clamps are convenience and safety. The prospects are parents of new babies.

Turning to the chart, you start with BASIC STYLE/TONE. Since child care is a serious matter to parents, and since the product advantages are rather straightforward, you might start by adopting a rational tone. With that in mind, move to the next column, FORMAT, and start down the list.

The execution might be a simple product presentation or explanatory demonstration that shows a mother easily diapering her baby while a voice-over announcer describes the product and its advantages.

Since the product has obvious advantages over safety pins, you might try a side-by-side demonstration that compares one mother diapering with clamps while another uses conventional pins. At this point you might jump over to the next column, PRODUCTION TECHNIQUE, to see if there is some way to add more visual interest. Under opticals and images you might select a split-screen technique that could contrast the two diapering mothers simultaneously. You could then jump back to the first column and consider a humorous tone and create "The Great Diaper-Fastening Race" with Pat Summerall and John Madden doing the play-by-play (or "pin-by-pin") commentary.

Instead of a competitive side-by-side demonstration you might move on to consider a before-after demonstration, showing how long it used to take (and how dangerous it was) to fasten diapers with pins and then contrast that with the new way, using modern plastic clamps.

By changing tone again (humorous) and adding a production technique (fast motion), the before scene could be portrayed like an old silent film comedy to underscore how silly and old-fashioned diaper pins seem today.

Moving down the format column again, you might explore a torture test demonstration. If the product lives up to it, you might show how firmly the clamps hold by fastening a huge diaper on a baby elephant. (In doing so you move into another change of tone, to humorous or exaggerated.)

Diaper clamps certainly solve some of the problems created by diaper pins. By focusing on the problem/need (unfortunate results of not using the product) you might show a new father with his fingers all bandaged from repeated jabbings of diaper pins. Maybe coin a name for this problem and announce the end of "new-father fingers."

Or maybe you could think up some ridiculous alternatives, like cutting leg holes in a big sponge or taking some metal clamps from the workshop, to humorously show what parents tried to use to avoid the perils of diaper pins before plastic clamps were invented.

Next in the format column is slice-of-life. A commercial could portray a new mother fumbling with diaper pins until her neighbor, stopping by to admire the new baby, suggests that she try new plastic diaper clamps. (You could even cut away to an animation/diagrammatic technique for an animated demo of how plastic clamps are designed to hold more firmly than pins.) The new mother is dubious but promises to give them a try. To her delight they work! The next time she sees her helpful neighbor she jokes about what an expert diaperer she is now.

This might be a product that cries out for presenters. Maybe it requires a salesperson-spokesperson, like the president of Acme Diaper Clamps, extolling the social benefits of this important child care advancement. Maybe you should use an authority-spokesperson, like a pediatric nurse or a mother of ten who has done more than her share of diapering. You could consider using a satisfied user-spokesperson who talks very directly and sincerely about how happy she is to have discovered diaper clamps or a celebrity-spokesperson, a well-known actress from the cover of *People* magazine who just had a baby.

Next, consider the possibility of a continuing character, either live action or animation, to speak for or symbolize the product's advantages. You might use a make-believe nanny (like Mary Poppins) who magically arrives in the nursery to help new parents with their diaper-pinning woes. Or you might create an animated baby (overcoming the difficulty of getting real babies to speak on camera) who is tired of being jabbed in the bottom with diaper pins and who comes to the aid of real babies who face a similar problem.

Next, consider testimonials. Maybe try a hidden camera interview with older mothers who "grew up on pins" but are surprised and converted by these amazing new diaper clamps. Or you could use vignettes of different moms and dads extolling the virtues of clamps from their own personal experiences.

Moving from testimonials to a pure vignettes format you might try a series of humorous scenes built around the disadvantages of diaper pins.

Most of the convenience benefits are parent benefits. But diaper clamps provide some baby benefits, too. They are safer than pins. So you might go back to BASIC STYLE/TONE and adopt a more emotional style that reminds parents how important the product is to the well-being of their baby. You might tell a story of a young couple enjoying every new aspect of caring for their first baby, especially these plastic clamps that cannot accidentally jab.

Maybe you could borrow a people/narration approach from the Michelin tire people and show adorable babies gooing and giggling while the announcer asks parents if they would dare risk jabbing, poking, or hurting their babies with pins when they could use safe diaper clamps.

You might build an emotional commercial around some musical treatment, perhaps a lullaby.

In the satire area, the diapering scene in the movie *Three Men and a Baby* might provide a jumping-off point for a diaper clamps commercial.

And so it goes. Tonality suggests a format, format suggests a production technique. Another production technique suggests another format, which in turn leads to another style of commercial.

The chart categories are arbitrary and deceptively tidy. Ideas do not often fit into the little boxes we would like them to, nor is the creative process as orderly or systematic as this or any chart might pretend. The two-directional arrow between idea and execution is a reminder that these two components are interdependent and usually difficult to distinguish from one another. The idea/execution can begin anywhere on the chart, but you should probably be more suspicious of one that begins with an esoteric production technique than one that begins with the desired emotional tone or basic appeal.

Once ideas for executions begin to surface in the minds of copywriters and art directors, the next step is to get them onto paper in a form that can communicate them to others.

Birth of the Storyboard

A TV commercial combines the power of words and pictures. It is the creative product of a copywriter and an art director. Copywriters write words, art directors draw pictures. It would appear that the creative process divides up into tidy areas of responsibility. In the early days of television advertising it often did. The writer, schooled in radio, ruled supreme. First came the words, then came the pictures. But a good television commercial is more than illustrated radio. A good commercial is good film. It draws on the power of visual imagery and cinematic structure to dramatically make its point. But before a commercial can become film, it must first be a storyboard.

A storyboard is the words and pictures of the idea. It is a diagram of the envisioned commercial that breaks down the action to be filmed into a sequence of drawings, each accompanied by a brief written description of the action and the copy or audio. It looks like an oversized comic strip.

There is no formula for creating storyboards. A storyboard can begin with an art director's vision or with a copywriter's script. It may begin as a visual idea to which words are added later, or it may take visual shape only after the structure of the sale or story has been written. Some copywriters and art directors work as a team, talking out the problem and building visuals and copy concurrently. Others prefer to work alone at first, testing false starts and half ideas on their own typewriters or drawing pads. An art dirctor may sketch out a visual treatment with only the vaguest notion of copy. A copywriter may turn out a script complete with scene-by-scene video directions accompanying the copy. More often the writer works with only a general visual style in mind and relies on the art director to work out the visual specifics.

The important thing to remember is that a storyboard, like the commercial it represents, is a combination of audio and video working hand in hand. It is strongly visual but rarely entirely visual. It requires the best of both—video and audio—and can begin with either.

HELPER LOOKS ON AS
GIANT TUCKS SPROUT
INTO HIS PEA POD.
SONG: UP IN THE VALLEY

MOVE IN AS HELPER
OPENS HIS BOOK AND SITS
DOWN.
OF THE JOLLY GREEN
GIANT

CU SPROUT
SPROUT: Read me about the
Giant's baby peas.

CUT WIDE AGAIN. HELPER
SMILES AS SPROUT NODS.
HELPER: Again, Sprout?

HELPER STARTS TO READ.
Well, once the Green
Giant . . .

RIPPLE DISSOLVE TO LIVE
ACTION. PACKAGE SHOWN
WITH FRESH-PICKED PEAS.
. . . froze tender baby Le
Sueur Brand peas . . .

DISSOLVE TO COOKED
PEAS POURING FROM
POUCH. SUPER: "BUTTER
SAUCE."
. . . in a flavor-tight pouch
with his special butter sauce.

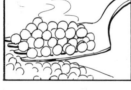

CU AS FORK LIFTS PEAS
They tasted so fresh and
buttery,

BACK TO ANIMATION AS
HELPER FINISHED
BEDTIME STORY.
. . . his baby peas made
people happy ever after.

CUT TO CU OF HAPPY,
SLEEPY SPROUT.
SPROUT: I love a story where
the heroes are little.

CUT TO PACKAGE WITH
GREEN GIANT IN
BACKGROUND.
SONG: HO HO HO GREEN
GIANT

(Fig. 8-2. Sample Storyboard)

Storyboards Are Like Layouts, Only Different

There is a temptation to treat a storyboard as you would a layout for a print ad. The two perform essentially the same function. But a storyboard demands more imagination from the person who sees it. An art director's layout can be a very accurate representation of how the final printed ad will look. Illustration, headline, body text—all the elements can be arranged and presented just as they will appear after production. But a storyboard does not bear this same close relationship to the finished commercial. Film has properties that cannot be duplicated on paper. Therefore the person who creates the storyboard, as well as the person who must evaluate it, must be able to look beyond the board itself and imagine it translated into film. And this is not an easy task.

Because the storyboard is such a poor substitute for a produced commercial, some creative people view it as a burden. Some have spoken out against storyboards as needlessly constrictive, as a step that precludes creative contributions from directors, camera operators, and editors. Here is how one agency executive described the shortcomings of storyboards in *Broadcasting* magazine.

Beyond the selling words, pictures and ideas, there is a "fourth" dimension: a kind of total impression that not only underscores the words, pictures and ideas, but which turns out to be an experience itself . . . that spreads its wings over the entire commercial and helps win friends and influence sales.

Second only to the basic selling idea, and far more vital than isolated words and pictures, this total impression is something that no storyboard can deliver.

In fact, the storyboard tends to kill it. We are looking at a print interpretation of a motion picture idea. And we are looking at it in a logical series of pictures with captions on a frame-by-frame basis. What's more, we are forced to accept what a talented artist can do with a drawing pencil in the suffocating confines of a little box measuring a few inches wide by a few inches deep.

Neither the artist nor the still camera can capture the essence of the idea as it will emerge on a fluid piece of film. There is a distortion of values, too, because we illustrate "pretty girl goes here" and "pretty package goes there" and it has nothing to do with the true dimensions of time and space as they will occur in the finished commercial.

These weaknesses in the storyboard could be dealt with if we all looked at it with true understanding that it was just the merest hint, the vaguest blueprint of what we would try to achieve on camera. They could be dealt with if we mutually agreed that the writers, producers, directors and cameramen (all cognizant and appreciative of the selling thrust and the advertising idea) had complete license to dance around the storyboard, to stray from it, to bring new values to it, and to use film to fulfill what the storyboard can only hint at—and very dimly at that.[1]

A Necessary Evil

Rare is the storyboard that does justice to the idea it represents. Storyboards lack the production values that make the finished commercial work. Drawing storyboards gobbles up an art director's time (time that might be better spent conceiving even better ideas). Storyboards constrict the creative input of the film director. Storyboards require a polished presentation to be understood by clients who must then commit thousands of dollars to produce them. One might well ask, why bother? Whatever injustice they might do to the magic of film, storyboards nevertheless perform some very important services.

The Storyboard Helps Test the Idea

The mere process of reducing a stroke of divine inspiration to storyboard form can be very revealing to the creators. It can help them uncover flaws in the structure of their idea that may have been glossed over in the mental image. It forces the writer and art director to think in concrete terms about what each scene should do, what should go into it, how the scenes connect and flow, and how well the commercial really communicates. It can help them see if they really have a workable, producible idea—or just a wonderful vision.

The Storyboard Helps Get the Idea Approved

Commercials are made for advertisers. They pay the bills and take the consequences. And very few advertisers are prepared to dish out over $100,000 for a copywriter's dream. Advertisers have a right to know what they are getting, or getting into. A storyboard can let them know.

An idea is only as good as its ability to communicate to the audience. And there has to be an idea in a commercial regardless of fancy film techniques. Although lacking the richness and subtlety of a motion picture, a storyboard usually contains enough of the basic idea to enable someone to recognize it. If the idea is good, it will be noticed and approved. If not, so be it. The storyboard that weeds out weak ideas early has justified its existence.

---

1. Alfred Goldman, *Broadcasting,* May 1, 1967.

The Storyboard Helps Get the Idea Produced

A frequent criticism leveled against storyboards is that they restrict the opportunity for the creative filmmaker to contribute to the end product; ideas get frozen too soon, and the studio must carry out the instructions of the storyboard to the letter. Certainly a bad storyboard will lead to a bad commercial. And there are certainly talented production people who would like to contribute their expertise before the idea gets nailed down. But you rarely hear complaints about a good storyboard, one that is a carefully thought-out execution of a solid idea. A good director can always improve on a good storyboard.

A storyboard can help head off problems. If a shot is impossible (too expensive), it can be spotted in the storyboard, discussed, and if need be, changed to a more practical shot. It is much easier to change a storyboard than to reshoot a commercial (and explain the extra costs to the client).

Finally, the storyboard serves as a guide to those who must actually produce the commercial. It helps the film studio accurately bid on the commercial (estimate what it will cost to produce it). It suggests casting, props, sets, and locations. And it keeps production people all "cognizant and appreciative of the selling thrust and the advertising idea."

The Script

The script is the copywriter's storyboard. It is a scene-by-scene breakdown of the commercial, consisting of a verbal description of the pictures (video) and the dialogue or sound accompanying them (audio). The audio—copy—is broken down to show which words go with which visuals. This provides an approximation of the length of each scene. To facilitate the reading of scripts and storyboards, the video and audio directions are customarily typed in all caps. Copy is typed in caps and lower case. This permits the person who is reading the script to scan the copy for the sense of the idea without getting bogged down in stage directions.

The video description in a script should be explicit, but simple. You do not want the reader (or writer) to get lost in technical jargon. But neither do you want to omit vital information that explains exactly what you envision, information that fills in around the single frame the storyboard shows.

Theoretically, a script would be written both sides at once. That is to say, the writer should always be concerned with how the pictures and words work together and how each scene fits with the next. But too often this interrupts the flow of copy. Copywriters usually think the pictures and write the copy without taking the time to describe each scene in detail. Then they go back and fill in the details. Initially, the copywriter needs only enough script to take to an art director. During the inevitable give-and-take of the creative team process, the pictures (and probably the words) are likely to change. Once the commercial has been worked out to the satisfaction of both, the final script is prepared. The final script for Fig. 8-2 appears on the next page.

Script for Jolly Green Giant Commercial

HELPER LOOKS ON AS GIANT
TUCKS SPROUT INTO HIS PEA
POD.
SONG: UP IN THE VALLEY . . .

MOVE IN AS HELPER OPENS HIS
BOOK AND SITS DOWN.
SONG: . . . OF THE JOLLY GREEN
GIANT

CU SPROUT
SPROUT: Read me about the Giant's
baby peas.

CUT WIDE AGAIN HELPER
SMILES AS SPROUT NODS.
HELPER: Again, Sprout?

HELPER STARTS TO READ. Well,
once the Green Giant . . .

RIPPLE DISSOLVE TO LIVE
ACTION. PACKAGE SHOWN
WITH FRESH-PICKED PEAS.
. . . froze tender baby Le Sueur Brand
peas . . .

DISSOLVE TO COOKED PEAS
POURING FROM POUCH. SUPER:
"BUTTER SAUCE."
. . . in a flavor-tight pouch with his
special butter sauce.

CU AS FORK LIFTS PEAS
They tasted so fresh and buttery,

BACK TO ANIMATION AS
HELPER FINISHED BEDTIME
STORY.
. . . his baby peas made people happy
ever after.

CUT TO CU OF HAPPY, SLEEPY
SPROUT.
SPROUT: I love a story where the
heroes are little.

CUT TO PACKAGE WITH GREEN
GIANT IN BACKGROUND.
SONG: HO HO HO GREEN GIANT

Commercial Lengths: Sixties and Thirties and Fifteens

Commercials come in many lengths, from flashbulb-quick ten-second IDs to rambling two-minute sales pitches and infomercials. It would be nice if the creative person could simply choose the length that did the best job of telling the product story. But there is the troublesome matter of budgets. A sixty-second commercial costs more to broadcast than a thirty-second commercial; a 30 costs more than a 15. When a media planner can spend less money to expose a commercial to more people, more often, he or she has achieved efficiency. The pressure for efficiency in an environment of increasing costs has been squeezing the commercial into shorter and shorter lengths.

In the golden days of television advertising, the sixty-second commercial was the rule. Today it is the exception. Today 60s have become the yachts of television advertising. If you have to ask how much they cost, you probably cannot afford them.

The best that a copywriter can hope for is a thirty-second commercial, which took over from the 60 as the standard length in the mid 1960s. But even the 30 is being pressured by the efficiency bargain of the 1980s—the 15. The 15 offers cost-conscious advertisers a cheaper way to reach their audience. Unfortunately, it also means more commercial clutter for that audience. As the *Wall Street Journal* observed,

> Until recently, a two-minute commercial break usually consisted of three or four ads; now there are often five different spiels strung together. Indeed, by late 1986, the number of network ads in an average week exceeded 5,300, reflecting the fact that about 20% were 15 seconds long. The year before, about 5,000 ads were shown during an average week, and just 9% were 15s.[2]

The hue and cry over the threat (opportunity?) of the 15 seems to be a simple case of history repeating itself. Creatives lamented the passing of the 60 with predictions that campaigns would shrivel up and disappear, unable to tell their product stories or stir consumer emotions in a mere thirty seconds. To be sure, there are times when the mood, imagery, and pacing of a 60 cannot be compressed into half the time. It became harder to launch new products, new characters, and new campaigns. But concepts tightened up and a lot of extraneous information and images that had weighed down some 60s disappeared. After a steady diet of well-crafted 30s, viewers now greet some 60s with impatience and wandering attentiveness.

The fact that most advertisers survived the creative constrictions of the move from 60s to 30s should not in itself be taken as assurance that a broad-scale move to 15s would be as smooth. All the arguments made against those early 30s are being made again against the 15. But now they seem more valid. For many kinds of commercials fifteen seconds is too short.

> It's hard enough to tell a story in 30 seconds. . . . Sometimes a 60 doesn't even translate to a 30 very well. I think 15s don't allow a good creative director or editor to tell a story.[3]

The advocates of 15s over 30s (as the advocates of 30s over 60s did before them) point to their performance as well as their economy. On such copy-testing criteria as recall and message communication, 15s are said to be about seventy percent as effective as 30s. (During the 30s vs. 60s debate, 30s were found to perform about two-thirds as well as 60s on recall measures.) In both cases, the shorter units were priced fifty percent cheaper

---

2. Ronald Alsop, "More Companies Squeeze Ads into Bargain 15-Second Spots," *Wall Street Journal,* January 29, 1987.

3. Jack Feuer, "15-Second Spots Take Hold," *Adweek, Commercial Production* (October 19, 1987): C.P. 32.

than the longer units. Since the cost savings were greater than the loss in performance, shorter commercials represented (and represent) attractive values. This assumes, however, that recall is a true measure of a commercial's effectiveness.

Making 60s into 30s (and Vice Versa)

The sixty-second commercial is a luxury few advertisers can afford. Still there are times when a minute is needed, such as important new product introductions, complicated demonstrations, complex copy strategies, emotional stories, and flagship image commercials. But because 60s are so expensive to run, advertisers usually want to make a thirty-second version to run with it or after the 60 has established itself. (Similarly, most of the 15s that are produced have thirty-second "parents.") These stepchildren of longer commercials are called lifts (because thirty seconds is lifted from the 60). Lifts are seldom as satisfying as the original.

There may be some production economies that justify lifts, but they are not as defensible from a story point of view. If the story is flabbily written, it may well survive being cut in half. But if the 60 is tightly written and carefully constructed, its thirty-second version will come up short, in more ways than one. The 30 should be treated as a thing unto itself. It demands special disciplines, special respect, and special effort.

> They (most copywriters) think 60 and write 30. And that's a big mistake. Because it usually ends up too confusing. By the time they strip away half the idea, the bare bones that are left make you wonder just what the writer had in mind in the first place. The little nuances, even the silences, that help a dramatic idea come alive have to be sacrificed. Everything has to be spelled out. No room is left for the viewer to participate in the commercial. All of a sudden, we're talking *at* people instead of playing *to* them.[4]

A wise but rarely followed rule is not to write a 60 until you have written an effective 30. But writers tend to write long. What may start out as a 30 easily becomes a 35 or 40. It is easier to expand it to a 60 than to cut it back to a legitimate 30. (One of the positive side effects of the 15 has been the availability of forty-five-second units. This is usually all the extra time a writer schooled in 30s needs to tell a more complicated product story.)

Be especially wary of sixty-second dramas. They need time to breathe and can be hard to cut. So can songs and jingles. It is tough to build a thirty-second commercial around a sixty-second song. Some commercial formats cut down more easily. A vignettes approach can usually make the same point in half the time. Presenter commercials condense to the degree that the copy story itself can be compressed.

Here are two examples of sixty- and thirty-second scripts that are edits of the same ideas, messages, and story situations. See for yourself what has been left out of the 30 (or added to the 60).

---

4. Tony Isidore, *Advertising Age* (September 24, 1973): 24.

9-LIVES

<u>:60</u>   <u>:30</u>

ANNCR: 9-Lives presents Morris.

SFX: (MORRIS SNORING)

WOMAN: Morris!   WOMAN: Morris!

MORRIS: Huh?   MORRIS: Huh?

WOMAN: Surprise! Little Albert   WOMAN: Little Albert's come to
         from next door is going   visit.
         to spend the week with
         us.

MORRIS: Oh joy!   MORRIS: Oh joy! Little dum-
                                                     dum!

WOMAN: Isn't he cute?

MORRIS: Cute, she says! Dumb
         is more like it. If the
         world was flat he'd be
         the first one to fall off
         the edge.

WOMAN: Sweeties, . . . time for   WOMAN: Look, Sweeties! 9-Lives
         din-din.   Kidney, Liver, Super-
                                                     Supper. Let's have
                                                     Tuna and Liver for
                                                     din-din.

MORRIS: Watch this! Yech! She   MORRIS: Hmph! Look at him go!
         says "din-din" and he's   He hasn't learned the
         off like a shot. Dum-   cat who doesn't act
         dum hasn't learned the   finicky loses control of
         cat who doesn't act   his owner.
         finicky loses control of
         his owner.

WOMAN: Now, what shall we   WOMAN: Here you are!
         have? 9-Lives Kidney,
         Liver, Tuna, Super-
         Supper.

(continued)

	:60		:30
MORRIS:	Man! Those 9-Lives goodies are getting to me.		
WOMAN:	Here you are, Tuna and Liver!		
MORRIS:	Hey, look at that kid eat! I'd better get over there myself before it's all gone. Move over, Albert! (EATING SOUNDS)	MORRIS:	Hey! I'd better get going before it's all gone. Move over, Albert! (EATING SOUNDS)
ANNCR:	9-Lives. The nutritious foods cats really like . . . even Morris.	ANNCR:	9-Lives. The nutritious foods cats really like . . . even Morris.
MORRIS:	Albert, when it comes to 9-Lives you're not so dumb!		

MAYTAG

:60	:30
Who says you can't have a washer in your own apartment?	Who says you can't have a washer in your own apartment?
Not Maytag!	Not Maytag!
Introducing . . . the New Maytag Porta-Washer!	Introducing . . . the new Maytag Porta-Washer!
It doesn't care where you live. Stores in a closet, almost anywhere.	Stores almost anywhere. It's portable!
The Porta-Washer needs no installation. Just roll it up to a sink.	No installation. Just roll it up to a sink.
In this new kind of Maytag, we've teamed up a washer and spin dryer.	
Washes a load in four minutes . . . spin dries in one.	Washes a load in four minutes . . . spin dries in one.
And like all Maytags, it's a dependable workhorse.	
It even washes sheets.	
(SFX: SHEET SNAPPING)	
For a complete portable laundry, add a Maytag Porta-Dryer.	The new Maytag Porta-Washer. Add a Porta-Dryer for a complete portable laundry.
The perfect pair for your apartment or mobile home.	
Porta-Washer . . . Porta-Dryer.	
Only by Maytag . . . the dependability people.	Only by Maytag . . . the dependability people.

The Challenge of Fifteen Seconds

The odds against cutting a good 30 into a good 15 are even greater. A 15 is so short that it limits the format and style. Music commercials and slice-of-life suffer when squeezed into a 15. There is no time to build a set-up, situation, or mood. It becomes almost impossible to do stirring emotional dramas. (Shock, yes, but not sentiment.) The ideas that survive in fifteen seconds are necessarily simple and highly visual. Naturally it helps if the product itself is simple and unique.

The discipline of the 15 can have a positive effect on creative strategies. There is no time for complicated, multibenefit strategies or long reason-why support. (A 15 may have to choose between promise and reason-why.) This can bring sharper focus to the purpose of the commercial—something that will lead to better 30s and 60s as well.

If editing a 30 into a 15 results in boiling it down to its most important copy point and most dramatic visual image, you may end up with a strong 15. But if you just compress the 30 and rely on viewers remembering the longer commercial and filling in the missing information or imagery when they see the 15, you are asking for trouble. There may be advantages to having "parent-child" 30s and 15s delivering the same message, but only if each commercial is effective in its own right. Again, as was recommended with 60s and 30s, write the 15 first. When you do, if it is truly successful as a 15 you may find that expanding it into a 30 means adding superfluous material. (You cannot improve an effective poster or billboard by adding more copy. It works because of its simplicity and brevity, not in spite of it.)

The fifteen-second commercial is no doubt here to stay. In Japan, for instance, the 15 is the standard length, and Japanese advertising is among the most creative in the world. If you have to do them, do them right. *Adweek* reported at least two favorable reviews for 15s:

> Levi Strauss Co. used 15-second spots to focus on individual members of its famous street-scene spots, which have run for four years. The spots were so effective that "you'd get a lot of positive votes on the 15 from this agency and the client," says Pat Sherwood, senior vice president/group management supervisor at Foote, Cone & Belding, San Francisco, the agency for Levi Strauss.

> And Polaroid has just launched a series of 15-second spots through BBDO, New York, for its Spectra camera to "convey spontaneity and the quickness of instant photography in given situations," according to Polaroid spokesman Allan Verch. The commercials, he adds, were "15 seconds by intent."[5]

"Fifteen seconds by intent" is the key. As the 15 becomes a fact of life, creative people (and clients) need to approach them for what they are and for what they can do best. They need to approach them as original, free-standing commercials and not as simply pale shadows of parent 30s.

---

5. Jack Feuer, *Adweek* (October 19, 1987): C.P. 33.

Some Rules That Even Creative People Can Live With

Rules are the antithesis of creativity. The creative person lives to break the rules, to challenge preconceptions and the accepted ways of doing things, to stand out from the crowd by being different. But there are good rules and bad rules in advertising. A good rule is that a thirty-second commercial should have no more than twenty-nine seconds of copy. That is all it can physically accommodate. A bad rule is that you must show the product within the first five seconds of the commercial. This is arbitrary and built on the assumption that all advertising works one way. The rules you have to follow are a matter of law, time, and technology. The rules you need to challenge are those that are based on what has worked in the past. Too often successes of the past become the basis for formulas, guidelines, and rules for the future.

But times change. People change. Tastes change. The environment changes. Attitudes change. Advertising follows—and sometimes leads—these changes. Taboos of the past become the breakthroughs of the future. Suppose, for example, that all the evidence proved that tense, conflictful openings for commercials attracted more attention than positive, happy openings. And suppose that all advertisers acted on this knowledge and legislated that all commercial openings be tense and show conflict. In such an environment, the first advertiser who dared show a positive, happy commercial opening would stand out and attract attention.

This leads to rule number one:

Understand the rules you break.   Learn to distinguish between constriction and common sense. Understand the assumptions and evidence on which a rule is based. If nothing else, this will give you a sense of the odds you are up against as you set out to defy conventional wisdom. If conventional wisdom says tht someone speaking on-camera is more effective than voice-over narration, blindly following this rule could be as detrimental as heedlessly ignoring it. If you assume that speaking on-camera per se guarantees effectiveness, you may not bother to pay attention to who is speaking and what he or she is saying. And if you overlook the fact that someone speaking on-camera can be effective because it is personal and involving, you may forget to make sure that your rule-breaking voice-over commercial has compelling and involving visuals or some other element that will compensate for any lack of one-on-one contact with the viewer.

Creative people were born to be rebels. But they should be rebels with a cause. The idea is not simply to defy traditions, but to out-perform them. Follow the good rules, break the bad rules. But understand why the rule is there to begin with. There can be no formula for being creative. But here are some commonsense observations about advertising that is relevant, likeable, and watchable, as opposed to advertising that viewers will not bother to watch.

It avoids the clichés of the category.   It goes beyond the phony slice-of-life, the dull presenter, the unbelievable testimonial. It brings something fresh to the familiar. It makes the most out of production values.

It involves the viewer from the beginning. It never assumes the viewer is interested in what it has to say. It reaches out and captures attention. The viewer must think, "This is interesting. This could be important to me." It does not settle for shock value or attention-getting gimmicks. It relies on empathy, intrigue, relevance.

It keeps the product central. It never loses sight of its reason for being. The story it tells is a story about the product. The style of the commercial reflects the personality of the product. The drama is inherent, rooted in the product itself. Making sure that a commercial is all about the product is much different from making sure the product appears in the first three seconds.

It rewards the viewer. It avoids the cardinal sin of boring the viewer or wasting his or her time. It is human. It touches the emotions as well as the mind. It is honest and intelligent. It is likeable. It entertains as well as sells. (Faced with a choice between two salespeople offering products that are essentially identical in form and price, the consumer is more likely to buy from the friendlier, more likeable salesperson.) And importantly, it is relevant. It does not tell the viewer something that is of no use or importance.

It is simple. It makes itself easily understood. It sticks to one point.

It is visual. It plays to the strength of the medium. It lets the pictures attract attention, set the mood, demonstrate the product. It uses copy judiciously to complement and enhance the pictures.

Part **4**

Storyboard to Commercial

Chapter 9

Visual Storytelling

Understanding Video

Whether it is the art director sketching the frames of a storyboard or the copywriter writing a script, visualizing a television commercial requires discipline as well as imagination.

Visualizing the commercial requires thinking in the language of film. This involves more than just talking in the jargon of film; sprinkling your video descriptions with terms like *lap dissolve* or *crab dolly* will not automatically make you a better visualizer. Visualizing in the language of film means seeing each shot in your mind's eye as if you were the cinematographer or director. It means seeing exactly what goes into each shot and how each shot relates to the shots that precede and follow it.

Video means "I see." When you begin a script with "Open on shot of girl holding product," what do you really see? What kind of girl? What is she wearing? Where is she? What is she doing? Is she close to the viewer or barely visible? Is she moving or standing still? Whatever is on the screen at a given instant is all that the viewer sees; it is the only information the viewer has as to what is going on. The person who is visualizing the commercial must make sure that at each given instant the viewers see whatever they need to see to be able to understand what they are seeing and to be able to follow the story or sales message as it unfolds. Such things as the number of elements included in the image, the distance of objects from the viewer (camera), the angle from which the viewer sees the scene, and the movement that takes place can all affect how the viewers interpret and react to what they are seeing.

Visualizing the Shot

The basic visual element in a film is the shot. A shot is a continuous view filmed by one camera without interruption. Each shot is a take. A number of takes may be required to get one acceptable shot. A scene may consist of one shot or a series of shots taken from different angles and distances.

The copywriter visualizing the shot need not get into the details of composition and cinematography, but there are three important considerations:

1. The area included in the shot (long shot or close-up?).
2. The viewpoint (objective or subjective?).
3. The camera angle (is the viewer looking up or down at the subject?).

You need not be a Hollywood director to determine such things. You need only know the purpose of the shot—why it is included in the commercial and what it is supposed to tell the viewer. In the earlier example, "Open on shot of girl with product," what is the purpose? Is the shot intended to convey information about the product? Or is it more important that the viewer learn something about the girl, such as her personality or mood, that might be revealed by a facial expression or the way she is dressed? Or is it critical at this point that the viewer notice the setting?

The shot controls what and how much information the viewers receive at that particular instant. It can tell them what is important, what they are supposed to notice, and even how they are supposed to react to it.

> Choice of camera angle can position the audience *closer* to the action to view a significant portion in a large close-up; *farther away* to appreciate the magnificent grandeur of a vast landscape; *higher* to look down upon a vast construction project; *lower* to look up at the face of a judge.[1]

Area Included in the Shot

To help you visualize and describe what is to be included in any given shot, think of a continuum of shots from very far away from the subject to very close to the subject. Each shot is defined in terms of its subject matter—the size of the subject relative to the overall picture area. For example, a man filmed in a close-up would fill the same relative amount of picture area as an elephant in close-up even though the elephant is bigger. There is a term for each shot along this continuum, but the purpose of the terminology is only to provide a shorthand means of expressing what you see in your mind's eye.

Extreme Long Shot (ELS)
At one end of the continuum is the vast panoramic shot that shows a great area seen from a great distance. Such shots are often called establishing

---

1. Joseph V. Mascelli, *The Five C's of Cinematography* (Hollywood: Cine/Grafic Publications, 1965), 12.

(Figure 9-1. Range of Shots)

shots because their purpose is often to establish a frame of reference for the audience. Extreme long shots may be used to establish geographical setting or scenic beauty (as in western movies when a rider is shown against a spectacular landscape). A spaghetti commercial may open with a panoramic view of the Bay of Naples or another Italian scene. The extreme long shot may establish a complicated bit of action, such as an automobile race, or a mood or atmosphere, such as the empty streets of a city in the early morning or a busy city at the peak of rush hour. Extreme long shots may set the scene and give viewers the information they need to interpret or understand what follows. For example, a distant view of a tiny desert island in the middle of a vast expanse of ocean would help prepare viewers for the next shot of a man in ragged clothes walking along a beach. They know the man is not a Sunday afternoon beachcomber strolling near Malibu; they know the man is a shipwrecked survivor. In commercials, extreme long shots are used more for such information than for spectacle. The small size of the television screen does not lend itself to impressive panoramas with the same impact as the wide-screen movie.

Long Shot
The long shot is less panoramic and a little more specific than the extreme long shot. Setting could be established, but the viewer will be better able to pick out and relate to specific individuals within the shot. "The place, the people, and the objects in the scene are shown in a long shot to acquaint the audience with their overall appearance. A long shot may include a street, a house, or a room, or any setting where the event takes place. The long shot should be employed to establish all elements in the scene, so that viewers will know who is involved, where they are located as they move about, and when seen in closer shots as the sequence progresses.[2]

---

2. Mascelli, 12.

Medium Shot (MS or MED)

In a medium shot, people are filmed about waist high. Although more than one person may appear, the camera is close enough to capture gestures, expressions, and movement. The most common type of medium shot is the two-shot, in which two characters exchange dialogue. The two-shot permits you to show not only the person who is talking, but also the reactions of the person who is listening.

The medium shot is excellent for television because the action is contained in a restricted area and the figures are large and easily visible. It focuses on the action but retains enough suggestion of background to remind the viewer where the action is taking place.

Medium shots are good reestablishing shots. After a series of close-ups, a return to a medium shot will help reorient the viewer to the larger scene, action, or setting.

Close-Up (CU)

The close-up trims away all the nonessentials and focuses the viewers' attention right where you want it. It tells them what is important, what they should be noticing. Generally, a close-up of a person includes head and shoulders. Variations of people in close-ups include the medium close-up (approximately midway between the waist and shoulders to above the head), the head close-up (head only), and the choker close-up (from below the lips to above the eyes).[3]

The basic use of the close-up is to draw viewer attention to a significant detail, such as a unique product feature or the emotional reactions of an actor. Since this is the aim of the shot, backgrounds should be kept simple so they do not compete for attention. Usually the background is simply out of focus.

Although close-ups are dramatic shots in themselves, the key to their dramatic effect is often the way they are used in a sequence of shots. The two basic editing uses of the close-up are cut-ins and cut-aways.

A cut-in close-up is a close-up look at a portion of the preceding larger shot. It is essential that the cut-in be established by a longer shot so viewers are aware of its location in relation to the overall scene and are able to clearly understand what they are looking at. A cut-in close-up can be used: to heighten dramatic dialogue (by cutting in to a close-up of a person as he or she says something important or by cutting to a person reacting to what he or she hears); to isolate a significant detail (by cutting in to the product on the kitchen table to eliminate surrounding distractions); to magnify small-scale action (by cutting in from a shot of a man working on an assembly line to a close-up look at his hands performing a delicate wiring operation); to condense time by eliminating dull, repetitious action (by cutting in from a shot of a secretary beginning to type to a close-up of fingers on the keyboard, followed by a shot of the finished letter being rolled out of the typewriter).

The second editing use of the close-up is the cut-away. A cut-away close-up is related to, but not a part of, the previous scene. It depicts action happening simultaneously elsewhere—action either directly or indirectly

---

3. Mascelli, 32.

connected to the main narrative. Cut-aways can be used: to present reactions of someone off screen (after a shot of a boy wearing his Sunday best falling into a mud puddle, cut away to a close-up of his mother's expression as she watches from the window); to cue the viewer on how to react to a scene (from a shot of a tall stranger riding into town on a black horse, cut away to a close-up of a frightened storekeeper to stimulate similar apprehension in the mind of the viewer); to comment on the action by showing a visual analogy (from a scene of commuters crowding into a subway car, cut away to a close-up of sheep pushing into a pen); to motivate a piece of action (a cut-away to a close-up of an alarm bell ringing causes firefighters to scurry to the fire truck).

Extreme Close-Up (ECU)

An extreme close-up can focus attention on a detail of a detail, such as the name on the label of a can of soup. Tiny objects or areas, or small portions, or large objects or areas can be filmed so that they appear greatly magnified on the screen. Such shots are used for appetite appeal in food commercials (an ECU of a pat of butter melting over corn on the cob) or to indicate some fine point of product difference (an ECU of green crystals in a white detergent).

The purpose of categorizing shots from extreme long shot to extreme close-up is to provide a convenient shorthand understood by those working in film (who must eventually produce the commercial) and to help crystallize what otherwise might remain just a fuzzy mental image. It gives the copywriter a way to think about and describe what an art director draws. What you include in a shot—the distance from which you view the subject—does make a difference. As you move away from the subject, you include setting and atmosphere, but you sacrifice detail. As you move closer to the subject you single out details and tend to heighten drama and impact. To repeat, your decision should be based on the purpose of the shot and its relationship to the commercial as a whole. You need advertising sense and common, storytelling sense.

Viewpoint: Objective and Subjective

The unique quality of the motion picture is that the audience can be positioned anywhere to view anything from any angle. The situation is very different with a theater audience. There, seat location determines the distance and angle from which a person must view all the action. The ad person who visualizes the commercial must imagine how the viewer is going to see each shot because viewpoint can influence how the viewer will react to a given scene.

The camera viewpoint (and thus the viewpoint of the spectator) can be objective or subjective. The objective camera is impersonal. It records the action from the point of view of a sideline observer, someone unseen and uninvolved in the action. Because the camera (viewer) is unseen, the people being filmed never look into the lens. If they do, the viewer will feel like a voyeur caught in the act.

The subjective camera films the action from a personal, involved viewpoint. Viewers participate in the screen action as though it were a personal experience. They are placed in the picture, either on their own as active participants or by trading places with a person in the film and seeing the event through his or her eyes. One dramatic use of the subjective camera was the famous Cinerama roller coaster ride. The sudden insertion of a subjective camera point of view into an otherwise objectively filmed sequence can heighten drama or suspense by suddenly thrusting viewers into the place of the person they have been watching. When the camera is used subjectively, on-camera performers can look directly into the lens. The strength of on-camera presenters or spokespersons in commercials is that viewers feel the person they are watching is speaking to them personally.

Camera Angle

Another concern of the person visualizing the commercial is how camera angles can contribute to the visual impression of a shot. Apart from tricky angles, there are three basic ways to record a scene: 1) eye level, 2) looking down (high angle), or 3) looking up (low angle).

Eye Level
Eye-level camera angles present a view as seen by an observer of average height. Although it is possible to make such shots dramatic, as in showing a train racing head-on toward the camera, eye-level shots are generally less interesting than those from higher or lower angles.

Looking Down (High Angle)
High angle refers to shots in which the camera is tilted downward to view the subject. It does not necessarily mean that the camera is placed at a great height. Such shots can be a welcome change of pace from a steady diet of eye-level shots. They can provide contrast, variety, and dramatic interest for even commonplace scenes. High angles may be used for: technical reasons (to make it easier to follow or understand the action, just as it is easier to see a football game from high in the stands than from the bench on the field); aesthetic reasons (to present a more artistic picture, like the kaleidoscopic effect of the direct overhead shots of dancing girls in the Busby Berkeley musicals of the 1930s); psychological reasons—to influence how the audience reacts to the shot. "High-angling is excellent whenever a player should be belittled, either by his surroundings or by his actions. An important player who loses prestige or honor may thus be depicted as beaten down by circumstances, or natural elements, or terrain, simply by positioning the camera high, employing a wide-angle lens to look down upon him, and reducing his image to lowly insignificance in relation to the setting."[4]

Looking Up (Low Angle)
Low-angle shots are those in which the camera is tilted upward to view the subject. They need not be exaggerated "worm's-eye views." Low-angle shots can be used for psychological impact. Looking up at certain subjects, such as courtroom judges or church interiors, may increase the effect of

---

4. Mascelli, 39.

apprehension or awe in the viewer. Low angles can be very dramatic visually and compositionally. A foreground figure filmed at a low angle will appear to tower over the others. By dropping the horizon and eliminating background objects, people can be positioned against the sky. Such shots can intensify dramatic impact.

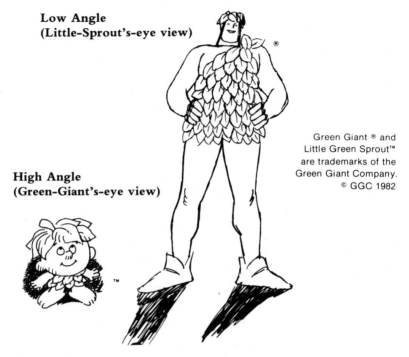

Low Angle
(Little-Sprout's-eye view)

High Angle
(Green-Giant's-eye view)

Green Giant ® and
Little Green Sprout™
are trademarks of the
Green Giant Company.
© GGC 1982

(Figure 9-2. Camera Angle)

The "Right" Angle

Camera angles can be helpful to underscore an emotional effect or to inject drama or visual interest, but like every other technique they can run away with themselves. If dramatic angles are used repeatedly and carelessly, they can begin to call attention to themselves and give the finished product a gimmicky look. Unusual angles must fit into the continuity of the commercial. The viewer should think, "What dramatic action!" and not, "What dramatic camera angles!" The "right" angle to use is the one that best contributes to telling the story or communicating the message.

Visualizing (and Describing) Movement

Movement is one of the big advantages that television commercials have over print media. Models can do more than smile and point at the product. The story can change locales, the commercial can build a rhythm and tempo. Editing—the joining together of individual shots—is one kind of movement. But there is also the movement that takes place within the shot or scene. One of three things can happen; 1) the subject can move (the camera simply records a man walking across a room); 2) the camera can move (the camera gradually draws nearer to a man who stands still in a room); 3) the subject and camera can both move (a man walks across a room toward the camera, turns, and the camera turns to follow his actions).

Suppose you visualize a man running. What exactly do you see? There are many ways this simple action can be visualized and described in the language of film. Is the camera objective or subjective? Do we watch him run or do we watch the road disappear under his feet as if we were running? Does he run past a fixed point in a blur? Do we watch him approach, pass, and disappear? Do we seem to be running alongside him? Does he run toward us? Away from us? Under us? Over us? Each specific action calls for a specific descriptive shot.

Side to Side

If the action you visualize and wish to describe moves from side to side, the descriptive camera moves are pan or truck.

Pan describes a move in which the camera pivots on a fixed point to turn and follow the action. The pan can be used objectively, as in following the action of a man running, or subjectively, as in panning around a room as though seen through the eyes of someone who just entered it. If the camera pans too quickly, the image blurs. Such blurred pans are sometimes used for effect, for example, to suggest speed (these are called swish pans or flash pans).

Truck describes the lateral movement of the camera when it is mounted and fixed to move parallel to the action without pivoting. Using this type of action you could film the running man as though you were running alongside him. Such shots, in which the camera tracks along to film action, are also called follow shots or tracking shots.

Forward or Backward

If the action you visualize and wish to describe moves forward or backward, the descriptive camera moves are dolly or zoom. The first involves moving the entire camera; the second is accomplished by adjusting a lens. To capture rising and falling action, the descriptive camera move is tilt.

A *dolly* is a platform on which the motion picture camera is mounted and can thereby be pushed toward or away from the subject. The term has been extended to describe the in or out movement of the camera—dolly in or dolly out. (Dolly and truck are often used interchangeably—dolly in/truck in—although truck is usually reserved for lateral camera moves.) Because the entire camera is moving during the shot, the dolly is generally slow. A faster move, from a long shot to a close-up, for example, would be to cut from one shot to the next, or to zoom.

A *zoom* is an in or out move accomplished by turning a special camera lens (called, not surprisingly, a zoom lens). This can be done at various speeds for various effects. For example, a chambermaid enters a hotel

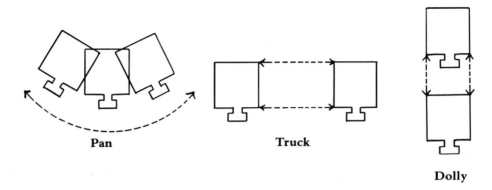

(Figure 9-3. Camera Moves)

room, sees a body under the bed, and the camera zooms quickly to a close-up of her terrified expression. During a zoom the image is out of focus, so the camera operator's job is to be sure the move begins and ends in focus.

In addition to moving horizontally, the camera can also tilt up or down. Such shots are used for catching important rising or falling action. Tilt shots are good ways to emphasize height. A cliff or building can be made to appear very tall by placing the camera near the base and slowly tilting it toward the top.

Movement: A Word of Caution

Movement is certainly desirable. A commercial that does not move risks looking dull and static. But a commercial that moves just for the sake of moving runs the equally dangerous risk of becoming frantic and confusing. A zoom might be very dramatic at the proper moment, but zoom after zoom would quickly strain both the eye and the mind. Each move, like each shot, should be evaluated in the context of the entire commercial. Cinematographer Joseph V. Mascelli offered this cautionary advice to those considering camera moves:

> Many cameramen and directors *mistakenly* believe that a moving shot contributes flow to the story-telling and speeds the screen action. In many instances, movement *slows* the screen story because it takes longer to come to the point! Unless the camera move is dramatically motivated, it is much better to shoot several static shots that may be straight cut, rather than a long moving shot which drags from one significant bit of action to another. . . .
>
> Use of shots . . . requires considerable forethought. This is especially important on static subject matter where the cameraman desires to inject movement by panning, tilting or dollying. The value of camera movement, in relation to the story-telling and editorial (film cutting) problems involved, should be employed only where justified—providing its screen length does not restrict the film editor.[5]

---

5. Mascelli, 162–163.

According to Mascelli, then, a camera move that is injected to prevent the film from seeming static may, in fact, contribute to the static feeling. What really gives a film a feeling of movement is not pans and zooms but the way the different shots fit together.

Transitions

A commercial rarely consists of a single shot or take. It is usually composed of series of different shots edited or cut together to make the whole. And the whole is greater than the sum of its parts. These changes from one shot to another can represent changes in the amount of area included (from long shot to close-up), changes in point of view (from objective to subjective), changes in camera angle (from eye-level to high-angle), changes in place or location (from exterior to interior), changes in time (from the present to much later), or combinations of these. It is the ability to make these abrupt changes smoothly that gives film its dramatic and flexible storytelling qualities.

Various transitional devices may be employed to bridge these jumps in time or space and to fit the pieces of the commercial into a continuous unit. The most common and direct way to join scenes is the cut. A cut is an instantaneous change of scene. The two pieces of film are simply spliced together; one shot ends and the other shot begins. If the shots do not relate, the effect may be jarring; but if they make sense in context, the transition is natural and unnoticed.

Opticals are mechanical operations performed in the lab to produce a variety of transitional effects and create a more noticeable change from shot to shot than a simple cut. These are added after the film has been edited.

Fade-In and Fade-Out

A fade-in is an optical transition in which a black screen gradually brightens into an image. It is used to begin a story or sequence. A fade-out is one in which the image gradually darkens to black. It is used to end a story or sequence. Fades may be of any length required to fit the dramatic tempo of the action. Generally, they are employed in pairs to mark a distinct change between scenes in time or locale.

Dissolves

A dissolve blends one scene into another. Technically, a dissolve is a fade-out superimposed upon a fade-in. The second scene appears before the first completely fades to black. Dissolves are used to cover a time lapse or a change in locale, or to soften a transition that would otherwise seem too abrupt or jarring. Dissolves come in a variety of forms:

- *Matched dissolves* are those in which the two connected scenes are similar in form, motion, or content (for example, between a wheel and a bottle cap, or between the flame of a match and a roaring forest fire). These are intended to make a smoother transition by making the image change seem less abrupt. But there is always a danger that the matching scenes will appear too obvious or tricky; when they do, the dissolve defeats its aim of a smoother transition.

- *Overlapping dissolves* are slower transitions in which the two scenes can be seen superimposed in the middle of the dissolve. This can create a dreamy, romantic, or arty impression. Overlapping dissolves are often used in succession to produce a montage effect.

- *Distorted dissolves* are those in which the blending images shimmy, ripple, shiver, shake, twist, turn, go in and out of focus, or are otherwise blurred. These effects can denote a sudden switch to a character's subconscious or suggest a drunken, doped, or other abnormal state of mind. Very often they are used to introduce a flashback or a dream sequence.

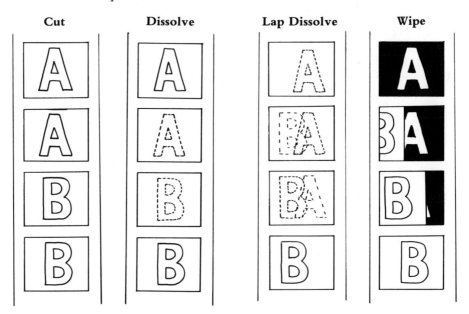

(Figure 9-4. Transitions)

Wipes

Wipes are optical effects in which the second scene appears to push the first scene off the screen. The wiping motion may be vertical, horizontal, angular, or circular, or may involve any of hundreds of special effects from keyholes to raindrops. Although there are many available, few are ever used—wipes are obvious transitions that produce a gimmicky look.

Sound Transitions

With all this emphasis on video it would be easy to overlook the audio. But sound, too, can help transitions. Voice-over narration, so common in commercials, helps to link sequences that are jumping about in time and/or space. Motion pictures have used overlapping sound in which the dialogue from one scene carries over into the next or the dialogue of the second scene begins before the picture changes. Dialogue may activate a cut from one shot to another. An officer shouts, "Fire!" and there is a cut to a shot of men firing their rifles. Familiar songs, such as "Chicago" or "I Left My Heart in San Francisco" may help establish locations.

Whatever the technique—cut, optical, sound—the purpose of transitions is to provide continuity, not to call attention to clever scene changes.

Cutting and Continuity

Cuts and dissolves are devices for getting from one shot to another. The act of piecing together separate shots to make a film is called cutting or editing. But as Kevin Brownlow wrote, "An editor's job is no more limited to joining up of scenes than a poet's to the rhyming of words Both are essential functions, but both are merely mechanical stages in a creative process."[6]

Editing determines the rhythm and pacing of the commercial. A perfume commercial, for example, may consist of a few lengthy shots joined by soft dissolves, in which each shot seems to melt dreamily into the next. A youth-targeted soft drink commercial, on the other hand, may consist of many short shots, quick-cut to a fast musical beat.

Editing permits the film storyteller to arrange material and control how and when the viewer sees it—whether it is a close-up or a long shot, whether a shot is on for an instant or a few seconds—and cram the entire thing into thirty seconds. We take the editor's tricks for granted. A steady diet of movies and television lets us absorb flashbacks and other manipulations of real time. But imagine yourself looking at a movie for the first time.

Back in the 1890s when motion pictures were in their experimental infancy, a movie consisted simply of a recorded event. Lumière set his camera up at a railroad station and filmed the arrival of a train. When the film ran out, the movie was over.

Another Frenchman, George Méliès, was the first to introduce narrative. He filmed a series of tableaux, each set against a single background. The camera was stationary and head-on, like someone seated in a theater watching a stage show. The only continuity between the individual tableaux was that they involved a central character.

In 1902, American film pioneer Edwin S. Porter produced *The Life of an American Fireman,* which combined previously shot footage of firehouse activity with a staged event of a rescue from a burning building. The different events, representing different times and places, were joined to create the effect of watching a single continuous event. Film continuity through editing was beginning to emerge. Events were linked, time was compressed. But the camera viewpoint still played a minor role.

---

6.   Kevin Brownlow, *The Parade's Gone By . . .* (New York: Knopf, 1968), 280.

It was D. W. Griffith who began to build impressions through a series of details. Whereas Porter cut for physical reasons (to shift from one location to another), Griffith used editing for dramatic reasons. He guided the viewer's reactions by selecting details from a larger scene (for example, a close-up of anxious, wringing hands to show suspense). He controlled the order and manner in which the viewer saw consecutive shots—the basis of film storytelling. He also used crosscutting; to achieve a chase, for example, he would take shots of pursuer and pursued and cut them together. (Porter would have filmed the chase as one contained, continuous event.)

Meanwhile, in Russia, editing was being pushed beyond storytelling. Instead of staging the action in long shot and inserting close-ups to heighten the dramatic effect, the Russian director Pudovkin believed a sequence could be constructed entirely from details. He and director Lev Kuleshov conducted experiments with disconnected shots to show how the emotional content of one shot could be affected by another. They took a close-up of a man whose face, according to Pudovkin, "did not express any feeling at all," and cut it together with three different shots—a bowl of soup on a table, a dead woman in a casket, and a child playing with a funny toy bear. Pudovkin wrote:

> When we showed the three combinations to an audience which had not been let into the secret, the result was terrific. The public raved about the acting of the artist. They pointed out the heavy pensiveness of his mood over the forgotten soup, were touched and moved by the deep sorrow with which he looked on the dead woman, and admired the light, happy smile with which he surveyed the girl at play. But we knew that in all three cases the face was exactly the same.[7]

Editing freed the filmmaker from the traditional concept of time, exemplified by the single continuous take in which the camera is turned on and records a complete action as it happens, where it happens. Editing can condense time. It can show the beginning of an action—a man walking toward a house—then cut to a shot of the completion of the action—the man on the porch of the house ringing the doorbell. Editing can extend time. It can take fragments of an action and overlap them so that the edited version takes longer than the real action. Editing can jumble time. It can cut from the present to a flashback of a remembered past event or to a flashforward, an imagined scene of the future. This compression and manipulation of real time is a necessity in a television commercial that must squeeze its story into thirty or sixty seconds.

Cineamatographer Joseph Mascelli lists four basic types of film editing: compilation cutting, continuity cutting, combination (compilation and continuity), and crosscutting. They all have application to television commercials.

1. *Compilation cutting.* This refers to editing in which the storytelling is really dependent upon the narration, and shots are merely cut together to illustrate what is being said. This is a common technique of

---

7. Kenneth MacGowan, *Behind the Screen* (New York: Delta, 1965), 235–36.

many explanatory television commercials. A voice-over announcer delivers the selling message while the pictures demonstrate.

2. *Continuity cutting.* This is the primary technique used in dramatic feature movies. In this case the storytelling relies upon matching consecutive scenes with no narrator to explain what is going on. Action flows from one shot to another. This may consist of various types of shots from various angles and cut-aways in which the action is not part of the previous shot. For example, a conversation between two people in a room may consist of a long two-shot, a succession of close-ups of each person, a medium shot of the two, and a cut-away to some action taking place outside the room that is directly or indirectly related to the main action.

3. *Combinations.* Combinations of compilation and continuity cutting are frequently used in commercials. A brief story or slice-of-life, utilizing continuity cutting, may open the spot and introduce the product, which is then explained through compilation cutting and by a voice-over announcer.

4. *Crosscutting.* This technique consists of combining two or more parallel actions in an alternating pattern. This may be used to join two events that are occurring at the same time but in different places (this is summed up by the familiar, "Meanwhile, back at the ranch . . ."). It may join events separated in both time and space. (A Dial soap commercial, for example, showed a man going about his daily activities and intercut flashbacks of him taking his morning shower, suggesting that this shower taken earlier was protecting him through each of these present situations.) Crosscutting may also join details of an action occurring at one time and in the same place. For example, the hair-color commercial—"The closer he gets, the better you look"—showed a man and woman running toward each other and then cut back and forth from one to the other as they got closer and closer.

Crosscutting may also be used to increase tension or suspense by alternating two simultaneous events as they move toward a climax, for example, a train and a car speeding toward a grade crossing. (A less dramatic example was a beer commercial that showed a man leaving his office for the tavern, entering the tavern, and walking the length of the bar to his usual place, crosscut with shots of the bartender drawing a beer and sliding it down the bar so that it arrived at the man's place at the same moment [almost] he did.) Crosscutting can make comparisons or contrasts between people, events, or products. (This is very useful, for example, in presenting "side-by-side" comparisons between Brand A and Brand B.) Finally, it can make comments or symbolic analogies. (For example, shots of a man at home drinking bottled water might be intercut with scenes of lush rain forests or bubbling mountain streams—the very fact that the two unrelated shots are cut together forces the viewer to see them as related.)

The editing of the commercial actually begins with the writer and art director. The writers edit as they write their dialogue and decide on the order in which information will be presented. Art directors, as they prepare a storyboard, move a step closer. They begin to visualize the actual shots, anticipating composition, camera angle, viewpoint. They try to vary their shots to maintain visual interest and to help the viewer focus on what is important in each shot. The viewer shoud not be aware of editing. The spot should flow naturally. If the information is being doled out to the viewer in proper sequence and in absorbable amounts, the actual editing sequence or rhythm (for example, CU to LS to CU) is of less concern. In other words, it is the content and appropriateness of the shot rather than size of field (LS vs. CU, for example) that is critical to smooth continuity. If each shot includes what it should, the viewer will not be conscious of the editing, much less disturbed by it.

However, if there is a breach in continuity, the viewer will be disturbed by it. Such jarring mismatches are called jump cuts. Jump cuts may result from failing to match action from one shot to the next so that a person appears out of place. Or if the amount of change from one shot to the next is insufficient, the cut will seem like a mistake.

(Figure 9-5. Jump Cut)

For example, cutting from A to B in figure 9-5 would be an insignificant visual change and would therefore be jarring, whereas a cut from A to C produces a different composition and would be smooth. There should always be a reason for cutting and changing the viewer's point of view.

A commercial is only thirty or sixty seconds long, so it is difficult to get too tedious in that time. Editing should keep the spot moving, but only to keep it interesting. Editors sometimes get nervous when they think one scene is running too long and look for ways to cut to keep it interesting. But a scene cannot be too long if something interesting is happening. If a character in a commercial is saying something relevant to the story and the product, there is no need to cut away to another shot or angle to hold the viewer's attention. Cutting should be governed by the dramatic content and not by the desire to balance or pace close-ups with long shots. Cutting is right as long as it advances the story.

The Art of Storyboardsmanship

Knowing and using television terminology will make it easier to make a storyboard. It is a language that film people understand. But it is not a language that advertisers (clients) understand. Not everyone can read storyboards with the same degree of sophistication. Forget about all those dissolves and ECUs. Just what is that storyboard supposed to represent? For someone accustomed to imagining finished print ads from layouts, imagining a finished commercial from a storyboard can be tricky. To minimize misunderstanding, there are some things to keep in mind.

Which Frame Should Be Shown?

A frame on a storyboard may represent a scene of many seconds. How well this frozen instant pasted onto the storyboard expresses the longer scene depends upon which instant you choose to freeze. Assume the scene you wish to describe begins with a medium shot of a man and moves to a close-up. What is the desired effect of this shot in the final commercial? Is it important for the viewer to remember the setting in which the man is first seen? Or is the dramatic impact to be the expression on the man's face at the end of the camera move? If the setting is more important, show the longer shot on the storyboard so that it is the visual effect conveyed. If the expression is the key ingredient, the close-up is the frame to show. If both are important, use two frames and show both. Include whatever is needed to tell the story and to convey the visual impression of the commercial.

How Many Frames Should Be Shown?

How long is a storyboard? The number of frames used in a storyboard depends on the length of the commercial, obviously, and also on its visual complexity. For example, a sixty-second commercial involving only an on-camera spokesperson in a stand-up pitch might be described adequately in four or five frames. On the other hand, a thirty-second commercial utilizing quick cuts or fast-paced animation may take many more frames to describe. The rule of thumb is use only the number of frames necessary to explain the idea/story.

This rule may have to be modified, however, when it comes to communicating the total impression of a commercial to someone unfamiliar with storyboards. A storyboard can distort the length and relative importance of a scene. For example, a scene that may take only a second or two of film time may take three or four frames to explain in storyboard form. Another scene may take five or six seconds of film time (and may include an important copy point), yet may be so visually simple that a single storyboard frame will describe it. The copy that accompanies the storyboard frames helps to indicate their relative length and importance, but visually (and a storyboard is essentially a visual aid) the impression may still be misleading. If the short-but-complex scene is there for entertainment (the necessary storytelling that involves the viewer, sets up the problem, or leads up to the introduction of the product-selling message) and the long-but-simple scene contains the sell, the overall impression of the storyboard is that of a commercial that sacrifices sell for fun, even though just the opposite may be true.

This is where a little storyboardsmanship can come in handy. If it is impossible to condense the longer scene, it might be helpful to visually stretch out the shorter scene by breaking one frame representing five seconds of audio into two frames of 2½ seconds each. This is not cheating. It is actually making the storyboard more representative of the final commercial. It becomes cheating if the extra frames pretend to represent extra scenes that could never be executed in the time allotted them. It also borders on cheating when extra frames showing the product are inserted to comfort a client who likes to think people will spend the entire commercial gazing at it.

The rule of thumb that said to include only the number of frames in a storyboard necessary to explain the story should perhaps be modified: *include only those frames that are necessary to convey the visual impression of the story*. However, if complicated scenes are fully diagrammed and then simple scenes are stretched out to compensate for them, you may face another danger—the storyboard will look so long and involved that it no longer seems to represent a nice, simple commercial.

The storyboard must also treat the line between being too vague to be any guide at all and being too specific or comprehensive to permit any creative interpretation in final production. If it is too sketchy or ambiguous, it risks being misunderstood by clients. If clients do not fully understand what the creative people are trying to achieve (or worse, if the creative people do not really know themselves), the chances are increased that they will be surprised, disappointed, or angered by the results. They may also be disappointed if the board is too specific and it turns out that things on the storyboard cannot be filmed as boarded. The boarded scene may not allow enough time to film the action or any of hundreds of other possible unforeseen production problems may force last-minute changes or compromises in the commercial.

What Form Should It Take?

Storyboards, like the ideas they represent, come in all shapes and sizes. The form they take depends upon the nature and complexity of the idea and also upon the immediate use the storyboard is to serve. Clearly, the needs of an informal internal review of ideas are different from those of a formal client presentation of recommended advertising. Each type of storyboard has its own special merits and shortcomings.

The Key Frame

The barest form of visualization consists of one or two key frames—pictures that suggest the visual mood or treatment of the commercial but make no attempt to diagram the story shot by shot. The key frames serve as a visual aid for the script, a jumping-off point from which the writer or art director can describe the idea.

The obvious advantage of this method is expedience. It permits the presentation of an idea without the time-consuming work of preparing a full-blown storyboard. But there are advantages beyond simply saving the art director time. Key frames leave room for the broadest latitude in execution. This may be very important when the commercial is essentially filmic, spontaneous, or experimental. In such cases a complete storyboard might even be misleading or misrepresentative. The creative person's verbal description of the desired effect or technique may come closer to representing the actual effect of the finished film than would a series of static drawings.

Key frames also carry a built-in danger. One person's creative latitude is another's ambiguity or uncertainty. A reluctance to fully storyboard an idea may result from a failure to have fully thought through the idea. It pays to be wary of the commercial idea that seems to rely too heavily for comprehension on some intangible mood or tricky production technique. Furthermore, different people may be imagining very different commercials from the same key frame. Everybody nods and says, "Terrific!" only to shake their heads later and say, "I didn't realize *that's* what you meant!"

The Rough Board

A rough board is a regular, full-fledged storyboard that lays out the commercial idea step-by-step in a series of explanatory drawings with accompanying copy. It is called rough because it need not be meticulously rendered and because its purpose is more often to demonstrate or explain the commercial idea than to provide an accurate blueprint for production or to make a dazzling presentation to a client. It is a working board, often the result of the first collaboration between copywriter and art director, and often prepared in haste. Despite its lack of artistic polish or production specifics, it is capable of communicating the concept and the continuity of the commercial. This is its advantage over a simple key frame; it shows the beginning, middle, and end. It comes to grips with the entire commercial as a unit. It shows what comes where and how all the pieces fit.

The Comprehensive Board

The only difference between a comprehensive and a rough storyboard is the degree of artistic finish of the drawings. Such boards are usually made for formal presentations. The people who must judge and approve commercial storyboards may not be very sophisticated when it comes to visualizing the end result. It helps them to visualize if the storyboard drawings are realistic, if the people in them look like real people instead of like rough drawings. Such presentation boards become a series of illustrations (or still photographs) instead of an artist's quick indications.

The drawback of the dazzling storyboard is that it may be viewed as a work of art in itself. Then there is a danger that the finished film will be a disappointment. By trying to very accurately represent how things will look on film, a tightly rendered storyboard may actually misrepresent the finished commercial and lead to such comments as, "Why doesn't the film look as good as the board?" Many art directors have unique and charming drawing styles. Their storyboards are gems. But this stylization will disappear when the action is recreated, using real people, real props, and real sets. The artist may cheat in the drawings and present things in a way that the camera cannot. If the charm of the commercial rests largely on the drawings or style of the storyboard instead of on the idea, expect trouble later.

The Shooting Board

Storyboards are usually created under the pressure of deadlines and end up filled with lots of "this-sort-of-things" and "you-know-what-I-means." They may get across the basic idea, but they are a long way from film. Even the beautifully rendered comprehensive storyboard with its carefully drawn pictures arranged in numerical order and neatly typed captions may not be producible.

Sometime after the flash of creativity and the excitement of the presentation, it is necessary to think seriously about production and turn the storyboard into a shooting board. A shooting board is one that works out all the little uncertainties and inconsistencies before production. It gets down to the nitty-gritty and plots out the action shot by shot, camera move by camera move. It applies much-needed objectivity and production know-how to the idea to make certain no problems (or at least as few as possible) arise in production. The shooting board is too often neglected—with all-too-frequent sad results. As one advocate wrote, "Properly done, a shooting board will tell you in advance whether or not a move or cut will work where you want it. And whether or not copy fits. You can avoid wasting an hour someday on the set trying to cut copy, when you discover you've 7 seconds of copy over an action that takes only 2 seconds."[8]

Presenting Storyboards

If a storyboard deprives a commercial idea of much of its form and excitement, the presentation of the storyboard can go a long way toward putting it back in. A good storyboard presenter can capture the mood, feeling, and flow of a commercial that does not always show up in the static drawings. Presenting a storyboard often takes more than a frame-by-frame reading of the video directions and audio. It takes some salesmanship and showmanship.

The Presenter

If at all possible, the person who created the commercial idea should present it. He or she is the only one who really understands the storyboard and what the commercial is trying to achieve. But just because the person can write does not mean he or she can present. If the creative person has trouble communicating to a group, he or she may accidentally kill his or her own idea.

If it is the account executive who must present the creative work to the client, he or she should have in advance a full understanding of the hows and whys of the storyboard. The account executive should try to feel it and not just read it. But he or she may have difficulty stepping out of character far enough to inject the needed showmanship into the presentation to

---

8.   Arthur Harris, "Your TV Needs a Shooting Board," *A.D. Assistant* (September 1967): 33-34.

convey the personality of the commercial. The creative person can waltz into the meeting, do his or her little song and dance, and then walk away. But the account executive has to stay around and discuss the marketing implications and the media plan.

The Presentation

How a storyboard is presented depends upon the idea, the audience, and the presenter. Ideas vary widely in complexity and dependence on execution. The more a commercial depends on execution, the more its understanding and appreciation depend on effective presentation. And, of course, audiences vary widely in their ability to understand and appreciate television ideas. Most of the jargon used by advertising and film people to describe commercial techniques means little or nothing to a client. Finally, the personality of the presenter will influence the presentation. The presenter should present the board in a way that is natural and comfortable for him or her. Not every copywriter can sing, dance, and do funny voices.

A storyboard lacks film's ability to communicate sound and pictures simultaneously. The presenter must try to bridge the gap between board and film. He or she must make sure the audience understands what is happening visually as well as what the copy is saying.

If the drawings make sense and if there is really coordination between words and pictures, it should not be necessary to have to explain what is going on before reading the copy. Simply start with the first frame, add any necessary description of the action, read the copy for that shot, and then go on to the next frame—just like telling a story. "This guy walks into the drug store and says to the clerk, 'I'm looking for a good after shave lotion.' The clerk smiles and reaches behind the counter and takes out the product and says, 'Here's just what you're looking for.'" And so on. Since advertising audiences are most interested in copy points, it might be a good idea to read the copy a second time after going through the board the first time with words and pictures.

If the visuals are very complicated it may be necessary to go through the video of the entire storyboard (without bogging down in mechanics and jargon) so that the audience feels the flow of the pictures. Then go back through and read the copy, pointing to the appropriate pictures so the audience can keep its place. It is like running a film twice, once silent and once with the sound turned on.

It is essential that the audience have the necessary information to understand each step as it comes along. Nothing is more deadly than to arrive at the punch line of a story and realize you left out the bit of information the audience needed to catch on. Start broadly and gradually focus in on the specifics. First comes the reason for the commercial, then the overall personality or mood. Then comes the visual description of the plot, then any specific visual techniques essential to the understanding of the spot. Finally comes the copy.

Sometimes a commercial is designed to build to a visual gag or surprise ending. To reveal this too early would spoil the fun for the viewer. If the entire board is spread out at the outset, the viewer can skip ahead and see the end coming, and this could drain some of the showmanship from the presentation. To avoid tipping off the gag you can cover the final drawing with a flap and then reveal it at the last minute, or the commercial could be boarded with one drawing per panel so that the audience sees it unfold one frame at a time.

One final truism: The simpler and clearer the idea and the storyboard, the easier it is to present. If the drawings make no sense with copy, if all the actions have to be explained in detail, you had better look again at the board to make sure all the necessary shots are included. If may be a good idea to take another hard look at the idea itself.

Demonstration Sound Tracks

A television commercial is more than just pictures. It is words, sound, and music. A storyboard does even less justice to the finished sound than to the finished look. The phrasing, rhythm, and tone of the announcer or character contribute to the meaning and interpretation of the words. And sound can add a dimension of meaning and reality even when no words can be understood—in the buzz of conversations at a cocktail party, the menacing murmur of a mob, or the bustle of a city street. A presenter cannot convey this feeling by reading.

This can be overcome by presenting storyboards along with taped sound tracks. This is especially true when the execution hangs on a musical treatment or multicharacter conversation. Of course, the track has to be a good one. A sloppy, homemade version may hurt the idea more than having someone explain it, because despite opening apologies and qualifications, the audience will tend to hear the recorded demonstration track as finished, and they will expect more.

When tracks are used to help present storyboards, they take the place of the presenter reading the audio. The presenter still describes the purpose, the personality, and the visual flow of the commercial before he or she plays the track. Then he or she just points to the appropriate frame as the track plays. When the idea relies heavily on music or a jingle, it may help to play a music-only track first to get the audience acquainted with the melody and then play a version with lyrics and copy added. Since it is harder to understand words when they are sung than when they are spoken, it might also help the sale of a new jingle to have the lyrics written out cue-card style so the audience can see the words as it hears them.

The advantages and drawbacks (and costs) of experimental sound tracks are multiplied when applied to storyboards on film (animatics or rough experimental films). Ideally, an experimental film would be the best way to present a film idea. It may be. But home movies can work against you, too. They may fail to capture the flair you had in mind—a flair professionals can capture. But the audience may view the test film as exactly what you intend. It may be harder for them to visualize the improvements that finished production can make than to visualize the improvements film can make over a storyboard.

Chapter 10

Does It Work?

The Storyboard Revisited:
Five Danger Signals

Although it is impossible to predict exactly when the big idea for a commercial will happen, a safe guess would be the night before it is due. As a result it usually turns out that copywriters are too busy writing and art directors are too busy drawing for anyone to stop long enough to work out the structural fine points of a storyboard that will become so critical later. Have the idea. Make the board. Sell the concept. All those rough edges can be ironed out in final production.

It is one thing to postpone details until the dust settles, but quite another thing to ignore them altogether. Vows to fix it later become mysteriously forgotten as soon as someone approves the idea. A storyboard hastily assembled under the gun of a deadline and presented as "the kind of thing we have in mind" may get approved on the assumption that all the little details will be worked out. Unfortunately, approval often casts mistakes in stone. The fact that no one commented specifically on the shaky parts of the storyboard is interepreted not as a gesture of good faith, but as a tacit order to keep hands off. "We can't change that! It's been approved!"

Something else happens as the storyboard travels the long, hard road to approval. It picks up little additions, deletions, suggestions, and changes along the way. The changes are always well-intended and always described as minor—a word added here, a sentence dropped there, a picture altered here, a legal requirement added there, and so on. The storyboard always ends up just a little different (and usually a little longer) than originally conceived. For the creative person, it can be like watching his or her automobile put through a car wash the wrong way. It enters spanking clean and shiny, but at each station along the line someone rubs on a little dirt or adds a tiny scuff mark until what finally comes out the other end needs a good washing.

A storyboard can be like sheet music prepared by a nonmusician. You can take the sheet, draw notes at various places, and if you show it to someone else who knows nothing about music, he or she will look at it and agree, "Yep, that's music." But show it to a musician and he or she will say, "That's not music, that's gibberish." You can take a storyboard with pictures all arranged and words typed neatly underneath them and show it to someone and he or she will agree, "Yep, that's a commercial all right." But show it to someone who understands commercial production, and he or she may say, "That's gibberish."

Few storyboards that survive for long are gibberish. But many contain the seeds of their own undoing. For all their style and surface charm they may not contain a real idea. If it does not have a concept, no storyboard will make a good commercial. But for the sake of discussion, assume that the storyboard contains an idea worth producing. What else might conspire against it?

It just might suffer from one of these five danger signals:

1. It's too long.

2. The opening is confusing.

3. The story does not track.

4. The words and pictures are out of sync.

5. The product message is not well integrated.

Problems in any of these areas will inhibit the commercial's ability to attract attention, hold interest, communicate its intended message, and positively affect consumers' attitudes toward the advertised product.

Timing: Beware the Sixty-Second Minute

Timing is sometimes treated in a rather cavalier manner during the early stages of creation and presentation. A sixty-second commercial that is sixty-five seconds long may make for a very persuasive presentation, but it will never get on the air. Before any storyboard goes into production it should have a stopwatch put to it—to time both its overall length and the length of individual scenes or important pieces of action.

Forget about pictures for the moment. Read the copy, flat out. If you can read your 60 in exactly sixty seconds, you are in for trouble. (Even if you get it down to fifty-eight seconds, the actual amount of audio time in a filmed sixty-second commercial, because picture precedes sound, you're in for trouble.)

Most commercials contain too many words. They do not rely enough on the visuals. A good director and good actors can add interpretation and dramatic timing to a commercial. All the subtle looks and double-takes that can express humor, happiness, pathos, or other emotions take time. If an actor or announcer has to read the copy with barely a pause for breath just to bring it in on time, it is not likely he or she will add much flavor to it. When the commercial is screened, everyone will grumble about the shoddy direction or how flat the actor seemed. But in most cases the blame rests with the writer. It is much safer to underwrite, that is, to use fewer words than you think you can squeeze in. This will give the director, the actors, and the announcer some room to work in. The result should be a more naturally paced, relaxed commercial.

In addition to timing the overall length of the copy, it is important to time individual scenes or sequences with an eye to what will be happening visually. Is there a long, complicated bit of action to accompany just a few words of copy? Or is there a big chunk of copy to go with a short, relatively uninteresting visual sequence? Before everybody gets onto the set to act out the action called for by the storyboard, make sure there is enough time to accomplish it. Even something as simple as a camera move may be impossible in the short time allowed by the storyboard.

Compare and evaluate the visual richness and significance of the various shots. See if the copy lets you maximize the good visuals and minimize the less exciting shots. For example, here is a line from a commercial for frozen strawberries: "Try them for dessert, or for breakfast, just the way you'd use fresh fruit." According to the storyboard, "try them for dessert" was to accompany a glamorous shot of strawberries in a fancy dish in a lush table setting. The rest of the copy went with a rather perfunctory shot of the berries being served on corn flakes. By simply juggling the sentence order, the attractive dessert scene could have been lengthened and the less interesting shot of the dish of cereal could have been shortened ("Try them for breakfast, or for dessert, just the way you'd use fresh fruit.") The commercial as a whole would have been visually stronger. It is much easier, and much less expensive, to rearrange panels on a storyboard and rewrite copy than it is to rerecord the sound track or reedit the film.

Time Compression: The Wordy Writer's Last Resort

Time has been a frustration to advertiser and creative person alike. Advertisers brimming with information about their product would love to have more time for their message. Creative people striving to tell product stories often find they run out of time before they run out of copy. Then along came an electronic technique called time compression and this tantalizing managerial implication was reported in the *Journal of Advertising Research:*

> It (time compression) could be useful when advertisers wish to tell a more complete story than would otherwise be possible in a 30-second commercial. It would, in fact, be possible to transform a 30-second commercial into a 38-second commercial.[1]

---

1. James MacLachlan and Priscilla LaBarbera, "Time Compressed TV Commercials," *Journal of Advertising Research* 18.4 (August 1978): 14.

Beyond simply squeezing more copy into a commercial, there was academic evidence that implied that effectiveness might be increased. (Faster commercials in the studies were found to be more interesting and better recalled.)

Essentially, time compression is a process that "electronically removes blank spaces between and even within words—some as short as 20/1,000ths of a second—and then splices together a shortened version that has no apparent 'Donald Duck' change in voice pitch or speed. The video portion is then speeded up to match the sound track, making the action a bit snappier."[2] (The equipment used to compress the track is manufactured by Lexicon, Inc., and that has become the term used to refer to the process, as in, "The commercial is running a little long, let's lexicon it.")

Luckily, there has been no concerted effort by advertisers to compress commercials so that additional information can be added. The last thing most thirty-second commercials need is an additional eight seconds of copy. Most have too many words to begin with. Copywriters would be better advised to cut eight seconds out and make a relaxed 22 than to rely on the lexicon to squeeze their fat 30s into an acceptable length. Telling some copywriters about the existence of time compression is like telling a teenager he or she absolutely has to be home by twelve o'clock . . . or maybe ten after. Count on both to use every second possible.

Most of the practical use of time compression has been in postproduction when it is discovered that the edited commercial is running a few (not eight!) seconds long. Rather than settle for a shorter, but less satisfying take, time compression can bring the spot in on time. Time compression is there if you need it, but the whole idea is to plan not to need it.

The Opening Shot: Obviously . . .

The opening shot of a commercial is critical. During these first few seconds viewers decide whether or not to continue watching attentively. They decide quickly if this is for or about them and whether or not the commercial is intriguing or interesting. It is often at this point that viewers either get with the story or fall out of step. Lose them here and they will never catch up.

In the interest of efficient storyboarding (getting by with as few drawings as possible), the first frame sometimes becomes a catchall for introducing several things at once—characters, setting, and props. The assumption is that if the key ingredient is stuck in there somewhere, the viewer will notice it. But viewers will notice what they want to notice, not just what the creative team hopes they will. It is up to the copywriter and art director to make sure viewers notice what they are supposed to notice in each shot. This means leaving out the nonessentials and using copy to focus attention on what is significant. Decide what the opening shot should show. What do

---

2. *Psychology Today* (June 1979): 37, 98.

you want the viewer to see first? The overall setting? A sign on the wall? A man at the desk? Whatever is important should be prominent in the shot so that the viewer looks at it.

Beware of any shot on a storyboard that, as it is being described or presented, leads the presenter to say, "Obviously . . ." "Obviously, the man is upset." "Obviously, the room is a mess." "Obviously, it's snowing outside." If the presenter had not pointed out the obvious, would it have been obvious to you just from looking at the picture?

(Figure 10-1)

Suppose a storyboard opened with this frame: OPEN ON MAN SEATED AT DESK READING. BEHIND HIM IS WINDOW AND WE SEE IT IS RAINING OUTSIDE.

Everything is there, as promised. And the video directions make it all sound fine. But without the video directions there is nothing in the picture (figure 10-1) that would guarantee that we would see it was raining outside. What, exactly, is the viewer supposed to notice first?

(Figure 10-2)

Is the important thing about this shot the fact that the man is reading? (As in, "Obviously, the man is engrossed in his book.") If so, crop out the distracting background so that attention is focused on the man reading.

(Figure 10-3)

Is the important thing the fact that the man is reading a particular book? (As in, "Obviously, he is reading a book about home repair.") If so, you will need to start or move much closer, so that the viewer can read the book's title, as in figure 10-3.

(Figure 10-4)

Or is the important thing that it is raining outside? (As in, "Obviously, it's a rainy day.") If so, start with the window to establish the fact that it is raining and then reveal the room and the man reading. Or recompose the shot to one that looks inside from out in the rain, as in figure 10-4.

Again, the first few seconds are vitally important. Make sure they are doing what you want them to do.

Structure: Leading the Viewer by the Hand

As discussed earlier, a storyboard does not bear the same relationship to the finished commercial as a layout does to a finished print ad. Primary among its many differences is that a commercial is structured in time, the print ad in space. The print designer arranges the various graphic elements—headline, illustration, body copy—into a form that guides the reader's eye through the page in the desired order. Readers know from the size, color, and position of the elements which they are to look at first, second, and so on. If everything were the same, elements would fight each other for attention and the reader would be confused.

A television commercial must be designed the same way, but in time. Through the selection and arrangement of shots the viewer's attention must be guided from beginning to middle to end.

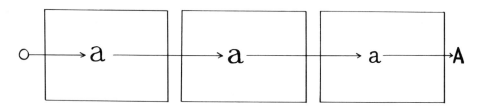

(Figure 10-5. **LEADING THE VIEWER'S ATTENTION. Ideal Version**)

Figure 10-5 is a diagram of four successive shots in a commercial. *A* represents the intended message. The goal of the commercial is to hold viewers' attention on a straight-line course to arrive at *A* by controlling the meaning they take from each shot (represented by *a*).

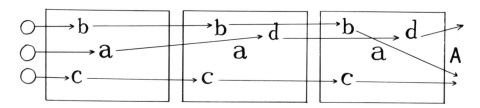

(Figure 10-6. **THE VIEWER'S WANDERING ATTENTION. Usual Version**)

However, figure 10-6 illustrates what usually happens. Again, *a* represents the intended meaning of each shot, but *b, c, d,* and *e* represent other possible interpretations. Some of these are unavoidable, traced more to what different viewers bring to the viewing experience (different beliefs, attitudes, backgrounds) than to the content. But others are the result of poor planning—extraneous or misleading elements in the shots. Once viewers are permitted to wander off course (away from *a*) into other interpretations, they may never get back on and may end up with different conclusions and impressions than those they were supposed to have.

(Commercial copy test results are packed with evidence of this phenomenon in action. Respondents repeatedly fail to play back what the advertiser intended.)

No commercial will ever elicit the same response from everyone who sees it, but this is the goal to work toward. Shots should be selected and arranged in a way that minimizes the number of possible interpretations and holds the viewer on a logical, steady course. And when the visual alone cannot do it, the copy should help out.

(Figure 10-7. COMPOSING SHOTS TO FEATURE WHAT IS IMPORTANT)

Compare the two versions of the short storyboard sequences in figure 10-7. In the first version, essentially one continuous master shot, the shots are of little help in leading the viewer to what is important. It relies entirely on the copy. In the second version, the compositions are more selective in what they present to the viewer. The first frame establishes the two characters, the second shows the product as it is named, and the next two highlight the characters' reactions.

Every shot in a storyboard should be composed and framed in a way that tells the viewer what is significant about that shot. Every shot cannot communicate everything at once. Your job is to feed viewers visual information piece by piece so that they have everything they need to understand the next piece.

Consider the opening of the cartoon storyboard in figure 10-8, which shows a frightened caveman tiptoeing out of his cave past a sleeping giant rooster.

(Figure 10-8. Two Storyboard frames)

The first frame shows a close-up of a caveman tiptoeing out of his cave and then cuts wide to see him sneak past the rooster. But frame two is deceptive. The caveman would have to enter from the left and cross the frame to reach the position shown. For one thing, this action would take precious seconds. Is there enough time? But more importantly, the viewer's attention would be divided between the caveman and the rooster.

(Figure 10-9. Three Storyboard frames)

A clearer staging of this sequence (figure 10-9) would open with an establishing shot of the rooster sleeping beside the cave entrance. When the caveman appears, the viewers' eyes are drawn to him (having already taken in the rooster). Frame three is a cut to a close-up of the caveman tiptoeing away from the rooster. The viewers now know why the caveman is tiptoeing (which they did not know in frame one of the original version), and they are ready to direct full attention to what he is doing and saying.

Each shot in a commercial builds on the shot that precedes it. It takes a very careful analysis to make sure shots build properly. Often the writer and art director are too close to their story to spot structural flaws. A scene that is perfectly clear to them (after all, they thought it up) may be confusing to the viewer. They may omit a shot or a sentence of copy that the viewer needs to fully understand the story. When this causes the commercial to go flat at the end, it is like the poor man who ends his joke, notices no one is laughing, then suddenly remembers that he forgot to mention that the guy in the joke had a parrot on his head.

Picture sequence is not the only thing that can go awry. The copy order, when words are misplaced, can cause the viewer to miss a beat or two. For example, in the opening of an insurance commercial, the company used a spoof on headache remedy commercials to talk about rising homeowners' insurance rates. A spokesman identified as the House Doctor stood before a graph and delivered the following copy:

DOCTOR: As you know, the homeowners' blues are sweeping California. This epidemic is the result of homeowners' insurance rates being raised throughout the state. Now, if you wish to avoid the dull, depressed feeling . . .

Despite what the House Doctor says, the people in California do not know that the homeowners' blues are sweeping their state. They do not yet know what the homeowner's blues are because the copywriter invented the term. But there is a good chance they know that homeowners' insurance rates are being raised. Once reminded of that they would be better able to understand what is meant by the homeowners' blues. As in this version of the copy:

DOCTOR: As you know, homeowners' insurance rates are being raised throughout California. [that is why] The state is being swept by an epidemic of the homeowner's blues. . . .

In this version, information pertinent to the point the commercial hopes to make is provided to the viewer, and the homeowners' blues, intended as a wry comment on the situation, become just that. Having thus established the existence of homeowners' blues, the subsequent sentence ("Now, if you wish to avoid the dull, depressed feeling . . .") is in a more logical place.

Audio-Video Integration

The television copywriter must continually check on two things: 1) Is the copy itself structured clearly? (Are the words in the right order? Do they make sense? Do they build to a logical conclusion?) 2) Does the copy work with the pictures? One thing that sometimes leads a writer to jam too many words into a commercial is the failure to take into account the power of the visual. Of course, if the visuals are lazy or ambiguous, all that copy may be needed to bail them out.

A good commercial should consist of an interplay of words and pictures. Time permitting (though it rarely is), there should be no need for copy to barrel along uninterrupted for the entire length of the spot. Sometimes the copy should let the pictures work by themselves. This visual-verbal interplay can be illustrated by the diagram in figure 10-10, in which the commercial is analogous to a two-part tape fed into a computer. The picture is one part, the sound track the other part, and the viewer's brain is the computer.

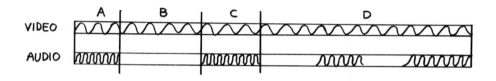

(Figure 10-10. WORDS AND PICTURES WORK TOGETHER)

A. Scene one opens with both picture and words. The picture that might otherwise be ambiguous is put into context by the words. Each (words and picture) contributes equally to establish the proper context in the viewers' minds.

B. Now the viewers know what they are seeing. The picture is in its proper context, so now the words can drop out for awhile and let the picture carry the whole load.

C. Now the words come back to hold things on a steady course, to keep the viewer from drifting away from the thought that you want the picture to convey.

D. Words and picture can then proceed in a back-and-forth, give-and-take manner. Instead of words flowing steadily for the entire commercial, they are used to punctuate, reinforce, and direct. In this essentially visual medium, they let the visual work.

Much is made of maintaining a close correlation between the audio and video portions. You cannot say one thing in the picture and another in the copy; one must reinforce the other. And they can reinforce each other without being redundant. If the words simply repeat what the picture is saying, there is less opportunity for the viewer to become involved. Instead, words and pictures should supply related, but not identical, bits of information that viewers can put together in their minds.

When in doubt about the ability of the picture to communicate alone, add the needed words. It is better to err on the side of explicitness.

(Figure 10-11)

Consider again our omnibus opening frame of the man reading at a table in front of a window. The visual is loose and vague. If we wanted the viewer to notice that it is raining outside, the copy could say, "It's a rainy day." This would help direct the viewer's attention to the window to notice something that might otherwise be missed. This is desperation audio reinforcement because the picture itself does not "say" rainy day; it "says" man reading.

(Figure 10-12.)

If the picture were staged to feature the rain (as in figure 10-12) and the copy said, "It's a rainy day," it would reinforce the picture, but it would be redundant. We can see it is a rainy day and we do not need someone to tell us so. The copy has a chance to add to the picture, perhaps by telling us how we should react to this rainy-day scene. For instance, "It's the day of the company picnic." We begin to get the idea that the man inside reading had planned to be outside playing.

Viewers may be confused if the words and pictures do not mesh. The picture must show what the words say. The mere presence of copy will not do the job. For example, if you are advertising a first-aid cream and you show a close-up of the cream squeezing out of the tube while the announcer says, ". . . and it doesn't sting," you may not fully communicate that no-sting idea. But if the picture shows it being applied to a child's wound while the child smiles, that same copy will reinforce the picture and better communicate the message.

Titles and Supers: A Short Digression

Super is short for *superimpose* and refers to those words, so dear to advertisers, that are superimposed over a scene in a commercial to reinforce a selling point. When there is a title or copy supered over a scene, the audio and video should match exactly. If viewers read "WORKS TWICE AS FAST" while they hear the announcer say, "is faster-working," the message is thrown out of sync and becomes more difficult to grasp. In addition to making sure that the audio and video reinforce each other, here are three other common sense guidelines:

1. Make the title legible. The viewer must be able to read it; this means it must be on the screen long enough to read. The typography should be clean and simple and it should be separated clearly from the background.

2. Make the title fit the scene—and the screen. The composition of the shot should be planned to accommodate the super. And the words should fall within the area of TV cutoff.

3. Make the title appropriate. The words should be relevant to the commercial idea, and the treatment should be appropriate to the content and style of the commercial.

The first step is to decide what to super. Supers should not be used indiscriminately. The fewer, the better, and the shorter, the better. In the case of new brands it may be advisable to super the name. In other cases the super is usually the key theme or copy point. But make sure the words fit the commercial and that the story builds to the same conclusion the super states. For example, if the commercial has not demonstrated that your brand works twice as fast as Brand X, supering "works twice as fast" will come as a surprise, not a reinforcement.

The second consideration is how to super. This involves the choice of lettering or type style, the method of bringing the super onto the screen (All at once? One word at a time?), and the arrangement of words and the composition of the scene.

Type style.   Legibility comes first and the basic rules of typography apply: simple, classic letter forms; caps and lowercase are usually easier to read than all caps. After legibility comes appropriateness. Choose a style that fits the thought. Old-fashioned suggests one style, modern suggests another. But don't go too far. Viewers have had enough snow-capped "frozens." And if it comes down to a choice between mood and legibility, stick with legibility.

Presentation.   Supers are quite versatile when it comes to making their appearance. They can pop on all at once, phrase by phrase, word by word. They can fade on gradually. A lengthy title may be rolled up or crawl a line at a time, like an unwinding scroll. Or they can animate on in any of a variety of tricky effects. Once on the screen they can bounce, wiggle, or dance.

TV cutoff.   The home TV screen loses about ten percent of the original picture area of the film due to the shape of its picture tube. This loss occurs around the edges of the picture, so unless a title is carefully planned there is a chance a word or letter may be lopped off.

(Figure 10-13)

As figure 10-13 shows, the safety area is the live area within which a title can read without loss. *Cutoff* refers to the picture area outside this live area. (The total area of the screen is also referred to as a 12 field. The safety area is an 8 field.)

Composition.   The words should be arranged on the screen in a logical, easy-to-read manner. This is no place for wild layouts. Words should be properly letter spaced. Leave adequate spacing between words to keep them from running together. If you must break a sentence, break it by thought. "WORKS TWICE AS FAST," if it must be broken into two lines, is easier to grasp as

WORKS
TWICE AS FAST

than as

WORKS TWICE
AS FAST

Color. Unlike print ads, in which reverse type is frowned upon, television commercials most often use white letters against all but the very lightest backgrounds. If color is used, make sure there is enough contrast in value for those viewing in black and white. Supers are not always viewed against solid backgrounds. The composition should be framed to eliminate busy background elements where the title is to be supered.

Product Integration

It is possible to have a crystal-clear opening that attracts the viewer's attention, compose and arrange the shots in a logical sequence, have the words and pictures interact in such a way that the viewer knows just what is going on, yet still get into trouble. Each of the pieces should fit together for one purpose: to tell the viewer something about the product. It is not enough to have an interesting story about people or cartoons or cats that incidentally mentions the product and its selling message. The story must revolve around the product. The conclusion it builds to should be a conclusion about the product. Advertising researchers call the manner in which the product is woven into the fabric of the commercial product narrative integration. Call it what you like, but make sure your commercial has it.

The advertiser's ready solution to making sure the commercial is about the product is simply to make sure the product gets screen time and gets it as quickly and often as possible. There are many rules aimed at registering the product in the viewer's mind. "Show the package in frame one." "Mention the brand name in the first five seconds." But what is more important than how soon, how long, or how often the product appears is the context in which it appears.

Few products are so intrinsically interesting that their appearance on the screen is enough to command rapt attention. The viewer has to be mentally prepared for the product's appearance. Very often this means establishing, through the characters and action, a need or desire for the product. Then when it appears, it is in a particular context the viewer can relate to. For example, a not-very-compelling commercial for facial tissues might open on the package (note appearance in first frame and within first five seconds) with an announcer saying, "These new tissues are very soft. So when you have a cold and your nose is sore, they will feel very nice."

A (slightly) more compelling commercial might open on a man with a cold looking miserable and longing for relief and the announcer saying, "When you have a cold and your nose is sore, you want a tissue that is very soft." Then, as the viewers nod in agreement, the product appears. "These new tissues are very soft."

Besides setting up the product's introduction by creating a need or desire, the commercial can pave the way dramatically by piquing the viewers' curiosity or building suspense or anticipation. An animated commercial for some new frozen raspberries began with a cartoon Paul Revere character riding into town and shouting, "The berries are coming!" He dismounts at the church tower, races upstairs, and shouts again from the tower, "The berries are coming!" Then he races back downstairs, out the door, and smack into the package of frozen berries. "They're already here," he says. The entire sequence had one purpose: to prepare the viewer, in an amusing way, for the introduction of the product. When it appeared (later than the first five seconds), it was at a point of high dramatic interest.

To test your storyboard for product narrative integration, try telling the story of the commercial. If you can tell it without mentioning the product, you have more work to do.

Storyboard Analysis: An Example

This chapter has focused on the structure of the commercial as represented by the storyboard. It has assumed the presence of a solid selling idea and has dealt with how to make sure the idea gets across to the viewer. This involves making sure the copy is clear and orderly, that the copy and pictures work together, and that pictures are composed and arranged in a logical order. It anticipates the final production of the spot by making sure there is time to accomplish what you intend to accomplish and by making sure you get all the shots you need to communicate the idea.

This sort of analysis takes clinical objectivity plus an understanding of how film works. It is very difficult if you are the copywriter or art director who created the storyboard. It is part of you. It must be right. This kind of self-editing demands a willingness to challenge everything you have created. You may conclude that what you have is the best solution possible. But if you conclude this after testing all the alternatives, you will feel even better.

To illustrate how careful analysis may lead to an improved commercial, a storyboard for a Maytag commercial is shown in figure 10-14. The commercial is based on the long-running campaign theme of dependability, as symbolized by the lonely repairman. Jess, the Maytag Repairman, is a continuing character who is always fighting boredom because Maytag washers and dryers never break down. In this commercial he describes a dream to a younger repairman, Mike, who decides that dreaming is the only way they will ever see any action.

A good idea. But is it working as well as it could? Look at the board carefully.

1

EST. REPAIR SHOP. JESS
WITH DREAMY LOOK.
YOUNGER REPAIRMAN
WORKS JIGSAW PUZZLE.
(SILENT PULL-UP)

2

CLOSE-UP OF TWO.
JESS: Boy, did I have a dream
last night . . .
MIKE: Yeah?

3

JESS STARTS TO GET
EXCITED.
JESS: Maytags were busting
down two-forty!

4

JESS GETTING CARRIED
AWAY.
JESS: Filters fizzling! Pumps
going pfft!

5

CUT TO CU OF MIKE'S
REACTION.
JESS: (VO) Washers stalling!
Dryers quitting!

6

TWO SHOT. RELIVING
DREAM, JESS GRABS PHONE.
JESS: Everybody calling! And
us Maytag repairmen weren't
lonely anymore.

7

CU MIKE, WIDE-EYED.
MIKE: Beautiful!

8

MIKE SWINGS HIS LEGS UP
TO DESK TOP TO GET INTO
SLEEPING POSITION.
JESS: (VO) Hey, what're you
doing?

9

JESS REACTS AS MIKE
PULLS CAP OVER EYES.
MIKE: Sleeping. I could use a
dream like that.

10

JESS DOES LIKEWISE.
ANNCR: (VO) Not all
Maytage repairmen are the
loneliest guys in town.

11

CUT TO WASHER AND
DRYER.
ANNCR: (VO) But we're
trying.

12

ADD LOGO. SUPER: "THE
DEPENDABILITY PEOPLE."
ANNCR: (VO) Maytag. The
Dependability People.

(Figure 10-14. How Can This Storyboard Be Improved?)

Frame #1 is another of those all-inclusive shots designed to introduce the characters, their attitude (daydreaming, working a puzzle), and the setting (Maytag repair shop). To accomplish all this the board allows only the 1½ second pull-up before the start of sound and then cuts to a closer two-shot for the dialogue. It would be better to pick an establishing shot that can be held longer, until after the dialogue starts, so the viewer can more fully absorb what is happening.

The copy with Frame #3 ("Maytags were busting down two-forty!") tries to be colloquial or picturesque at the expense of clarity. Why risk confusion? Better to say "everywhere." Also, why all the extreme action? Jess should show enthusiasm, yes, but more mental stimulation than body action. A simpler staging would call for both characters to remain seated.

Frame #5 cuts from a CU of Jess alone to a CU of Mike's reaction. It is time to draw Mike into Jess's enthusiasm for the dream, but by putting more of the copy with the two-shot it would be easier to show his mounting interest. Staying on a two-shot for the entire dream description and showing Mike's reaction to Jess sets up a cut to a CU of Jess for the key, culminating line, "And us Maytag repairmen weren't lonely anymore." Furthermore, the action of Jess using the phone to pantomime "everyone calling" is unnecessary and confusing and should be eliminated.

Frame #7, the CU of Mike's reaction, is also unnecessary. We have shown his involvement with the dream earlier. And the line, "Beautiful," is really too short to fully express his feeling. Cut it and save the time.

Frame #8 can be changed to a two-shot. Having just done Jess's climactic line in a CU, we can cut back to a two-shot to see Mike do something that shows he has a new idea. Instead of immediately swinging his legs up he could clear away the jigsaw puzzle (remember it?). Jess then follows suit as the announcer's copy comes over.

Figure 10-15 shows how the restaged, restructured, and rewritten storyboard would look.

Can Your Storyboard Pass This Test?

By way of summary, here is a checklist of some of the things to look for in a preproduction analysis of your storyboard:

- **Is there a single central message or idea?** It is never too late to ask again if you are asking your commercial to do what it does best—communicate one simple idea. Thirty seconds is not enough time to develop a catalogue of sales points. At best these underdeveloped points will be throwaways. At worst they may detract from the central idea by complicating the commercial.

- **Is the message you want to communicate explicitly stated?** Do you have a set of words you want consumers to remember? Are these exact words in the commercial? If you insist on an implicit statement of your claim or idea, be prepared for a variety of consumer responses in addition to the one you hope for.

(PULL-UP)

JESS: Boy, did I have a dream last night . . .
MIKE: Yeah?

JESS: Maytags were busting down everywhere! Filters fizzling.

JESS: Pumps going pffft! Washers stalling! Dryers quitting! Everybody calling!

JESS: And us Maytag repairmen weren't lonely anymore!

(CLEARS AWAY PUZZLE.)
JESS: Hey, what are you doing?

MIKE: Going to sleep. I could use a dream like that.

ANNCR: (VO) Not all Maytag repairmen are the loneliest guys in town.

ANNCR: (VO) But we're trying.

ANNCR: (VO) Maytag. The Dependability People.

(Figure 10–15. Maytag Repairman Storyboard, Revised)

- **Is there enough time?** Too much copy restricts dramatic interpretation and defies good direction. Is there enough time for actions and expressions? Is there enough time to complete the moves and actions called for on the storyboard? Are there too many shots for the time available?

- **Does the opening shot really set the stage?** Does it show all that is essential, but only what is essential to the understanding of what follows? In the interest of saving drawing time, has too much been crammed into the first frame of the board? Should its action be broken down into more frames to make priorities clear? Just what should the opening shot convey? Is it framed to convey that alone, or does it open the way to viewer confusion by showing nonessential background details? Will it be on long enough to establish what it is supposed to establish?

- **Do the opening seconds involve the viewer?** Does the commercial attract attention in a way that is relevant to the viewer and the product? Do viewers recognize the situation portrayed as being about them and their problems? If the commercial is a problem-solution format, is the problem clearly set up?

- **Do the shots progress in a logical order (or illogically logical order)?** Does each successive shot advance the story and add to the viewer's knowledge of what's going on? Do any shots feel out of place? Do you feel a need at any point in the storyboard to pause and go back a few frames to reexamine something you missed the first time through?

- **Are the pictures explicit, simple, and single-minded?** Do they make sense without the words? Or are they intentionally vague? If the pictures are vague, does the accompanying copy give them the intended meaning? Is the viewer's attention directed where it should be?

- **Do the words reinforce the pictures, or are they merely redundant?** If the words simply repeat what the picture is saying, there is less opportunity for the viewer to become involved than if the words and pictures supply different but related bits of information that the viewer puts together.

- **Are supers in sync with the audio?** Do they say the same thing at the same time? Rarely can you get away with showing one set of words on the screen while saying something else.

- **Are the words clear and meaningful in themselves?** Is there a colloquialism or pet slang expression included whose meaning may not be clear to a majority of viewers? How much comprehension are you willing to sacrifice in the name of style and cleverness?

- **Are the words clear and meaningful at that point in the story?** Are there words, expressions, gags, or copy points that depend for their meaning or impact on something that has not yet occurred in the story? Occasionally, during revisions, key set-up lines get juggled out of position or cut.

- **Is the copy structured to maximize the visuals?** Are rich, exciting, or complicated visuals on the screen long enough (accompanied by enough copy or allotted enough time) for the viewer to appreciate or understand them fully? Are dull, static visuals on longer than they deserve to be? Would a rearrangement of copy help strike a better balance?

- **Could the viewer tell the story of the commercial without mentioning the product?** Tell the plot in your own words. Does the product fit naturally into the narrative? Does it solve the problem or settle the issue between the characters? Or does the product come in from left field? Is the story just an irrelevant attention-getter?

- **When does the product enter?** Advertisers like to see their product on stage early. But it is more important that the product enter at the right moment than at the first moment. Has the viewer been prepared to meet the product? Has interest been piqued or a problem set up?

- **If it is a 60 could you cut it to a 30?** If not, ask yourself if the idea is simple enough. If it is, look at what you cut out and ask yourself how much the extra thirty seconds is really adding to the idea.

- **Is the commercial story believable?** If not, is the selling message believable within the unbelievable or exaggerated story? Are the characters real people? Are they consistent? Do they always speak and act as they should? Are the right lines given to the right people? Do the stupid people act stupid and the smart people smart? If characters do change, is the motivation for their change explained? Is it convincing? Is it the result of experience with the product?

Chapter 11

Is It Legal?

The End of Misleading Advertising

In an advertising agency conference room the lights had just come up after the screening of a recently produced commercial. The agency lawyer, referring to a scene in the commercial that was under discussion, said the commercial was legally unacceptable as it stood. There were protests from the producer that nothing had been done in this film that had not been done many times in the past. The lawyer held his ground. The scene had to be reshot. An observer, with tongue in cheek and mock horror on his face, gasped, "You mean this is the end of misleading advertising?"

It was indeed. These days an advertising copywriter can scarcely look up from the typewriter without bumping into the chin of someone looking over his shoulder. Committees and commissions and special interest groups are watching commercials more closely than any consumer ever has. Codes and guidelines abound. Lawyers are trying to decipher court cases and government rulings to try to understand exactly what is acceptable and what is not. They are reviewing copy to make sure every claim is supportable and everybody's rights are protected. Lawyers are even present on the set when a commercial is produced, making sure the demo that ends up on film is a true and accurate representation. This is a far cry from the days when advertising seemed to be limited only by imagination, taste, and a sense of morality. In 1980 David Ogilvy wrote,

> I look back at some ads I wrote 25 years ago, which I felt were honest at the time, and I shudder and think, my God, if I wrote that today I'd be put in jail.[1]

---

1. David Ogilvy, "Ogilvy Reflects on Changing, Constant Ad Rules," *Adweek* (May 12, 1980): 40.

Who Watches Commercials?

If consumers feel threatened by sinister or devious television advertisers, they should be comforted to know they are not alone. Looking out for their interests are agencies of the U.S. government, representatives of the broadcasting industry, the self-policing watchdogs of the Better Business Bureau, and various consumer groups who complain to these agencies.

The Federal Trade Commission

Biggest of the big brothers watching advertising is the Federal Trade Commission. Created by the Federal Trade Commission Act in 1914, the FTC drew its power from section five, which stated that "unfair methods of competition in commerce are hereby declared unlawful." The first commissioners interpreted the act to cover deceptive advertising.

In 1938 Congress passed the Wheeler-Lea Act amending the FTC Act to read: "Unfair methods of competition in commerce and unfair or deceptive acts or practices in commerce are hereby declared unlawful." This change gave the FTC power to act whenever deception of the public was involved, regardless of the effect upon competition.

In 1975 the Magnuson-Moss Federal Trade Commission Improvement Act granted the FTC power to issue trade regulation rules with respect to "unfair or deceptive acts or practices in or affecting commerce." The commission no longer deals on a case-by-case basis but can issue rules affecting an entire industry. Rather than having to prove an act is or has the capacity to be false, deceptive, or misleading, the commission need show only that the advertising is in contravention of a trade regulation rule and the advertiser can be fined.

The FTC consists of five commissioners appointed by the president, but the actual investigative work and preparation of cases in the advertising field is carried out by a staff of lawyers and consumer specialists under the Bureau of Consumer Protection.

> When the FTC believes a deception has occurred, its staff drafts a proposed complaint. If this is accepted by the commission it may be publicly announced, often naming the advertising agency involved, in addition to the advertiser. Negotiations toward settlement are offered at this point, and many succeed. If no settlement is indicated, a formal complaint is issued, and hearings are conducted before an administrative judge who issues a decision. His decision can be appealed to the full commission and is subsequently reviewable in a court of law.
>
> The FTC's normal sanction is a cease-and-desist order which, in addition to stopping a practice, can impose a variety of required actions including, in appropriate instances, corrective advertising, and restitution to consumers found to be cheated.[2]

---

2. "The New World of Advertising," *Advertising Age* (November 21, 1973): 147–48.

Since 1938 the FTC has had specific authority over the advertising of foods, drugs, and cosmetics. This area of regulation is shared with the Food and Drug Administration. The FDA controls contents and labeling.

> While the FDA is confined to the "label," its role is broader than the word implies. If it finds that a claim in an ad is not supported by the information on the label, the FDA can proceed with a "misbranding action."[3]

Food advertising, and there is a lot of it on television, receives considerable attention from the FTC, especially when product claims imply health or nutrition benefits. A lengthy trade regulation rule specifies when a product can be described as nourishing, wholesome, nutritious, how and when energy claims can be made, the conditions under which the nutrients in food can be compared, and more.

Whatever the product category, the basic concern of the FTC is the truth of the claim and its substantiation. The burden of proof or substantiation has been placed clearly on the advertiser and its agency. Both share liability for any false, misleading, or deceptive advertising. Besides claims and claim substantiation the FTC is also alert for any demonstrations that may be deceptive and any commercials that use testimonials or endorsements.

In addition to the FTC there are other government agencies that may influence the television advertiser. The U.S. Postal Service, which denies fraudulent advertising the use of the mails, is also concerned (along with state governments) with control of lotteries. The Securities and Exchange Commission regulates advertising that offers securities to the public. The Civil Aeronautics Board has authority to prevent unfair or deceptive practices in the air transport industry. The Federal Communications Commission, which licenses TV and radio stations, prohibits private lotteries, fraud, and obscenity and requires disclosure of all commercial sponsorship.

The National Advertising Review Board

Another advertising watchdog is the National Advertising Review Board. The NARB was established in 1971 for "the self-regulation of national advertising and to sustain high standards of truth and accuracy." The NARB reviews complaints brought by the public and competing advertisers and also matters brought by its own investigative arm, the NAD (National Advertising Division of the Council of Better Business Bureaus). In its own policy statement adopted January 20, 1972, the NARB explained the issues it expected to consider:

> The adequacy of substantiation, including research data, to support an objective claim for a product or service.

> A testimonial involving the competency of the testifier as a regular user reflecting average experience.

---

3. "New World of Advertising," 149.

A claim with respect to a bargain price savings for a product or service.

The matter of fair or honest reference to a competitor or a comparison of products.

Substantiation for guarantees and warranties and whether there is adequate disclosure of pertinent information about these.

Advertising directed to children where misrepresentations not misleading to the adult mind could have the capacity to confuse or mislead the immature and impressionable mind.

The NARB will also issue, from time to time, special reports. One such report, released on March 17, 1975, analyzed how the advertising industry portrayed women and concluded it had "not gone far enough in reflecting women's changing status in the modern world."

The Networks

Any commercial that is to be broadcast on the networks (or on more than one of their owned and operated stations) must be cleared by each network's broadcast standards department. Clearance by one network does not guarantee clearance by the others. To avoid producing a commercial that cannot run, scripts must be cleared before production. The networks may take two weeks or so to respond to submitted scripts. They may request additional information or support for copy claims. They may request changes that must be discussed and resolved.

The networks also have guidelines for advertising to children that cover a broad range of concerns from copy to production techniques. For example, commercials advertising to children must avoid exhortative language ("Try this." "Look!"). Children cannot be directed to "Ask mom to buy. . . ." The networks place much emphasis on safety. They prohibit the portrayal of any dangerous behavior that children could imitate. Small children in commercials often must be supervised by on-camera adults. Commercials should not portray antisocial behavior. The list goes on and on. "Batteries not included" is a familiar example of guidelines in action.

Theoretically, if all the people involved with creating advertising copy understand what the product does and does not do, and if they clearly state those product attributes, there should be no problem with government agencies, networks, and review boards. Copywriters rarely set out to willfully deceive. But it is becoming easier and easier to trip over a rule or tread on a toe and end up with copy that is unacceptable or even illegal. It is therefore important to seek legal advice early in the game, certainly before a commercial is produced and, ideally, before an idea is sold. Any legal problem caught early is a little problem. Any legal problem discovered later, after the commercial has been produced, or worse, aired, is bound to be a big problem.

Know the rules. Make no claim you cannot substantiate. Clear copy in advance. If symptoms persist, see a lawyer.

Copy Claims (You Can't Say That!)

When a lawyer reviews a piece of advertising copy, he or she looks first for the thing the networks or FTC will look for: the claim. All claims must be truthful. And there must be reasonable support. A claim may be either express or implied.

Express Claims

Does the copy claim that the product is made a specific way, does a specific thing, provides a specific benefit? Any claim explicitly stated is an express claim and needs to be substantiated. The nature of the substantiation naturally depends upon the nature of the claim. "Contains Z-1" can be documented with laboratory data supplied by the manufacturer's research and development department. A performance claim ("lasts for weeks") will require field research. "Tastes like homemade" may require tests with consumers in which the taste of the product is compared to a homemade version.

This does not mean you need a volume of test results to say something nice about a product. "Tastes really great!" is regarded as simply puffery. But the line between embellishment and deception is not always clear.

> The courts have traditionally taken the view that an advertisement must be written so that it will not deceive "the trusting as well as the suspicious, the casual as well as the vigilant, the naive as well as the sophisticated." While the commission [FTC] has long stopped short of putting a literal interpretation on statements that represent nothing more than bragging, it has cautioned advertisers that "puffery" will not be an acceptable explanation for any statement which could be regarded by the public as a performance claim.[4]

Because of the demands of substantiating research, the superlative *-est* has practically disappeared from the advertising vocabulary. It is too difficult to support the claim that your brand is best. Even the comparative *-er* is an endangered species. Copy is riddled with modifiers that tone down the totality of a claim while trying to preserve the spirit of it. No toothpaste, even clinically-tested fluorides, could claim "prevents cavities." There are too many variables. Instead, it claims "helps prevent cavities." This means that the toothpaste, used after every meal and in conjunction with regular dental checkups and careful eating, is one of several things that contribute to the prevention of cavities. But clever wording does not get you off the hook. If the commercial, through the way the copy is presented, leaves the net impression that the toothpaste alone prevents cavities, it will be held to be deceptive.

Implied Claims

So the next thing a lawyer will look for, in addition to or in the absence of any express claims, is the presence of any implied claim. If a commercial

---

4. "New World of Advertising," 147.

sings, dances, acts out, or alludes to something it never comes out and expressly states, it may still be making a claim and that claim will still have to be supported.

Sometimes a supportable claim ("contains Z-1") may imply an unsupportable claim. For example, if the product that contains Z-1 is a soap and the commercial claims it leaves you smelling fresh for hours, and Z-1 is only a coloring agent, the commercial may be misleading.

Comparative Claims (Looking Out for Brand X)

Another thing a lawyer will look for is to see if the copy makes any comparative claims, a stated or implied superiority over a competing brand. For a long time the networks would not approve commercials that named names. The FTC, however, felt that comparative advertising should be encouraged because it could be more informative and useful for the consumer. It is now allowed, often done, and always carefully examined. The following guidelines are a composite of those of the American Association of Advertising Agencies and networks:

- The intent, connotation, and net impression of the ad should be to inform and never to mislead, deceive, discredit, disparage, or unfairly attack competitors or competing products or services.

- When a competitive product is named or identified in any manner, it should be one that exists in the marketplace as significant and actual competition.

- The competition shall be fairly and properly identified but never in a manner or tone of voice that degrades the competitive product or service.

- The advertising should compare related or similar properties or ingredients of the product, dimension to dimension, feature to feature, preferably by a side-by-side demonstration.

- The identification must be for comparison purposes and not simply to upgrade by association.

- Competitive product testing should be done by an objective testing source using generally accepted scientific and technical procedures and utilizing the best possible test for proof of the claim.

- The claims made must fairly and accurately reflect the tests utilized.

- The advertising shall disclose any limitations of the test or results involved and shall set forth significant and measurable differences only.

- The property being compared should be significant in terms of value or usefulness of the product to the consumer. The word *significant* shall be used in accordance with standards of statistical validity.

- Comparatives delivered through the use of testimonials should not imply that the testimonial is more than one individual's thought unless that individual represents a sample of the majority viewpoint.

Demonstrations (Waiter, There's a Marble in My Soup!)

Once all the claims and comparisons are accounted for, the lawyer will examine any creative devices and techniques, especially demonstrations.

During the early golden days of television, commercial makers took certain liberties with the products and props they filmed. They did this for two reasons. The first was the desire to portray their client's product in the most favorable light possible. The second was to make technical compensations for what the camera could not capture on film. Just as performers on the old black-and-white TV shows wore blue shirts to look like white shirts because real white shirts were too bright under TV lights, so did commercial producers build mock-ups for the camera to recreate what was difficult or impossible to film. On one memorable occasion a shaving cream manufacturer wanted to dramatize how its product soaked and softened whiskers. The commercial claimed this shaving cream was such a good moisturizer that it would shave sandpaper. To demonstrate this on television they made a simple mock-up: sand affixed to a Plexiglas surface that the razor zipped clean without difficulty.

The FTC took exception, and in a now-famous case that went all the way to the Supreme Court, its opinion prevailed. The mock-up was deceptive. Viewers were shown one thing and told they were seeing something else. As it turned out, actual sandpaper had to be soaked in shaving cream for ninety minutes before it softened enough to be shaved.

The rules for a TV demo are that it must be typical, relevant, and true. Viewers must be seeing what they believe they are seeing. The demonstration must truthfully show how a product actually performs. The demonstration must represent normal conditions of product use. It should be able to be duplicated by consumers in real-life situations. The benefit demonstrated must be important to consumers. It must demonstrate a feature that is relevant to the way the consumer is likely to use the product.

In a very dramatic TV demo a can of antifreeze was punctured with an ice pick. The fluid squirted out for a few seconds and then stopped. The antifreeze had sealed the leak. The implication was that it would perform similarly in your car's radiator. Unfortunately, there is a difference between cans and radiators. The demonstration did not duplicate actual flow rates and pressures of a car radiator. It was held to be misleading.

In a demonstration comparing a stainless steel razor blade with a chrome blade, an advertiser showed photographs comparing the amount of corrosion to each blade after five shaves. The steel blade looked horrible by comparison. However, the demonstration did not prove superior shaving performance.

Packaged-food advertising presents a particular problem because consumers do not know what they have until they open the package. They can easily check out a commercial for an automobile by looking at the car for themselves. If the commercial made it look longer and lower than it actually is, they will know that before they plunk down their money. Not so with packaged products. What is inside may come as a surprise if the commercial represents it too glamorously.

Food photography has always been an exacting art. In commercial production an entire day will be spent lighting and filming a few seconds of footage designed to make the product appear as mouth-watering as possible. It is not unusual to see the camera operator arranging cereal flakes with tweezers to get rid of a shadow or glare or to add drops of "dew" to vegetables with an eye dropper. All this is fussy, but legal, unless it begins to misrepresent the product. Marbles placed in the bottom of a bowl of soup to make the vegetables visible at the surface went too far. This misrepresented the amount of vegetables in the soup. The product must be shown exactly as it will be experienced by the consumer.

Everybody wants the commercial to have production value. It should be dramatic, artistic, creative. But it must be creative within definite guidelines. Not that this should be cause for lament. The guidelines are simply intended to ensure that any claim a commercial makes is capable of being substantiated and that any demonstration of the claim is accurate and truly representative of what the product can do.

Testimonials (I Am Not an Actor, I Am a Real Person)

The demonstration is not the only technique likely to attract legal scrutiny. Another is the testimonial or endorsement. In a testimonial commercial, a consumer or an actor or actress presents his or her own beliefs or experience with the product or service advertised. (This personal endorsement is different from actors or actresses used as spokespersons presenting the advertiser's opinion about its product.)

Testimonials must accurately reflect the testifier's beliefs. Endorsements cannot be taken out of context in a manner that distorts their content. And the testifier may be asked to sign a testimonial affidavit confirming the truthfulness of his or her own statements.

Testifiers cannot make any statement about the product that cannot be independently supported. They cannot make claims just because they believe them to be true.

When the testimonial is that of an expert, the requirements are that the expert's qualifications must support the expertise he or she is represented as having. If the commercial implies that the endorsement was based on a comparison, then it must be based on an actual comparison, and the endorsed product must be at least equal overall to competing brands.

There are still other restrictions that come into play when a celebrity is used in a commercial aimed at children. For example, the celebrity cannot offer products associated with his or her real-life occupation. A professional baseball player cannot advertise baseball bats to children.

Rights (and Wrongs)

Once assured that the copy claims are supported, that the creative techniques are relevant and not misleading, and that the copy does not disparage the competition, the lawyer will then look to make sure there has been no violation of people's rights.

Advertising copy is governed by the laws of defamation, libel, and slander. No untrue statements may be made about other persons, nor may they be held up to contempt. Moreover, the use of an individual's name, picture, or statement without his consent is an invasion of the right of privacy and grounds for action for damages.[5]

Copyrights

Any creative person must be very aware of the distinction between inspiration and plagiarism. A picture that triggers an idea or a song that fits a new set of lyrics may lead to trouble. You cannot use someone else's photograph and translate it into art without that person's permission. You cannot use a poem or song lyric, or part of it, or even do a close parody of a poem or lyric without permission. Original work must be original. If it is not, it must be licensed or purchased. Even coming too close to the style of a particular artist can lead to litigation.

The only nonoriginal music that can be used without permission or payment is that which is in the public domain. *Public domain* means it has not been copyrighted or its copyright has expired. But just because a song is old or familiar does not mean it is in the public domain. Sometimes a certain arrangement of public domain music may be copyrighted.

Personal Rights

You cannot use people in advertising without their permission. If they are famous, they have a right of publicity, which means they are entitled to profit by the use of their name, likeness, or testimonial. In recent California cases, this right of publicity has survived the grave, so do not assume that if the actor is dead you can use his or her character in advertising. Even with ordinary people you need permission. They have a right to privacy protecting the use of their name, likeness, or testimonial.

These personal rights may extend to people's property as well. Use of a recognizable home or famous piece of property as a setting or prop might infringe a right of privacy or publicity or create an implied testimonial from the owner.

Special talent contracts must be negotiated for celebrity talent. A lawyer should negotiate and write a license for use of licensed characters. For private individuals, the producer should obtain a written release for the commercial.

Trademarks

In addition to guarding against infringing upon someone else's trademark, the television copywriter must take steps to protect those of his or her client. When actor Robert Young went around in commercials inviting people to "have a cup of Sanka brand coffee," it was not because some writer liked the sound of it. It was to protect the name *Sanka* as a brand name, or trademark. Trademarks are words or symbols that identify the

---

5. John S. Wright, D. S. Warner, and W. L. Winter, Jr., *Advertising* (New York: McGraw-Hill, 1971), 771.

goods or services of their owner. Trademarks cannot be used without the owner's permission. Examples include product names and logos, characters, and slogans. If a trademark is not protected it may lose its exclusivity.

> Shredded wheat, aspirin, linoleum, cellophane and many other erstwhile trademarks have passed into the public domain for one reason or another. Exclusive ownership in many cases was lost because the marks were held to have become the common name of the product. Others were ruled to have been wrongly used, inadequately protected, or abandoned.[6]

While every company wants its brand name to become a household term, too much familiarity breeds contempt for the trademark. So brand names must be handled carefully in copy. The legal department of the company whose trademark is in question will determine what specific use may be made of its specific trademark. But there are some general guidelines:

> A trademark is an adjective. Do not use it as a verb or noun. A trademark is not *a thing* or a *kind* of thing. It is a *brand* of thing. To maintain this proprietary status (the objective of all protective measures), the trademark should always be associated with the generic name of the product. "Ask for WAMSUTTTA sheets." Do not use as a possessive. Say "The wonderful smoothness of WAMSUTTA sheets," not "WAMSUTTA'S wonderful smoothness."[7]

To the poor writer trying to trim his TV copy down to twenty-eight seconds of natural-sounding dialogue, the inclusion of *brand* and other necessary modifiers is often awkward and annoying. But it is a small price to pay to protect the millions of dollars invested in a registered brand name.

Four Red Flags

Four of advertising's favorite words are sure to catch a lawyer's eye.

New

In the eyes of the Federal Trade Commission a product is only new for six months. After six months of national advertising, *new* words have to come out of the commercial. Introductory commercials that envision a longer-than-six-month life often produce a non-new version at the same time.

---

6. Charles A. Holcomb and Sidney A. Diamond, "Trademarks . . . Orientation for Advertising People" (New York: American Association of Advertising Agencies, 1963, 1964, 1971), 3.

7. Holcomb and Diamond, 16–17.

Free

An item must be truly free to be advertised as free. This seems reasonable. But this means there can be no hidden costs or increase in price of accompanying goods to offset the cost of the free item. Any conditions (such as, "buy one, get one free") must be clearly disclosed.

Best

Best can be a powerful claim or puffery, depending on its use. An unqualified *best* claim may require proof that the product excels against all competitors with regard to all relevant product attributes.

Guaranteed

There are very explicit regulations involved in advertising warranties and guarantees. You cannot imply a warranty or guarantee unless such actually exists.

Honesty Is the Best Policy

In spite of what the anguished cries of its critics might lead you to believe, advertising in general (and commercials specifically) is not a dark conspiracy to deceive, beguile, and mislead the public. In addition to the agencies, boards, and bodies looking out for their interests and legal rights, consumers have their own common sense and built-in ability to take advertising with the proverbial grain of salt. Lawyers are busy making sure that advertising obeys the letter of the law. But advertising has more than a moral and legal obligation to be truthful. It has a very good business reason. A prospect deceived is a prospect lost.

Chapter 12

Producing
Commercials

From Storyboard to Answer
Print: An Overview

After the storyboard has been massaged, revised, and approved for production, the difficult part is over. And the other difficult part begins. Now somebody has to deliver what the storyboard promises. It is time to turn the idea into a commercial.

The first step is to obtain bids, or estimates of the cost of production. Copies of the script and storyboard are submitted to several production houses, chosen on the basis of their past work, personnel, style, or specialty. Along with the script and storyboard goes a set of production notes in which the writer or art director who created the commercial describes its purpose, style or tone, and specifics on casting, props, sets, and techniques. In addition, the studio is made aware of required delivery dates and the various elements it is expected to supply. The studios evaluate the commercial submitted to them and estimate what it will cost them to produce it—and make a little profit in the process. On the basis of the submitted bids the agency makes its recommendation. Agency commission and other costs are added, and this gross bid is submitted to the client for approval.

Representatives of the agency—usually the writer and/or art director, along with the agency producer—meet with the studio personnel (producer, director) to discuss and plan the upcoming production. The storyboard is reviewed shot by shot. Props, settings, locations, wardrobes, and other details of production are discussed. The talent who will perform in the commercial is selected The purpose of this preproduction discussion is to clear up any misunderstandings about the action, style, or attitude of a particular scene and the commercial as a whole. This helps head off many costly problems or delays that might otherwise occur in the actual shooting.

Finally, the actual production begins. Filming proceeds scene by scene (although not necessarily in the order the scenes will follow in the finished commercial). Sound may be recorded at a separate recording session and may provide the exact timings to which visuals must be coordinated (as in animation), or sound may be recorded simultaneously with the pictures during the filming. Acceptable takes are processed and screened the next day by the director and producer. This footage is called rushes or dailies. The approved takes from the dailies are then edited and assembled in sequence in a rough cut.

When all the shooting and recording are completed, the two elements are viewed in an interlock. The edited picture is run in synchronization with the sound track, which is still a separate element. Revisions in editing or color can be made more easily (economically) at this point. Once approved, the sound track and picture elements are combined onto a single piece of film and any needed opticals (effects such as dissolves and supers) are added. This first combined print is called an answer print. It is screened and approved by the agency and then transferred to videotape for release to the various television stations scheduled to air the commercial.

The Bidding Process

The first client approval a commercial storyboard receives is not usually a go-ahead to produce. It is first approved for bids. The advertiser still wants to know how much the commercial is going to cost to make.

Criteria

The agency creative people and the agency producer huddle to review the requirements of the job and to decide which of the hundreds of available studios (independent film or tape action houses) should be asked to submit bids.

In evaluating studios, they consider the following factors:

- **Studio talent and personnel.** A studio may have a particular director or cameraman who is especially good at shooting fashions or children or food.

- **Past performance.** A studio's sample reel showcases the commercials it has recently produced. Such reels can be requested and reviewed. If the studio has produced work for the agency in the past, there are further considerations, such as their performance in meeting schedules.

- **Particular strengths and weaknesses.** A studio may be especially noted for a certain style or type of work—animation, stop motion, special effects.

- **Costs and financial history.** Are their charges in line with other studios or justified in terms of the finished creative product?

- **Location.** Sometimes cost or logistics will influence the decision. Shooting close to home may be more economical and make production control easier to maintain. The studio may be closer to a desired location or have a better pool of talent and technicians.

After discussing studios and directors and screening their reels, the producer and creative team narrow down their choices to three that will be asked to bid on the job. Although it is likely that there will be individual preferences, there should be an agreed-upon willingness to shoot with any studio asked to bid on a job. This makes competitive bidding truly competitive, with the job going to the studio with the lowest cost.

To further guarantee that the bidding process is accurate and competitive, it is essential that each studio have the same information on which to base its bid.

Where the agency producer really earns his keep is in the bidding process. The more accurately and fairly he communicates the specs, or physical requirements, of the commercial to the studios selected to bid, the more realistic will be the bids.[1]

If one studio is told one thing and another studio is told something else, their bids will reflect these discrepancies. One may think a job can be shot in one day. Another may be told something that makes them realize two days are required. Another thing studios need in order to bid realistically is time. If the studio is given too little time to bid and if the agency has too little time to thoroughly review the bids, the chance of errors (and extra expenditures) increases. The studio needs time to clarify any uncertainties in the storyboard and possibly offer alternatives.

What Goes Out to the Studios

Each studio should be sent the following:

- **Script and storyboard.** It is important that the studio bid on the final, detailed storyboard and approved script. Last-minute copy changes and revisions in staging may affect timings or the number and type of shots needed. It does not help anyone if the studio bases its estimate on one storyboard only to discover later that it is being asked to produce something else.

- **Production notes.** A storyboard is rarely self-explanatory. It does not include all the details of production the writer or art director has in mind. It helps if the writer includes along with the storyboard any additional information relevant to the production of the spot as well as a sense of the style or mood being sought. There is no standardized form for these remarks, but here is a checklist that suggests some of the areas of concern.

---

1.   Arthur Bellaire, "Where the Producer Really Earns His Keep—the Bidding Process," *Advertising Age* (March 4, 1974): 36.

GENERAL STATEMENTS

- OBJECTIVE: What do you expect this commercial to communicate?

- MOOD/ATMOSPHERE: Light or serious?

- ANIMATION: Full or limited? Any particular style?

- MAJOR COPY POINTS: In order of importance.

VIDEO DIRECTION

- CAST SELECTION: Age bracket, character description; name; examples of types; if possible, special qualifications.

- SETTINGS: Keep general.

- WARDROBE: Keep general.

- DIRECTION OR PACING

- PRODUCT: Special notes on handling.

- COMMERCIAL PROPS: Other than product. Includes premiums.

- TITLES AND LETTERING: Size, style, and positioning.

- LOGO OR SIGNATURE: Style and handling.

- SPECIAL EFFECTS: Keep general.

- OPTIONAL CUTS: Are they indicated on script or storyboard?

AUDIO DIRECTION

- IS THERE MUSIC? What kind—library, original?

- MUSIC AND SOUND EFFECTS: If sample tape is being sent, how closely should it be followed?

- TYPES OF ACTOR VOICES DESIRED: Give examples.

- TYPES OF ANNOUNCER VOICES DESIRED: Give examples.

- **Specifications.** In addition to the copywriter's interpretations and elaborations of the storyboard that give the studio a better idea of what is expected of it, the studio also needs to know all the specifics it should figure into its costs. This includes:

    Schedule and delivery dates. What is the air date (the ultimate deadline) for the commercial? When are the various in-production approvals required? Most of the problems and extra expenses in production arise when there is not enough time to do the job the way it should be done. The reasonableness of the schedule gives the studio a good clue as to the future pressures, such as overtime.

Contractual elements to be supplied. How many prints are required? Tape transfers?

How is the commercial to be used? Network? Spot? On-air test? Usage determines the rate at which talent must be paid.

Music. What is needed and who is to do it, studio or agency?

Product/packages/artwork. Will the agency supply product for the shoot? What about color-corrected packages, titles, and other artwork or specified props?

Besides all these written materials, the studio should have the opportunity to discuss the commercial with the agency producer. Any storyboard is bound to contain ambiguities. It may appear to call for a shot that is "impossible" (very expensive), and that would naturally inflate the bid. Studios often complain that they are asked only to estimate storyboards as they are, not for suggestions on how to simplify or improve them.

The studio may not succeed in changing the commercial, but all such questions should be clarified and resolved. If a suggested change is adopted, however, the agency should relay the change to other studios bidding on the job so that everyone is working with the same specifications.

The Estimate

If you have ever wondered why commercials cost a lot of money to make, consider all the things that must go into a typical production.

- **Preparation.** For studio jobs this includes preproduction meetings and obtaining props. For location jobs, it may cover extensive scouting for locations.

- **Set construction, dressing, and striking.** How many sets are called for? How elaborate are they? Expenses include design, construction, studio rental, and disassembly when the shoot is over.

- **Locations.** Considerations include accessibility, travel (for crew, talent, agency, equipment), and payments to outside people for permission and assistance.

- **Shooting days.** How long will it take to film the commercial? Talent and crew must be paid, and unions watch the hours very closely. Facilities and equipment must be rented.

- **Equipment rental.** How many (and what kind of) cameras, lights, dollies? How long will they be required? Any special equipment like cranes or helicopters?

- **Crew costs.** How large a unit is necessary? This includes camera operators, lighting technicians, prop people, and stagehands, and may require other specialists, such as makeup artists, hairdressers, stylists, home economists, teachers (if children are used), drovers, or animal trainers.

- **Director's fee.** The director, whether staff or free-lance, often receives more than union-scale payment. The same may be true of certain cameramen.

- **Sound recording.** Sound crew (and equipment) for the shooting? Studio rental for postrecording?

- **Film stock, developing, and printing.** How much footage is likely to be shot? How much will be printed?

- **Costumes, wardrobe, props.** Who supplies them? Bought or rented?

- **Animation.** How much is called for? How complex is it?

- **Artwork, lettering.** This covers the cost of preparing titles or other graphic elements called for.

- **Color correction.** Any modifications to the product or package that are not supplied by the agency?

- **Editing.** Is the studio to finish the picture or just to shoot, print, and deliver dailies? If the studio does not have its own editing facilities, this work must be subcontracted.

- **Opticals or special effects.** Are there complicated (and expensive) techniques called for in shooting or postproduction?

- **Overtime.** Adequate planning should eliminate the need for this. When necessary it involves double pay or more to union workers.

- **Contractual elements.** The cost of prints, tape transfers, or other required elements.

- **Talent payments.** How many principals or players (featured performers who receive residual payments in addition to initial session fees)? How many extras? Who pays the talent? (Residuals are the agency's responsibility, but session fees are part of the studio's costs.) Any casting or audition fees?

- **Music.** Fees paid to the contractor for composing, arranging, and recording an original music track (plus studio time, musician payments). Or the cost of obtaining stock music. (Usually music is the agency's responsibility.)

In addition to studio costs (and mark-up) there are additional costs that the agency adds (the former is called net cost, the latter, gross). Talent payments and music costs are usually included here, along with the costs of shipping product photostats, artwork, or color correction costs not covered by the studio, travel expenses for agency people covering the production, contingencies or reserves to cover the inevitable surprises, and the agency commission (usually 15–17.65 percent). In the case of location shooting, an additional weather contingency is usually included in case bad weather prevents shooting and talent and crew must be paid.

The Preproduction Meeting

After the estimate has been approved, the wheels of production can begin to turn. The first step is a meeting with representatives of the studio, the agency, and the client to review, once again, all the details of the storyboard. The preproduction meeting has a very ambitious goal: to anticipate and solve in advance every problem likely to occur in the ensuing days of production. At the very least it should result in a mutual understanding of what is expected in the commercial about to be filmed.

Participants

The participants in such a meeting include the following:

- **Agency creative team.** The copywriter and art director are the people closest to the commercial. It is they who best understand its content, mood, style, and intent.

- **Agency producer.** In some agencies the creative person is the producer. In others a specialized producer is assigned. The producer provides creative interpretation as well as a grasp of the technical aspects of production. Capturing the intent of a storyboard on film may not be as simple as shooting it as boarded, especially when one must adhere to a budget. The producer must balance artistic considerations with cost considerations. The producer is also the person responsible for all the details and logistics of production and serves as the communication link between the studio and the agency.

- **Account executive and/or client.** It is the client (or sometimes an agency counterpart) who best understands the product and the marketing objectives of the commercial. The client carries final approval and should have a clear understanding of what he or she expects from the commercial. Arthur Bellaire noted the following reasons the client should attend the preproduction meeting:

  To help protect savings already made by assuring himself that all plans are within the approved budget; or to approve or reject a newly proposed expenditure not covered in the budget.

  To become more aware of what will actually happen during shooting. Storyboards seldom tell the full story.

  To act as technical advisor to agency and studio, particularly with regard to product handling, subtle legalities, and matters of company policy.

  To absorb a preview of the shooting in the event he cannot attend.[2]

- **Director.** The director is the key creative person once production begins. A good director should contribute heavily to decisions on

---

2.   Arthur Bellaire, "Production Can Run Smoother—If the Client Plays His Role Right," *Advertising Age* (April 2, 1973): 36.

casting, sets, locations, and the structure and shooting of the commercial. The preproduction meeting is a time for directors to express their views as well as gain an understanding of what is expected from them.

- **Studio producer.** He or she is the studio's counterpart of the agency producer. His or her job is to organize the production and attend to all the details that affect the budget and schedule.

- **Other concerned parties.** Depending upon the nature of the commercial (and where the meeting is held), there may be other people who will contribute. (The set designer or art director, the prop person or stylist, a home economist if it is a food commercial.)

The preproduction discussion begins with a detailed review of the storyboard and proceeds to examine every major production element.

Action. Does everyone involved in the production understand exactly what the commercial is trying to do? Does everyone agree on the overall style and mood? Do the copy and action called for fit in the allotted time? Does the story track? Can the shots called for be physically accomplished? Have the camera angles and moves been anticipated? Is there an easier or better way to do it?

This last point is key. The storyboard should not dictate the way the commercial is finally filmed. A director is chosen on the basis of what he or she can bring to the production. The director should have an opportunity to make those contributions. But there is a reverse side to the coin. There are frequent opportunities to be seduced in the name of art and led away from the original purpose of the commercial. Production value must be weighed against advertising value. Each shot must be judged on its contribution to the commercial as a whole and not treated as a thing of beauty unto itself. In a simple tabletop food commercial, for example, how important is it to the shot of the product in a dish to arrive at that dish by means of a sweeping camera move up and over a bouquet of daisies? Would it be better to cut to the dish and spend those seconds looking at the product?

Copy approval and clearances. Double check to make sure everyone is working with the final script with all its revisions. Has the copy been approved by the client? Does it have legal approval? Does it conform with network requirements? Are all copy claims supportable? Are all demonstrations faithfully performed and legitimate? Advertising is under increasing fire these days. The importance of watching legalities cannot be overstated.

Locations. If the commercial calls for location shooting, has the best location been selected? Does it afford you the light you need? Is it accessible? Regardless of whether it is private or public there are clearances involved. Have the necessary permissions been obtained? You cannot preplan a sunny day, but be sure to take weather into consideration.

Sets. If you are shooting indoors, the set must be designed and constructed. Does the design fit the requirements of the commercial? Can the action called for be accomplished in the set? Can the set be constructed within the budget? Can it be disassembled and stored for future use if need be?

Lighting.   This is the realm of the cameraman and director, but everyone should be in agreement on the general mood and on any special lighting effects called for. It is up to the studio to be sure the necessary lighting equipment is on hand for the shooting.

Props and product.   Have the necessary props been obtained? Will they be on the set in time for the shooting? Has the product package been color corrected? (Product packages right off the shelves are usually not suitable for use in commercial production. The packages have to be cleaned up and color corrected before they are filmed. Unnecessary copy ("Net Weight: 8 oz.," for example) is removed to simplify the package and increase legibility. Airbrushed mock-ups may be made to ensure that the colors are sharp and will translate onto film and hold up during photographic reduction and duplication. Since certain dark colors may go black when filmed, they need to be lightened. Other value relationships are adjusted for maximum contrast and legibility. These specially prepared packages are called heroes and are handled very carefully during preproduction and the actual shooting.)

If a technical expert is needed to assist in handling or preparing or operating the product (for example, a home economist or a hair stylist), have such arrangements been made? Is there sufficient product on hand for shooting?

Titles and artwork.   Have all the necessary titles, supers, and other artwork been ordered? Who is to prepare them? What is to be delivered to the studio—Layout? Finished art? Slides? Will the artwork read on film? Do titles and supers fall within the safe area of the TV screen? Have the scenes on which supers are to appear been planned and composed for the supers? Has copy for supers been approved and legally cleared?

Wardrobe and makeup.   Is special makeup required? How long will it require to apply? Who will apply it (talent or makeup artist)? Is there an area provided for makeup application? (This may be a problem on location.) Is a hairdresser required before or during production? What costumes are needed? Who will supply them (talent, studio, rental, purchase)? Have costumes been approved? Have arrangements been made for changes, fittings?

Music and sound tracks.   Has a music track been prepared? Is music to be recorded? If so, have facilities been contracted for? If stock music is to be used, have the rights been obtained and fees paid? In what form is the music track to be delivered to the studio? Are sound effects called for? How are they to be obtained? When are they to be mixed with the rest of the track?

Shooting schedule and delivery dates.   Does everyone involved know when and where the shooting is to take place? Is it clearly understood when the agency will see rough cuts, interlocks, pencil tests, answer prints?

Talent and Casting

One of the most important parts of preproduction is the selection of the talent to appear in or be heard on the commercial. Talent includes actors, actresses, announcers, people with pretty or steady hands, sports stars, celebrities, children, and animals. You might not consider a hand model to be talent, but as an article in *New York* magazine noted: "A performer named Greg Fortune, for instance, can pour a perfect head of beer. . . . It is said that Fortune can walk on a set in the morning, ask the director, 'How much foam?' and pour within centimeters of the desired height, for take after take."[3]

Principals and Extras

Commercial talent comes in two varieties, principals (or players) and extras. Principals are recognizable performers who are paid both for their performance (session fee) and for the re-use of the commercials (residuals). *Recognizable* includes anyone whose face is seen on camera and who speaks or is featured or identified with the product. This also covers real people who appear in testimonial or hidden camera commercials. Extras are not recognizable and are not usually paid re-use fees, but rather are paid once on a buy-out. The differences becomes very significant when it comes time to pay the bills. Talent re-use payments can sometimes add up to more than the cost of the original production.

Unions

Talent falls under the protective umbrella of three performers' unions: SAG, AFTRA, and SEG. The Screen Actors Guild (SAG) covers filmed commercials (and videotape commercials produced in film studios). The American Federation of Television and Radio Artists (AFTRA) covers live, videotaped, and radio commercials. Extras in either filmed or taped commercials belong to the Screen Extras Guild (SEG).

The explicit details of what talent can or cannot do and what and how they are to be paid are spelled out in thick, formidable union contracts that are nervously renegotiated every three years. Basically, there are three types of payments: 1) a *session fee* for the actual performance; 2) *re-use fees* (residuals) for the continued use of the commercial (in thirteen-week cycles, based upon how the commercial is used—spot, program, or dealer—and the size and number of markets it appears in); and 3) a *holding fee* if the advertiser wishes to retain the right to use a commercial.

The minimum payments for each of these situations as specified by contract is referred to as scale. Actors or actresses of star caliber may demand payments well above union minimums. Such overscale contracts must be negotiated separately.

---

3. Janet Coleman, "Hey, That Sounds Like What's-His-Name," *New York* (July 13, 1970): 36.

In addition to fees paid to talent, the unions' national contracts stipulate that a contribution (11.5 percent for SAG and AFTRA, based on gross compensation to the performer) be made to the pension and health funds of the respective unions.

Residuals: See How They Grow

Residuals (re-use payments) are determined by the number of times the commercial runs and the size and number of markets. Airing on programs in more than twenty cities qualifies the commercial as a class A program (New York, Chicago, and Los Angeles, because of their size and importance, count as eleven cities each), and a principal gets paid every time the commercial runs.

To get an idea of how it adds up, both for the talent and the advertiser who is paying the bills, consider the example of an on-camera principal whose commercial qualifies as a class A program. He or she is paid $366.60 for the first use, $122.70 the second time, $97.35 the third time and each time thereafter until the fourteenth time. From then on he or she receives $46.65 each time.

Use	On-Camera Rate per Use	Cumulative Total
1	$366.60	$ 366.60
2	122.70	489.30
3	97.35	586.65
4	97.35	684.00
5	97.35	781.35
6	97.35	878.70
7	97.35	976.05
8	97.35	1,073.40
9	97.35	1,170.75
10	97.35	1,268.10
11	97.35	1,365.45
12	97.35	1,462.80
13	97.35	1,560.15
14 and every use thereafter	46.65 each	

(Figures effective until February 6, 1991)

Nice work if you can get it. And not only are performers paid when the commercial runs; they even get paid when it does not. For each thirteen-week cycle, starting from when the commercial is filmed, the advertiser must pay each principal a holding fee equivalent to a single-session fee ($366.60) for the right to use the commercial.

Obviously, talent can quickly drive up the cost of production. Three or four people on camera may not seem like a lot until it comes time to pay the residuals. Look carefully at the commercial to make sure you need all the people indicated. If you do, the next question is: Who should they be?

Casting Criteria

Casting really begins with copywriters. As early as the first draft of the script they should be writing for a particular type of character, voice, or personality. They should know the audience they are trying to appeal to and the type of character likely to gain its empathy. Ideally the commercial would be cast before it was written so that the tone of the copy would be sure to fit the personality of the person delivering it. But it rarely works that way (unless you have a continuing character or spokesperson). Instead, the writer and producer must review the copy and try to select the type that best fits it and is consistent with the objective of the commercial's target audience. Here are some considerations to keep in mind:

- **Pretty people vs. real people.** The people in commercials are no longer idealized stereotypes. The trend is toward performers who are human and convincing. Unless the beauty of the performer is to make a point (in a fashion or cosmetic commercial), it may be distracting and undermine believability.

- **Exposure vs. overexposure.** Experience and a long list of credits are comforting. You know you will get a professional performance. But everyone is looking for this year's Brooke Shields, the new face, not someone instantly recognized as the girl in the Alka-Seltzer commercial. If a performer is too familiar, he or she may be distracting and lose credibility as a "real person."

- **Models vs. actors.** If the talent is expected to interpret rather than read copy, make sure he or she is trained to do that and not just to pose. There is more to acting than looking good.

- **Appropriateness.** You may come across a face or character or delivery in an audition that sweeps you off your feet. Be sure to step back objectively and ask, "It's great, but does it fit this commercial?" At the same time, do not be blinded by preconceptions. A good actor may suggest an interpretation better than the one you had in mind. It may even be worth a rewrite.

- **Togetherness.** Dialogue takes two people. How do they work together? Some performers have a way of sparking each other and getting more out of a performance as a team than either could individually.

- **Past performances.** The producer and/or director may know how a particular actor or actress works and takes direction. Listen. Retakes can be expensive.

Casting Procedures

These are the final steps to take before rehearsing and then shooting the commercial:

- **Set talent criteria.** Review the script and storyboard and determine the number and type of characters needed. Consider age, appearance, and the performance that will be required.

- **Select a list of candidates.** Ad agencies usually maintain talent files, directories that include the composites of models, actors, and actresses as well as a stock of audition tapes, films, and records. Furthermore, there are talent agencies. Contact them and tell them your needs.

- **Hold an audition.** The agency or studio casting director will call in the most promising candidates for an audition. It is difficult to make an audition seem like anything to the talent but an inquisition, but it should be as relaxed as possible. After having had a chance to review the script, the talent is shown in and introduced to those holding the audition—the agency producer, studio producer, director, and copywriter. Someone, usually the director, explains the part and the interpretation or characterization sought. (Obviously, there should be a consensus at this time as to exactly what interpretation is being sought.) The actor or actress then reads the part. If the commercial is essentially dialogue, call in candidates for both parts so that they may read together. If facilities permit, videotape the audition. It may take several readings before the talent starts to warm up to the script or really understands what everyone is looking for.

- **Check on availability.** At the conclusion of the audition the talent is asked about availability and possible product conflict. Are they free to make the shooting date? Are they presently appearing in any commercials for competing products?

- **Make final selection and notify.** At the end of the casting session everyone compares notes and discusses the possibilities. If the auditions have been videotaped, it is possible to review the performances. (Videotaping the casting session also permits review and approval by those not able to attend the session itself.) If no agreement is reached, it may be necessary to call back certain performers or perhaps to call in additional candidates. This is no time to compromise. Make sure you get the talent you want.

After call backs and after the final selection is made, the talent is notified, told once again the time and place of the shooting, and instructed as to what wardrobe to bring.

It is just about time to make the commercial.

Producers and Creatives

Back in the early days of television, agency creative departments tended to divide along the print-TV line. The creative action was still in print, and the TV departments worked off in a little corner under the direction of a few visionaries.

But as television grew in importance as an advertising medium, the heavy creative types moved in for a piece of the action, and the walls around the TV department came tumbling down. The creative person who came up with the advertising concept for the commercial grew reluctant to turn over the execution of his or her idea to the trained television producer.

Still, the ability to conceive a creative idea did not necessarily carry with it the ability to translate it into a complicated technical art form like television. So a rather tenuous team system emerged consisting of creative person and producer. They worked together, but each was secretly convinced the other was destined to subvert the successful production of the spot. The creatives viewed the producer as a necessary evil retained to handle the tiresome paperwork and logistics. The producer viewed the creative as an unwelcome guest on the set, without the grace to keep quiet and let the professionals save his or her idea.

It raised an interesting question: Who should be charged with the responsibility for commercial production—the writer or artist who conceived the idea or the producer trained in the ways of film production?

One school of thought holds that writers should write (and artists should draw) and only producers should produce. This is based on the assumption (too often correct) that most approved scripts and storyboards are unproducible as is and must be revised or restaged before they can be successfully converted into commercials. But too often the producer, with professional objectivity, suffers from not being fully aware of the advertising/client problems wrapped up in the job. Certainly the first criterion of production should be to do it right. But occasionally the advertising interpretation of *right* differs from the pure production interpretation.

The other assumption of the producers-should-produce school is that producers know how to produce the commercial better than the writer. Chances are their knowledge of the film medium and the mechanics and logistics of production will be greater than those of the copywriter. But the most important aspect of television commercial production is not how a film works as film, but how it works as a commercial. Taste and advertising comunication savvy are traits to be cherished above just knowing how to operate a camera.

Some writers are better producers of their commercials than are producers. And some producers are better writers (rewriters) than writers. Any system should be flexible enough to permit the better person to prevail. A skilled writer/producer should not be compelled to turn over a commercial to a less skilled, though more technically trained, producer. Nor should a skilled commercial producer be saddled with the judgment of a production-ignorant writer who refuses to have a creation tampered with.

It is up to each—writer and producer—to be more sympathetic toward the problems and judgments of the other. The writer should learn what works and what does not. The producer should recognize that advertising considerations take precedence over art.

Production People: Who's Who (and What They Do)

A typical set is usually crowded with people, only one or two of whom seem to be doing anything. But each of them has a very specific function.

The size of the unit varies with the size and complexity of the job. A basic film unit consists of a director, cameraman, electricians, and stage hands. If it is a sound shoot, a mixer to work the recording equipment and a boom man to handle the microphone must be added. Although the atmosphere appears relaxed and informal, there are very distinct areas of responsibility.

Director

Directors rule the set. They direct the talent and the camera. In commercial production directors very often serve as their own cameramen, directing the lighting of each shot and operating the camera. Or they may hire a cameraman and concentrate on the staging and action. It is directors who interpret the storyboard. They must understand staging and composition. They must be able to interpret dialogue and communicate with the talent. And they must understand all the technical demands of lighting and sound.

Naturally it helps if the director understands advertising and the purpose of the film he or she is creating. There is always a danger that because a director's background and interest is creative filmmaking, he or she will let beauty take precedence over commerce. An interesting angle, camera move, or some other piece of dramatic business may contribute to making pretty film without contributing to (and sometimes hindering) the making of better advertising. This is a reason to have a good producer on the set, not a reason to go with a less artistic director.

Commercial directors, despite their protests and denials, do tend to get typecast as specialists. Some are noted for their lighting, others for the dialogue or people commercials they have made, others for their action or food photography. It is important for the advertiser (and the agency) to know exactly what it is after and then select the director most likely to deliver that quality and not try to impose a look or style on a director that is contrary to his or her instincts or unique talents.

Assistant Director (AD)

In larger productions assistant directors may handle the administrative and organizational details. Their job is to handle the crew and see that the production runs smoothly. They call for quiet during sound takes, and as the title suggests, assist the director with the action.

Cameraman (First Cameraman)

The cameraman is the key technical artist after the director. Cameramen have a star system of their own and contribute heavily to the success of the production. The cameramen are responsible for movements and settings of the camera and for the lighting of the scene to be shot. He or she is the key to the composition and look of each shot.

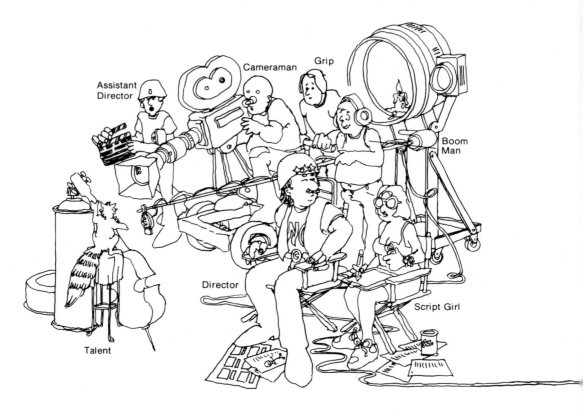

(Figure 12-1. Who's Who on The Set)

Camera Operator (Second Cameraman)

Acting on instructions from the first cameraman, the camera operator carries out the preliminary adjustments to the camera and monitors the scene during shooting. He or she may pan, tilt, and otherwise operate the camera.

Assistant Cameraman

This job includes loading the camera magazines and changing film; keeping the necessary records of scenes, takes, and footage exposed; changing, inspecting, and cleaning lenses and camera mechanisms; slating scenes and operating clapsticks when shooting in sound.

Gaffer

Gaffers are the chief electricians. Under the camera operator, they are the ones responsible for lighting the sets. Gaffers do not usually handle lights themselves, but they are skilled in the art of placing lights and using devices for softening, directing, and redistributing light. The gaffer's first assistant is called best boy.

Juicers

Juicer is a slang term for all electricians under the gaffer (because they handle the power, or juice). These may include lamp operators, who handle big lights; spot men, who are assigned to spot lights; and dimmer men, who install, operate, and strike lighting instruments.

Grip

A grip is a stagehand who "grips" and pushes the camera equipment, moves sets, and does incidental carpenter work. This includes laying tracks for the dolly and pushing it at the required speed, mounting and moving the camera, moving wild walls of the set, and doing the many other manual jobs related to production.

Prop Man

The prop man handles properties, furniture, and set decorations. He makes sure they are on the set for the shooting and moves them about at the direction of the director.

Script Girl (Script Clerk, Script Supervisor)

Primarily responsible for checking dialogue during filming, the script girl notes the details and timings of each take. Her notations are given to the editor as a guide. She also checks on the matching of details as sequences are filmed. She may also serve as prompter for the actors.

Others

Different kinds of commercials require additional personnel. For example, home economists are an important cog in the filming of food commercials. Their job is to obtain, cook, and prepare food for the camera. Commercials involving on-camera performers also require the services of makeup artists, wardrobe mistresses, hair dressers, and stylists. Jobs requiring especially elaborate sets may necessitate the use of a set designer or art director. Jobs filmed on location may require teamsters, wranglers (if horses are involved), and perhaps a helicopter pilot for that spectacular overhead shot.

What They Do (And Why It Takes So Long)

Once the visitor to the film set has recovered from the shock of the mob scene of people and equipment and has settled back into a canvas chair to observe the shooting, his or her next question is, "Why doesn't something happen?" Something is happening. Slowly and deliberately. Even though a shot may account for only a few seconds in the final commercial, it still takes hours to prepare.

Breaking Down the Shots

During the preproduction meeting agency people discussed with the director each frame of the storyboard and arrived at the number and type of shots needed. If there are differences of opinion as to the best way to shoot a particular shot, it may be shot several ways and the one that works best selected. These variations in shooting a scene may include a change in camera angle, shooting with or without a camera move, or a complete change in composition or action. For protection it is always recommended to shoot one version as boarded, since this is what was approved and what is expected.

When shooting dialogue, as in a slice-of-life commercial, it is common practice to shoot a master scene of the entire action of a sequence from a longer camera angle and then to repeat short segments of the action in medium or close-up. The final sequence can then be cut together in a variety of different ways.

When the storyboard has been broken down and the number of required shots determined, the director then decides the order in which the shots will be taken. This again requires preplanning. If a performer is in only half the shots of the commercial, the director will try to shoot these first so the actor may be released and not have to be paid for the time he or she is standing around. The director also wants to shoot all the shots using a particular set or lighting arrangement or camera angle at one time, since it takes a long time to change any of these. It is also necessary for those who are preparing items for shooting—the home economist who is fixing food, the makeup artist who is readying the talent—to know when things will be needed. Everything on the set costs by the hour or day, so the fewer hours it takes to shoot, the better.

Setting the Camera

What activity there is during the long preparations for shooting revolves around the camera. It must be set in the position that will give it the desired angle on the scene and then framed so that its field of view takes in all that it should (but no more). The field of view is determined by the lens.

Focal length refers to the distance from the surface of the film to the optical center of the lens. Lenses vary from short focal lengths (which photograph large areas, with the result that objects seem farther away) to long focal lengths (so-called telescopic lenses, which include a smaller area but seem to bring objects closer). Focal length affects perspective, the feeling of depth. For example, a head-on shot of a horse race through a telescopic lens makes it difficult to tell which horse is in the lead. A zoomar (zoom) lens is one with a continuously variable focal length within a certain range. Adjustment of the zoom lens simulates the effect of the camera moving toward or away from the subject.

Depth of field describes the range of distance within which objects are held sharp, or in focus. The smaller the focal length of the lens, the greater the depth of field. A lens with a longer focal length (such as a telescopic lens) has a smaller depth of field. When the subject moves toward or away from the camera, it is necessary for the camera operator to follow focus. Focus becomes a technique for directing the viewer's eye to what is important in a scene, or even to lead the eye from one object to another. For example, in a shot of a man sitting at a desk, the telephone and other foreground objects on the desk may be out of focus. The viewer's eye is drawn to the man. When the telephone rings, the camera operator may focus on the telephone, allowing the image of the man to blur. This draws the viewer's eye to the telephone.

Every detail of the shot—camera angle, field size, focus, zooms, camera moves (dollies, pans, tilts)—must be carefully thought out in advance and rehearsed between director and camera operator. All of this must be worked out with another consideration in mind: lighting.

Lighting

Nothing seems more maddeningly slow to the observer than the arrangement and setting of lights. There are lamps everywhere you look. They come in every shape and size and have fascinating names: baby, brute, broad, junior, inky. For every lamp there is an attachment to soften, sharpen, screen, or diffuse the light. By the time they are all finally in place around the set, there hardly seems room for the camera or the talent.

The theory and practice of film lighting, which could fill volumes, is unnecessary for anyone not actually involved in production. But it helps the observer of a commercial production, whether writer or client, have a general idea of what is going on and a more specific idea of what he or she expects to end up with. For it is lighting that will determine, along with the composition of the shot, the visual impression. Lighting will influence mood and drama as well as clarity.

There are three basic categories of studio lighting—key lighting, fill lighting, and backlighting. Each has a specific purpose and each must be planned with the others in mind.

The key light is the primary light source. (See figure 12-2.) It establishes the overall lighting pattern. It is usually a strong light (brute) directed at the subject to produce well-defined shadows. Lighting referred to as high-key is that in which the set is brightly lit with very few dark areas. It implies a bright, cheery mood, but if pushed to extremes can convey a barren, washed-out feeling. Low-key lighting produces an overall dark scene and may suggest a mood of menace or mystery.

What generally affects the lighting mood is the proportion of light from the primary source (key light) relative to the amount from the secondary source (fill light). Fill light is softer light used to reduce contrast and fill in the shadows thrown by the key light. The more fill lighting, the softer (lighter) the shadows and the less range from light to dark. Greater use of key lighting will produce sharper contrast, darker shadows, and a wider range from light to dark.

The third category of lighting is called backlighting. It is placed behind the subject and tends to pull the subject from the background by illuminating the back edge surfaces of the subject. (This is also called rim lighting.)

A separate light may be used to light the background or set in addition to the lights used for the subject matter. This is called a set light. Occasionally a scenic element will have a shadow pattern on it to relieve its blankness. This is created by a cookie (from the Greek word *kukaloris*), an irregularly shaped and patterned object placed in front of the light.

Along with the basic categories of lighting, the camera operator may use small spotlights to beam highly concentrated light on a particular subject in a scene. Or he or she may fit a cone-like attachment called a snoot over a light source to direct its beam. Barn doors are hinged flaps on a lamp used to cut off light from the camera and control the beam. Those screens or nets that fit over the front of the lamp to cut down the brilliance are called scrims. Scrims, cutters, and flags are used to eliminate troublesome hot spots (kicks or burns)—highlights that are too bright (such as might be caused by a bright spotlight reflecting off a shiny silver teapot). To mask light completely the camera operator may use a gobo, a black cutout of wood or cardboard. It is held in place in front of the light by a century stand, an upright pole-like stand with an adjustable arm and clamps. Excess light falling where it should not is called spill.

Etiquette and Jargon on the Set

Once the set has been dressed and lighted and the camera properly set, the director may call for a rehearsal. In the case of a tabletop commercial, a rehearsal may involve nothing more than a hand model dipping a spoon

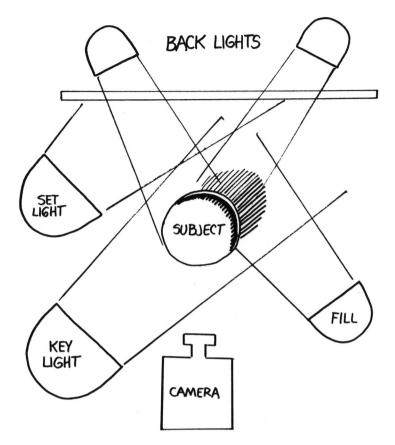

(Figure 12–2. Basic Types of Lighting)

into a stand-in dish or product. Tabletop commercials or inserts (footage to be included in a commercial) are filmed silently, or M.O.S. (an expression which came down from the early days of Hollywood when a certain foreign-born director would say, "Ve vil shoot dis scene *mit out sound.*")

To get into proper position the model may have to stand on wooden boxes called apple boxes—either a large one (full apple) or small one (half apple). The product may be set up in front of a limbo background consisting of a colored paper sweep.

In the case of a shot involving actors, a rehearsal means a run-through of dialogue and action as well as any camera moves. It is at this point that the director and the agency producer get their first look through the camera at the action and final compositon of the shot.

There is a definite channel of communication on a film set. The director is the only one who gives instructions to the talent or the crew. The agency producer makes comments or suggestions to the director. If there is a copywriter or client on the set who thinks an actor is misreading a line, he or she mentions it to the producer, the producer tells the director, and the director tells the actor. At each step along the way the criticism or comment is subject to review and discussion before being passed on to the next level. This may sound needlessly structured and formal at first, but chaos would reign if several different people were giving directions all at once.

All the members of the crew work within informal but very explicit jurisdictions. Union contracts make the duties of the gaffer and the grip very clear. Technically, camera operators do not move lights to correct their composition. They tell one of the electricians to move them. If they want a bowl of soup moved an inch camera left, this is the job of the grip or prop person.

When there is to be a long break in the action, the director or assistant director gives the word to save the lights. The set lights are turned off, and a work light (ordinary light) is turned on.

Silent Shoot

When a silent shooting is ready to proceed, the lights are turned on, the talent takes their places, and any stand-in package or product is replaced with the hero (color-corrected package or dressed and styled product). The director's cues are "Ready!" to prepare everyone for the shot and "Roll camera!" to instruct the camera operator to start filming. The assistant director then slates the take (by holding a slate on which is written the job, the scene, and the take number in front of the camera). Later, in editing, these slates will guide the editor in finding those takes noted as acceptable in the log. "Action!" instructs the talent to move. If the action includes a camera move, the cue may be more specific, such as "Ready . . . zoom." This tells the camera operator to turn the lens a predesignated amount. The familiar cry, "Cut!" means the end of the take. Action stops and the camera is shut off. If the take looked satisfactory to the director and the camera operator, the director instructs the script girl or assistant camera operator, whoever is keeping the camera report or log (record of information pertaining to the day's shooting, such as number of takes, footage, and takes selected for printing), to print it. This means that the take will be processed and viewed in the following day's screening of dailies or rushes. For obvious economic reasons, only successful takes are processed. If there is some doubt about the effectiveness of previous takes, an extra take of the scene, called a cover shot, may be taken. Between takes it may be necessary to reload the camera. The assistant camera operator uses a changing bag for this—a portable darkroom that permits him or her to unload and load the film magazines.

Sound Shoot

When shooting with sound, there are some additional steps taken and some additional terms heard. The microphone is a very sensitive and nondiscriminating instrument. It picks up every sound it is exposed to (unlike the human ear, which is able to tune out unwanted noise and concentrate on only what it wants to hear). The basic problem of direct sound recording is to record all the sounds pertinent to the scene and to eliminate extraneous sounds. This requires a perfectly quiet set during the shooting. Everyone must wait patiently while trucks drive by outside or airplanes pass overhead. Even the noise of the camera must be eliminated. Sound cameras are enclosed in special soundproofing cases called blimps.

"Quiet on the set!" tells everyone nearby to stop talking and moving around. "Bells!" signals the ringing of a warning bell that tells everyone in the vicinity of the stage that a sound take is in progress. The mixer, seated at a recorder listening through earphones, indicates that the set is quiet. The camera and recorder roll and the mixer's call of "Speed!" indicate that recorder and camera are in sync and running at the desired rate.

The assistant camera operator steps in front of the camera with a slate and clapsticks. He or she says, "Beauty Shop sixty; scene two, take one!" to identify the scene on the sound track. He or she slaps the sticks together to provide a visible cue-point in the picture and corresponding audio cue on the track from which sound and picture can later be synced, or synchronized. The director's cue, "Action!" starts the talent. "Cut!" followed by the sound of the bell indicates the take is over.

Each room or studio has its own sound or presence. Just as you sound different singing in the shower than in a living room, voices sound different when recorded in different places. For consistency in the sound track, all the recording should be done in the same place. If later, during editing, it is decided to insert a longer pause between two speeches, the space inserted should be the same as other pauses in the track. Blank tape would be noticeable. Therefore, at the end of a session, the sound engineer usually records several sections of studio silence (room tone) for possible use in edition. He or she also records a wild track. This may be later mixed with the original material if it becomes necessary to replace a particular reading in a take.

To avoid surprises at the screening of the dailies, many shoots include videotape equipment (VTR) that permits the instant playback of the take filmed. Shooting of each scene continues until the director and the producer are satisfied it is covered.

When a particular set has served its purpose, the instruction is given to strike the set.

At the end of a long day of shooting the welcomed cry is, "That's a wrap!"

Making Tracks: Sound and Recording

Sound tracks may be recorded directly at the same time the picture is filmed or they may be recorded separately, either before (pre-) or after (post-) filming.

There are two methods of direct recording: single system and double system. In single-system recording the sound recording unit is built into the camera. The developed film contains both picture and sound track and can be projected immediately after processing. The obvious speed and convenience, however, is outweighed by poorer sound quality. Far better sound quality can be obtained through double-system recording, in which recorder and camera are two separate units run simultaneously by synchronous motors. The sound is recorded on magnetic tape as the picture is filmed. Since the sound and picture are on separate elements (until the sound is combined optically along the edge of the film at the answer-print stage), it is easier and less expensive to make changes in either one.

Voice-Over Recording

A great many commercials use a sound track that is not lip-synced to on-camera performers. Instead, a nonsynchronous, off-camera narration is recorded to accompany the picture. Such tracks may be prerecorded to provide exact timings to which the picture is later cut, or postrecorded, to fit a precut picture. When a commercial has a lot of copy and very clear-cut editing cues, prerecording is very helpful. In animation, the voice track is prerecorded and used as a guide to the animators, who then lip-sync their drawings to the track. (For a discussion of animation production, see appendix I.)

The simplest voice-over track is the straight announcer. A single narrator, be he or she announcer or actor, simply reads the copy to time, perhaps leaving holes for sound effects or music to be added later. (A reminder: The sound track for a filmed commercial is always two seconds shorter than the picture. A sixty-second commercial has a fifty-eight-second track; a thirty-second spot has twenty-eight seconds of audio. The first two seconds are silent pull-up, to compensate for the gap between picture and sound that results during film projection.)

The work of a skilled announcer is a thing of beauty. One copywriter praised a voice-over announcer: "He can read faster and sound slower than anyone else around." It takes a built-in sense of timing to know just how long to pause or to be able to pick up a second in a reading.

Music Tracks

A music track for a commercial consists of either a jingle or a background score. A jingle has lyrics, usually copy points set to music. A background score is usually instrumental and is used to accent or soften the voice track and to add mood and atmosphere to the commercial. The three sources for music are original compositions, popular songs, and public domain. Popular songs are often used with specially-adapted parody lyrics. The rights to use such songs must be obtained and a fee paid. Costs of such songs vary with their popularity and the exclusivity of the terms. Public domain (p.d.) refers to those songs that have been around so long they are no longer copyrighted. (But do not assume a song is p.d. just because it has been around a long time. You could be in for some legal surprises for copyright infringement.)

As pointed out earlier, the current trend in commercials is to use original, custom-scored music. Very few copywriters are songwriters. The copywriter may write lyrics to which a composer then fits the music. Or the copywriter may just suggest the type of treatment he or she wishes and the copy points or ideas he or she wants the song to convey. The actual composing and arranging of commercial music tracks is the job of an outside specialist.

The musician is called in to discuss, with the copywriter and the producer, the requirements of the job. They go over the storyboard and analyze the intent, mood, and general style. If the music is to be postscored, they may have a voice track or even a completed picture. In the case of animated commercials the composer usually works with a bar sheet, which breaks down the film frame by frame, showing the exact length of each syllable, word, and action. If there are any holes in the track left for a particular musical effect, these are discussed. Armed with these counts, the composer goes off and composes. He or she may return with a rough track to see if the composition meets with approval.

The Language of the Recording Session

The composer/musical contractor arranges for recording studio time and books the necessary musicians and singers. The composer goes over the score with the musicians. There are rehearsals and very often some minor rewriting to get the desired blend of instrumentation. The engineer arranges the mikes and gets a level (volume or loudness used for determining balance) for each instrument. The track may be laid down (recorded) in sections or stages, with additional instrumentation and vocals to be added (overdubbed). Each instrument is recorded on a separate track (up to twenty-four) so that it can be raised or lowered or dropped out altogether when the final track is mixed. The audio engineer operates a frighteningly complex console that can control the level of each track. The musicians wear earphones through which they can hear a click track, a recorded mechanical beat. (This assures that the recorded track will conform to the film. Film is projected at a rate of twenty-four frames per second. An 8-frame click would consist of a beat every third of a second.) After a take, the contractor-musician who is conducting the session may request a playback so that he or she and the musicians can evaluate the performance. If there is a mistake near the end of the take, the instrument or instruments that need to be rerecorded can be punched in at that point in the track without requiring the entire group to take it from the top.

Once the instrumental track is completed, the vocal track is added. The singer or singers, wearing earphones that feed them the click and as much of the instrumental as is helpful, record their part. After all parts are recorded, they are mixed in proper balance. The track is evaluated over the large studio speaker and then over a small monaural speaker to hear how it will sound under normal listening conditions. If there is announcer copy, it is usually necessary to dial down the music under the voice track so that the copy can be clearly heard. The multitrack master is left on file in the recording studio, along with the engineer's log detailing information pertinent to the session in case it becomes necessary to revive or revise the track. The track is then transferred to a mag track on 35mm film stock so that it can be synced with the picture. Very often the final composite track will not be made until later. Rather, music and voice tracks are kept separate until the final dubbing.

Dubbing

The final sound track may consist of three separate tracks: one with voices, one with music, and one with sound effects. The process in which the three are rerecorded and blended into one sound track is called dubbing. Mechanically, it is a relatively simple process. The tracks are synced and run at the same time the picture is projected. The volume of each track is controlled by the mixer. In this final mix the levels of the various tracks are balanced to the desired overall blend of voices, music, and effects. At this time special effects, such as echo, can be added, or additional voices may be overdubbed.

Looping

Sometimes it is necessary to add a lip-sync voice track after the picture has been shot. Perhaps extraneous noise on location made direct recording impossible, or perhaps it is later decided that an actor's reading was not clearly audible or was otherwise unacceptable. To make this new voice track, the picture and sound to be replaced are cut into loops and taken to a recording studio. They are projected over and over again while the actor listens and watches, then tries to read the line to exactly match the picture. When the new line has been recorded, the editor matches the new track to the original picture.

From Dailies to Screening Room

After each day's shooting the selected takes are processed and screened the next day for the director, producer, and editor. These are called rushes or dailies. Remember, much more film is shot than will ever appear in the final edited commercial. Most of it will end up as outtakes on the cutting-room floor.

Each take is longer than it will be in final form. This is to make editing more flexible. Extra footage at the beginning of the take is called heads; footage at the end of the take is called (you guessed it) tails.

As the film is screened, everyone agrees on which are the best takes or selects. Since each take has been slated, the editor will be able to pull out selected takes when the reels are broken down. The selected takes are assembled into a rough cut. This puts them into the sequence of the final version. Although the takes are in their proper order, they are not necessarily timed to final length. The rough cut can then be synced to the sound track (mag track) and viewed simultaneously. At this point adjustments can be made in picture or track to achieve the desired pacing and correlation of sound and picture. Scenes may be shortened, lengthened, rearranged, or removed altogether.

All this work is being done with a work print. The original material is never handled until the final version is agreed upon. At this time it will be conformed to the approved work print. Edge numbers printed along the edge of each foot of film outside the sprocket holes enable the editor to identify the film. These will later be matched against those of the original to assure exact duplication.

To indicate optical effects to be added later, the editor marks the film with a wax pencil, as figure 12-3 illustrates.

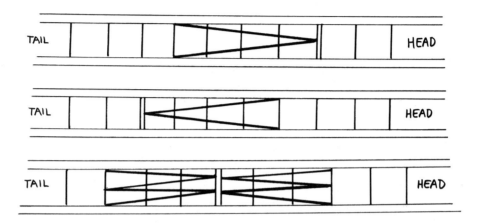

(Figure 12-3. The Film Editor Marks Transitions)

This rough cut is then screened in interlock form (in sync with the separate mag track) for approval. The sound and picture elements of the approved interlock are then combined optically, and special effects (dissolves, titles, mattes) are added to produce an optical print or answer print, at which time everyone sees the commercial in its final form combined on a single piece of film with the sound track now an optical stripe alongside the picture. Once the 35mm answer print has been approved, it may be transferred to videotape and/or reduced to 16mm prints for release to stations.

Chapter 13

Evaluating Commercials
Some Aids to Judgment

The Rise of Numbers

When advertising people sit around and swap tales about the good old days, they recall with particular fondness clients who reacted to copy more with their hearts than their heads. These brave individuals would look at the storyboards and then pound their fists on the conference room table and shout, "Now that's great advertising! Run it!" Some, of course, behaved the same way but concluded that the advertising was lousy and killed it on the spot. But right or wrong, they lived by their instincts.

You do not see many table pounders these days. The risks are high and the wrong instincts can come back and haunt you. Judging advertising is very subjective and the judges hunger for objective support. This is where copy testing comes in. Testing can provide some numbers. Although most marketing people would agree that advertising is more art than science, they like to be as scientific about it as possible. And so more and more copy decisions are being made with the aid of copy test results. When a decision maker pounds on the table and shouts, "Now that's great advertising! Test it!" it is not exactly a return to the good old days. What he or she is really saying is, "Now that's advertising that should test well." This is not a judgment; it is a prediction.

Because a test score is so tangible and objective, and because judgment is so intangible and subjective, it is easy for the former to undermine the latter. When advertising that was felt to be great goes off to be tested and comes back with low numbers, it will never again seem great. Everyone can agree in theory that recall, for example, is no proven indication of in-market performance, and that high recall was not the primary goal of the commercial, but a low recall score will taint it nevertheless. It is a little like being on a jury when the prosecutor introduces some highly incriminating but technically inadmissible evidence. After the murmur in the courtroom dies down, the judge rules that the jury should disregard what it just heard. But the seed of doubt has been planted.

Marketing people live with numbers. Numbers equate with performance. High numbers are good news; low numbers are bad news. Slowly but surely the number (test score) becomes the judgment. If that number measures only one aspect of a commercial, such as its ability to make people remember it twenty-four hours later, then that aspect becomes the critical criterion for success. When this happens, it can begin to exert a restrictive influence on the creative process. When copy decisions are based on recall scores, creatives may begin to design commercials for high recall and clients may begin to evaluate commercials solely on their recall potential. This often means falling back on the proven techniques of the past—formats and techniques that seem to improve recall. And before you know it, the tail is wagging the dog.

Research does not kill copy, people do. Properly used, copy research can provide valuable insights into how a commercial is working or not working. It might point out ways to improve it. If research is to be a valuable aid to judgment, it should be used to learn about the advertising, not to grade it.

The Dilemma of Copy Testing

The only reason an advertiser makes a commercial is to help increase sales. Therefore, the only meaningful measure of a commercial's performance is how it influences sales. The problem is, there are all these annoying variables. More things influence consumers to buy a product than just the style and content of a TV commercial. There are other advertising variables (such as media weight, share of voice, reach, frequency), other marketing variables (such as distribution, pricing, packaging, promotion), and outside variables (such as competitive advertising, word-of-mouth, social or economic factors). The "noise" of all these variables makes it very difficult and generally impractical to try to measure the direct effect of advertising on sales. It requires an in-market test, and that, of course, can only be conducted after the money and advertising have been committed. The commercial that everyone is so eager to prove effective is just one of many difficult-to-control variables.

At the other end of the research continuum are tests that are relatively simple to control. They can be conducted in laboratories with carefully screened respondents. Variables can be isolated and eliminated until you are examining just the aspect of a piece of advertising you are interested in. You could take two matched samples and expose them to commercial A and commercial B and count and compare their reactions. On such carefully controlled measures, commercial A might emerge as the clear statistical winner. But what does this victory have to do with sales? All too often, precious little.

Therein lies the dilemma. The more meaningful the measure, the less sensitive (and less practical) the test; the more sensitive the test, the less meaningful what is measured. To be truly valid, copy test measures would have to correlate with real-world sales results. Determining advertising's effect on sales involves an expensive, broad-scale, in-market test with dozens of difficult-to-control variables, only one of which is the commercial itself. Tests can be designed to examine parts of an advertisement, practically and with sensitivity. But the results may tell you next to nothing about what is likely to happen in the real world. Research works best in the laboratory, but advertising works in the marketplace.

Faced with this dilemma, researchers have turned to theoretical models of how advertising works to bridge the gap between what can be measured and the desired end results—effect on sales. If you cannot measure how a commercial will influence sales, at least measure its effect on consumers' attitudes that, other things being equal, may lead to an effect on sales. The most typical of these models is based on the classical learning hierarchy:

Attention/Awareness

Communication/Comprehension

Attitude Effect

Purchase Action

This theory led to the assumption that consumers must first understand the advertising, then they must remember it, and finally they must resolve to act on it. Armed with these criteria, researchers set out to measure advertising for clarity, memorability, and persuasiveness, assuming that a commercial with these qualities would perform in the marketplace.

As chapter 2 pointed out, however, there is growing evidence to support the long-held, commonsense view that not all advertising works the same way. The learning hierarchy seems most applicable to commercials that are logical, informational, based on real benefits and distinct product differences. It demands a high degree of involvement on the part of the consumer. But this involvement seems to be missing in many product categories where product differences are minor or nonexistent and behavior is more influenced by emotion than by logic. Copy test systems have not yet come to grips with the low involvement process.

Anyone looking to copy test scores as proof of a commercial's sales-building impact should bear in mind these cautions:

- There is no direct way to test copy for sales effectiveness.

- The theories behind copy testing are still tentative.

- Any test score reflects only a small portion of total impact.

- Certain measures may be inappropriate for some kinds of advertising.

The State of the Art: A Look at Two Commercial Tests

Even if you accept the traditional criteria (memorability/awareness, clarity/communication, attitude effect/persuasion) as measures of advertising effectiveness, you are still at the mercy of the ability of research to measure them accurately. For instance, at least three different approaches are used to measure awareness. One testing service asks respondents to recall brand names shortly after viewing commercials. Another waits twenty-four hours, gives respondents a brand cue, and asks them to recall the commercial. Another employs a recognition method in which respondents are given visual cues and asked to supply the brand name. Each of these approaches measures a different type of awareness (and may yield different results for the same commercial).

To further illustrate how the technique defines the measure, let's look at the procedures of two leading commercial testing services, Burke and AC-T (McCollum/Spielman).

Burke employs a day-after-recall method. The test commercial is exposed on the air in one of Burke's twenty-nine established test cities, so that it is viewed under normal conditions. The day after the commercial is aired, telephone interviews are conducted with viewers of the program that carried the commercial. The sample is drawn by a systematic procedure from telephone directories and usually includes two hundred program viewers. The general line of inquiry followed by the interviewer is designed to: 1) establish TV ownership, 2) determine whether or not the respondent viewed the test program, 3) determine whether or not the respondent watched the complete program, 4) determine the commercial audience (respondents who claim to have seen the commercial or program segments just before or after the test commercial), 5) determine what products the respondent recalls seeing advertised on the program (both spontaneously and brand-aided), 6) determine what the respondent recalls about the commercial, 7) determine what the respondents thought of the test commercial.

The McCollum-Spielman AC-T method consists of exposing respondents to test commercials in a clutter of other commercials and program content on TV monitors in a theater situation and then questioning them. Testing takes place simultaneously in three areas—East, Midwest, and Far West—with a sample of 100 to 125 in each audience.

A typical session begins with a standard taped introduction and some questions on demographics and brand usage. The first program consists of four five-minute segments of stand-up comedians with a seven-commercial clutter between the second and third performers. Of the seven commercials, four are test commercials and three are control commercials.

Respondents are then asked a series of questions about the program and about the commercials. These questions about the commercials constitute the clutter awareness and main idea measures.

A second program reexposes the four test commercials, each by itself, interspersed between four entertainment segments. After this second exposure respondents are asked questions about the programs and are then asked to state their brand choices. This brand preference postmeasure yields the motivation score.

With Burke the test commercial is seen at home under normal viewing conditions. But what is normal? What is the influence of such variables as the type of program in which the commercial is shown, the commercial's position in the program, and the time it is shown? AC-T controls these variables but may introduce its own bias due to the artificiality of the test setting, which may focus greater-than-normal viewer attention on the commercials.

The Burke recall score records the number of people (when aided with a product and brand cue) who could consciously recall the advertising the next day. The AC-T clutter awareness score measures the percentage of people who recall and write down the brand name of the product, unaided, within a specified time.

Beyond its basic recall score Burke also measures some internals, such as the number of people who can play back the selling message and the situational or visual elements of the commercial.

AC-T also reports a main idea score. Respondents are asked what they thought the commercial was trying to get across. AC-T's motivation score is a pre-post change measure based on brand choice before exposure to the advertising and after the second exposure to the advertising. Burke does not measure attitude effects or changes.

What Copy Tests Measure (and Do Not Measure)

Most of the copy testing services reflect a left-brain bias. They short-change the nonlearning hierarchy models of advertising effectiveness that are likely to operate for parity products with low consumer involvement. They reward the linear qualities of commercials (the verbal, logical, rational, informational) and neglect the nonlinear qualities (the emotional, sensual, nonstructured, experience-oriented, visual).

Testing copy in ways that create high involvement situations (forced viewing) and measuring copy with high involvement/learning hierarchy yardsticks (verbalized responses to verbal messages), may be forcing the copy to perform well on measures that have nothing to do with the real way the copy works. Such tests may be measuring how the copy does not work, not how it does work.

Memorability

Although no one has yet proved the theory that more memorable advertising is more sales effective, many popular copy tests are based on the assumption that sales power is partly a function of intrusiveness, the ability of a commercial to cut through a cluttered environment and be perceived (and later recalled) by the viewer.

Certainly a commercial must be sensed in some way by viewers, and these sensed effects must somehow persist or linger so that, combined with other influences, the probability of brand purchase can be increased. But there is considerable disagreement that this lingering influence is memory in the strict sense of the word. And there is disagreement on how to best measure this effect.

The most frequent test for memorability is day-after-recall (DAR). This technique involves identifying a small sample of the audience of a televised commercial, and then in next-day interviews, determining the proportion of respondents who can recall the commercial. Usually the respondents are given product or brand cues and then asked to prove their recall of the advertising by describing what they remember of it.

The verbal articulation that this technique requires makes it a cognitive measure, most relevant to commercials with logical structures and explicit product claims. When an advertiser has a benefit that is really important to the consumer, and when this information is integrated into a cohesive story line, the consumer is more likely to remember it. If, on the other hand, the advertising seeks to communicate something that is nonsubstantive, such as a mood, feeling, something sensory, or a user image, the DAR score may not reflect the commercial's true effectiveness. Commercials that evoke nonverbal responses may be strong in effect but less adequately describable in words. DAR would not measure, in any adequate way, the memorability success or failure of emotional or imagery-focused commercials. Since most commercials contain both verbal and emotional dimensions, the recall score will measure only a portion of the commercial's overall next-day memorability. Even the most nonverbal image commercial must be successfully exposed to viewers. The copy testing issue arises over how to prove attention. Is it the ability to dredge up and write down a brand name? Is it the ability to verbalize some unique aspect of the commercial? For some products and some commercials, not necessarily.

Clarity/Communication

After all that hard work to fashion the right creative strategy, and after searching for just the right words to express the benefit, it is a reasonable hope that your commercial will clearly communicate that message to the consumer. Research wants to know: Exactly what message was conveyed? Can the consumer play back the main idea of the commercial?

Clarity sounds like an undeniable good. But as seen through the screen of testing methodology, clarity is often limited to clarity of logic and reason, and not clarity of communication in the broadest sense. As tempting as it is to reduce advertising to questions of claims and messages, the fact remains that advertising also communicates through nonlinear, non-verbal means of symbols, imagery, and mood. In copy tests, communication usually reflects the ability of the respondent to organize thoughts, to distill and write down or describe a rational product message. This may ignore any nonverbal message or feeling that may have been clearly communicated to the respondent. Whether the advertising is linear or nonlinear, left brain or right brain, rational or emotional, it contains some message that you want communicated to the viewer. But is that necessarily a literal, verbal message that the respondent must be able to play back? In some kinds of commercials, comprehension is more like absorption (conscious or unconscious) of some positive feeling of the brand or its user.

Attitude Effect/Persuasion

Commercials are also tested for persuasion, or their effect on attitudes. Pre-post attitude shift is the most frequently used measure which purports to reflect the attitudinal effect of commercials. Typically, respondents are questioned about brand preferences, exposed once or twice to the test commercial, and then asked again for their brand choices. The difference between the two is taken as a measure of persuasion or attitude change.

The operating assumption is that if a commercial could persuade consumers who had been neutral or negative toward a brand to adopt more positive feelings toward it, they would be more likely to buy the brand in the future. Unfortunately, persuasion scores do not have an impressive record of being able to predict sales effectiveness. They seem instead to indicate the degree of consumer interest in product messages.

Is it reasonable to expect a single exposure to a single commercial for an established brand to change people's attitudes toward that brand? Attitude change is a gradual process, more influenced by campaign effect than by one exposure to a single commercial. If a well-known brand is being advertised, consumers probably already know a great deal about it. They may have used it in the past. It may even be in their homes. They have had time to build a complex body of information, attitudes, and beliefs about the brand. A pre-post persuasion measures assumes that a single thirty-second commercial will instantly and measurably alter this long-accumulated body of opinions and experiences.

Even more than in DAR testing, attitude testing depends heavily on the theory of behavior being used. It assumes that buying behavior results from attitude change. Chapter 2 discussed the mounting research that suggests that under certain circumstances (low involvement) and for certain kinds of products (those without critical, material difference, for instance), attitude change may not precede behavior, but may, in fact, take place only after purchase and experience with the product. Advertising for such products may not form or change an attitude, but may simply create a favorable predisposition to form an attitude.

Advertising, regardless of style, seeks to form, reinforce, or change consumer attitudes toward the brand. But it is overly optimistic to think that a single commercial exposure will accomplish it. Only after multiple exposures in a campaign is it likely that there will be a connection of a positive feeling or image with the brand, or that consumers will learn and believe the message. Evaluating certain types of advertising on the basis of one exposure may not reflect how that advertising will perform over repeated exposures. Low involvement, peripheral route, transformational, and affect referral theories (see chapter 2) all depend on repetition of exposure.

The Elusive E Factor

Tucked away in the back pages of many copy research reports, after the well-read recall, communication, and persuasion scores, is a collection of data referred to as internals or diagnostics. These are the numbers behind the numbers—the details of what respondents took away (or at least reported they took away) from their exposure to the advertising. Among these internals you may find reactions to the commercial—how they liked it.

Left-brain theorists do not put much stock in likeability, believing it is more important to be recalled than loved. They profess to believe that there are important nonverbal image-based elements, but they tend to regard these as a bonus, something to be counted only after the commercial has passed the basic tests of memorability, communication, and persuasion. But for advertising that plays more to the emotions than the intellect, advertising that romances the product experience or user, likeability may be a critical factor. If the advertising is the product experience and viewers do not like the advertising, it is going to be difficult for them to feel positively toward the product. Even for advertising that is linear and informational, there is evidence that the better-liked commercials are more likely to move consumers toward preference for the brand than are irritating, boring, or disliked commercials.

If a value of copy testing is that it applies objectivity to the evaluation of advertising, a detriment may be that it neglects subjectivity. It forces those who judge the advertising to *think* about it instead of *feel* about it.

Forget for a moment that you are an advertising expert and imagine yourself at home in front of the television set, with no copy strategy to tell you what to look for. The program ends, the commercial begins, and thirty seconds later it is all over. What was your impression?

Your first gut reaction will probably be "I liked it" or "I didn't like it," not "I wonder why they didn't introduce the product sooner?" Respond to the commercial first as viewer, then try to analyze why you responded as you did. This will be easier than trying to detach yourself so completely that you are worried about what viewers will think of it even before you know what you think of it.

There is something to be said for judging a commercial, at least initially, by listening to your own inner voice. How does it grab you? How does it make you feel? Although a personal, intuitive, emotional response is not the sole criterion, it does tap into a vein that copy research has trouble reaching.

A few years ago Vance Packard had the public trembling at the specter of subliminal hidden persuaders at work manipulating them to behave at the whim of the advertiser. From this scary, but long-since-discredited notion that a commercial could somehow make viewers want to buy something almost against their will and without even realizing it, we have somehow arrived at the opposite conclusion that a commercial can influence viewers only if they can accurately recall an explicit message. Commercials cannot influence people to such an extent that they behave against their will. But something about an effective commercial must move people in subtle ways, other than the rationality of its selling message.

Those who worry about the emotional impact of television commercials would probably be heartened by any move by advertisers to rely entirely on explicit, logical arguments in their commercials. By ignoring the emotional overtones that surround the message in favor of literal registration of its content, however, the advertiser would be overlooking television's greatest strength. Copy testing that chooses to ignore or discount the subtleties of style and simply count the noses of those who can play back specific, explicit messages may be rewarding the least important dimensions of the commercial.

An encouraging article in *Adweek* reported ". . . Researchers are looking for measurement techniques that rely less on the words and more on visual images and emotional triggers. Some of that research 'illustrates what creative directors in advertising agencies have known for some time: How you say something has an impact on the consumer that is at least as important as what is said. . . .'"[1]

There will always be some elusive aspect of a television commercial that defies statistical measurement, yet somehow separates not just the good from the bad but also the great from the good. Call it the E factor (E for elusive. Or emotional. Or executional.)—it is some emotional hot button that causes some commercials to hit a nerve and others to miss. It may be in the copy itself, in that unexpected combination of words that turns out to be just the right way of saying just the right thing to just the right people. It may be a tune or lyric that expresses not just the content, but also the spirit of the message. It may be in casting or in the performance of the talent. It could be in any one of these things, but most likely it is the combined effect of all of them, plus a measure of good luck. The E factor occurs when everything goes right: strategy, idea, execution, and production. Scripts and storyboards contain clues and promises, but you cannot be sure your commercial captures its E factor until it is finally produced.

It is the quest for this elusive quality that drives creative advertising people. It is this quality that separates so-so advertising from sensational advertising. And it is this elusive quality that makes creatives suspicious of research. They fear that the pursuit of numbers will eventually reduce

---

1. "Non-Verbal Messages in Ads Gain New Importance," *Adweek* (January 4, 1988): 23.

creativity to a formula that will lead to the same, safe advertising for everyone. Leo Burnett sounded the alarm in the 1950s:

> A lot of advertising today is being analyzed, engineered, researched and nit-picked within an inch of its life. . . . The result is a lot of expensive advertising that is irrefutably rational but hopelessly dull.[2]

And in 1965 William Bernbach told a Western Regional Annual Meeting of the American Association of Advertising Agencies:

> You are never going to analyze effectiveness into your work. You are never going to formulate the equation for a great idea and great execution. You are going to have to rely in large measure on the artistry, on the keen and sensitive intuition of your ad-makers, or you are going to have the sameness in all of your work that the public says is their greatest obstacle to noticing and believing your ads. Everybody is doing research, everybody is coming up with the same answers, and all ads are looking alike.[3]

Summary: A Few Things to Consider While Waiting for the Test Scores to Arrive

Copy testing has its place, but it is not as a panacea. It is easy to misuse and the reasons for its misuse are usually logical and often compelling. Judgment alone is scary. Judgment supported by research is comforting. Misery loves company.

Properly used, copy testing can reduce the risk of airing weak copy. It can help identify areas for revision and improvement. But the art of developing effective, brand-building, reputation-enhancing advertising remains a process of creative problem solving and it not always conducive to scientific analysis.

Any copy test is built on a theory of how advertising works. Most are built on the classic learning theory that favors the verbal and logical over the visual and nonlinear. But no single theory should be raised to universal truth. Recognize the shortcomings of each. Different commercials for different products under different circumstances work in different ways.

Copy testing can help when its purpose is enlightenment. It can shed light on parts of the process. But it can harm when it becomes an end in itself or when it is used rigidly or as a definitive answer.

---

2. Leo Burnett, *Communications of an Advertising Man* (Chicago: privately printed, 1961): 11.

3. William Bernbach, "Some Things Can't Be Planned," American Association of Advertising Agencies, Western Regional Meeting, Pebble Beach, California, November 3, 1965: 2.

What lay behind the hunches and intuitions of those table pounders who made their copy judgments without benefit of numbers? Probably some quickly formed answers to questions like these:

- Does the strategy make sense? Is it relevant? Is it based on what consumers desire from the product or product category?

- Does the strategy mesh with how consumers think and feel about your product? Does it overpromise? Does it undersupport your claim?

- Is the strategy focused on a single, clear, compelling idea and not just a catalog of selling points?

- Does the advertising grow out of the strategy? This means more than just being on-strategy or off-strategy. It means does the commercial transform the strategy into a living, breathing idea? Does it capture the uniqueness of the product?

- Is the product central to the commercial? This means more than seeing to it that the product appears within the first few seconds or that the package is shown at every opportunity. It means that all the words and pictures contribute to making the product more desirable and never wander off into irrelevance.

- Is the advertising entertaining? Do you like it? If people are bored they will not pay attention. They should be rewarded for watching. But they should be rewarded with entertainment that is relevant to the product, message, or image you want the commercial to convey.

- Are there powerful, evocative visual images? Does it make a strong appeal to the right brain? Strong pictures can communicate more powerfully and persuasively than words.

- Does the advertising have human values? Is it relevant to how consumers see and feel about themselves? Does it reflect their dreams and desires? Can they see themselves in the advertising (using the product)?

- Does the advertising treat the viewer as an equal? Is it intelligent and not condescending or insulting? Does it give the viewer credit for having a brain and a sense of humor?

- Is the advertising fresh and unique? Does it avoid the clichés of the category? Is it original and truly creative?

These are not questions that require a large sample of consumers, a battery of interviewers, and a computer analysis to answer. These are judgments you can make as you look at commercials. You are always looking for the E factor, that elusive touch of empathy, emotion, entertainment, even exaggeration, that moves people to respond to advertising. The next thing you know you are pounding the table and shouting, "Now that's great advertising!"

Look, ma, no research!

Appendix I

Animation Production

Writers of animated commercials may find their production even more mysterious than a shoot they can observe from a canvas chair on the set. They take their script and storyboard, discuss it with some people at the animation studio, record a dialogue track, and that is the last they see of the commercial until it is screened weeks later in pencil-test form. Somehow drawings get drawn and things get put together. And the process is considerably more complicated than those simple-looking moving drawings might suggest. This overview will cover the following stages: preproduction, recordings, track reading, direction and layout, animation, the pencil test, inking and painting, shooting, and editing.

Preproduction

As with any commercial, the production process begins with a careful reevaluation and discussion of the storyboard. The storyboard for the animated commercial is a much closer representation of the finished film than is one for a live-action commercial. It is possible to analyze the staging and compositions much more precisely, to determine what should happen in each shot and scene, and to decide what should be included and what should be omitted. Again, timing is critical. There must be enough time to accomplish the action or animation business that is called for. The animation director is just as concerned about characters' reactions and interpretations as the live-action director is about an actor's performance.

The preproduction meeting involves representatives from the agency (the creative team and the producer) and from the animation studio (usually the producer and the animation director assigned to the job). This is the time to reach agreement on the attitudes and actions of the characters, staging, and styling. The studio may have already done preliminary work designing layouts or characters. Key characters are rendered in different poses and from different points of view (to ensure uniformity of drawing). Such drawings are called model sheets. The agency may request the studio to submit a variety of different character models from which the final selection is made. A good character should be distinctive and appropriate to the commercial situation/story. It should also be simple and easy to animate. In addition to the way the character looks, it is important to decide how it sounds. Which leads to step two, recording.

Recording

The animated commercial usually begins with the sound track, specifically the dialogue track. (Music may come before or after animation, depending on the situation.)

Casting in animation consists of selecting voices that fit the cartoon characters. Specialized voice talents are often used—people with the ability to create distorted, funny voices. (The voice completes the process of distortion and exaggeration that is the root of cartooning.) Many recent commercials have used straight voices for a low-key effect. This may help establish greater realism (and may make the delivery of the copy clearer and easier to understand than if it were delivered by a squeaky or raucous cartoon voice. A low-key voice delivery may also be an amusing counterpoint to the exaggerated drawn character.

The recording session is no different from any other. The actors (voices) are called in, and, working from the script, they record the voices to time on quarter-inch magnetic tape. This voice track becomes the framework for the animation to which the drawings and actions must be synchronized.

The music track may be either prescored or postscored. If the music is to be an integral part of the commercial, it is often prescored and recorded ahead of time so that the animation may be drawn to fit it. The composer meets with the writer and the producer to go over the storyboard and discuss the mood, action, and character of the commercial. He or she then composes the score, sets the recording time, and arranges for the needed instrumentalists and vocalists. At the session the music track may be recorded independently or simultaneously with the actors (voice for characters).

If the music is essentially background atmosphere and does not figure significantly in the action of the commercial, or if you want to fit music to animation action yet undetermined, it is often postscored and recorded after the animation has been completed, or at least after the dialogue track has been recorded. The composer, in such cases, meets with the creatives and the producer to discuss the mood and intent of the commercial. If it is available, the film may be screened to see exactly what the action is. But the composer does not work from instinct or memory. He or she is given a bar sheet that diagrams the commercial frame by frame, showing exactly where each word of dialogue and each visual action occur. This provides exact timings, both overall length and any breaks or holes in the voice track where music might play a more significant role. With the bar sheet as the guide, the composer writes the score. At the session the track is recorded to a click track—a mechanical audio pulse that maintains an exact tempo and assures that the musicians end up where they are supposed to. The track may be played back against the screened film to make sure it fits. The taped music track is then turned over to the animation studio for final mixing and dubbing.

Track Reading (And the Exposure Sheet)

The dialogue track is transferred from quarter-inch tape to magnetically striped motion-picture film. The film sprocket holes serve to register the sound track with the eventual cartoon picture, but at this stage the film is blank. The film with the sound track is then put through a track reader, an electronic scanning device that is operated manually by the editor who is reading the track. He or she slides the film back and forth to determine exactly where words begin and end and makes notations in grease pencil on the film. The notated film is then run through a frame counter to determine at exactly which frame of film a particular sound or syllable occurs.

This information is then recorded (written) by the animator on a specially-prepared form called an exposure sheet (X-sheet). This sheet is ruled horizontally, each line representing one frame of film, each double line representing one foot of film. (Each page of the exposure sheet accounts for six feet, or four seconds, or ninety-six frames.) The sheet is also marked off vertically to accommodate other information relevant to the shooting of the film. Reading from left to right, this includes the video action, the sound/dialogue, cels and cel levels and backgrounds, and camera instructions (field size, camera moves, and effects). Exposure sheets are used by the animation director to indicate the action, by the animator for timing animated action and synchronizing lip movements with the dialogue track, and by the animation camera operator as a blueprint for how to shoot the film—which cels and backgrounds to be exposed for each frame, field size, and camera effects, such as zooms, pans, and cross dissolves.

Direction and Layout

The planning and supervision of the animated commercial is the job of animation directors. Guided by the storyboard, directors determine how the action will be staged and developed. They determine the field size and content of each shot, as well as camera moves, opticals, and cuts. They work with the animator to arrive at the desired attitude and personality of the characters. And they are available as work on the film progresses to view and approve the various stages of development. Since they are involved in every phase, good animation directors should be skilled in sensitive to each aspect—design, layout, animation, and editing.

Another key person is the layout person. The layout person is the animation equivalent of the live-action film art director. His or her job is to plan, sketch, and design the backgrounds and compositions of the various scenes. He or she is responsible for how the picture looks. The animation layout determines the basic composition of the scene. The layout provides the animator the limits within which the action must take place, where a particular character is in relation to other characters, props, and background elements.

After the director and layout person have staged and composed the scenes, it is time to begin the actual animation.

Animation

Animators are artists who draw characters in motion. Their contribution is the movement, action, and expression they bring to characters. They may work very loosely, leaving it to others to clean up the actual drawings. The animators draw the characters in extremes—key poses that show the outermost aspects of a given action. The intermediate poses needed to complete the fluid movement are drawn by assistant animators and in-betweeners. The number of assistants and in-betweeners varies with the complexity of the job, as does the number of drawings the animators make.

Bob Thomas describes the animator at work at the Walt Disney studio:

> The animator is given a rough layout that shows him the extent of the background, the size of the characters and props and the extremes to which they move, plus an exposure sheet which indicates the timing of the action and dialogue frame-by-frame
>
> He works at a board that is tilted at a forty-five degree angle. The center of the board is a large metal circle which can be rotated to place the drawing at any angle. Inside the circle is a glass rectangle that can be lighted from underneath. This allows the animator to place one or more drawings over a separate background and see how they combine on the screen. He draws on medium grade bond paper that is thin enough to be semi-transparent.
>
> At the bottom of the paper are two slotted holes and a round one spaced an equal distance apart. These correspond to pegs on the board. These pegs are standard throughout the studio, assuring that the animator's drawing will be in the same position when it is inked and painted on cells and placed under the camera.[1]

---

1. Bob Thomas, *Walt Disney/The Art of Animation* (New York: Simon and Schuster, 1958): 137-39.

The animator, assistant animator, and in-betweeners all work with paper and pencil. As the gaps between the extreme poses are filled in, it is possible to test for smoothness of action by flipping the drawings. These drawings become the masters, or working drawings, from which the final cels are prepared. But before the cels are inked and painted, the animation is checked in a pencil test.

Little Green Sprout™ is a trademark of the Green Giant Company © GGC 1982

(Figure I-1. PENCIL TEST TO INK AND PAINT. The Little Green Sprout as a rough drawing and as a finished cel)

The Pencil Test

The pencil drawings are combined (there may be several for each frame if the action and characters are sectionalized) along with the contours of background, strongly lit from underneath, and photographed. (Despite the strong underlighting, a pencil test is often difficult to read because the paper is a far cry from the inked, transparent cels. Plus, everything is linear. There are no flat areas of color to help various elements to visually separate.)

The rough animation on film is then run in sync with the sound track for analysis and approval. It is at this stage that the agency gets its first look at the commercial. If there are live-action inserts, these may be included, or blank film may be inserted to correspond to that part of the commercial that will be live photography. This is the time to spot flaws and make corrections and revisions. Changes become costly and time-consuming once the cels are completed. Once the pencil test has been approved, production moves to the next step: inking and painting.

Inking and Painting

Final animation drawings are traced onto thin sheets of clear cellulose acetate (called cels). The person who traces the animator's drawings onto cels with ink is called, appropriately, an inker. The lines may be drawn with quill pen or fine brush in a variety of weights and linear qualities, depending on the styling desired. The drawings may be transferred to cels mechanically (by Xerox or Ozalid systems). Since such processes reproduce the original pencil lines, the line quality is a little more rough and ragged.

The inked cels are then painted (or opaqued) in tempera colors on the reverse side of the ink lines. This avoids obscuring the lines. Background artists prepare the finished backgrounds, using the layout person's pencil layouts as a guide. The backgrounds are painted on opaque paper. The transparent cels with the characters painted on them are then laid over the backgrounds.

© Keebler Company 1982

(**Figure I-2. ANIMATION SET-UP. Cels are added to painted background for final shooting.**)

Shooting

Following the instructions on the exposure sheets, the camera operator precisely aligns the backgrounds and cel overlays on the horizontal table of the animation camera and exposes them, a single frame at a time. The animation camera is a special camera, usually mounted on a post or column, that tracks up and down. The camera is mounted on a bracket in such a way that it is always centered over a normal field corresponding to a standard animation drawing area. The camera is equipped to expose one frame at a time and to keep an accurate count of all frames exposed. It is during this shooting stage that special effects and moves are added.

Editing

Editing in animation does not mean cutting in the way it does in live-action films; this is all ploted out in advance. Animation editing is the final assembly of picture and sound track. The film is synchronized with the sound track. The animated portion of the film is combined with the work print containing live-action sequences, if there are any in the spot. Picture and sound track are still on separate reels. They are projected in sync (interlock) for review and approval by the agency.

An approved interlock means proceed to answer print. If titles or supers are called for, they are prepared and photographed on the animation stand for combining into the final print. The voice and music tracks are dubbed onto one final composite track. The negative is cut to match the work print and the final sound track is then combined with the picture and printed to achieve the finished product. The optical printer adds titles and optical effects to the animation and live action sequences as called for. This finished answer print is then screened and approved.

Varieties of Animation

The above production procedure describes the most widely used form of commercial animation—full or cel animation. It is the most fluid, flexible, and expensive form. But even in full animation there need not be twenty-four different drawings per second. The smoothest possible action would mean a change of drawing position each frame. Animators call this on ones. But most often the action is shot on twos. This simply means that a cel is held still for every other frame. This cuts the drawing work in half, saves money, and sacrifices practically no discernible quality in action. (Action on threes, however, would tend to skip and be "posey.")

Held cels is an animator's term for a cel that is held still for several frames during a portion of a sequence. These portions of a scene that do not move need not be redrawn for each exposure. This saves time, work, and money. Because it is more economical to do as little drawing as possible, characters are usually drawn on separate cels, so that only those in action need to be redrawn. As a result, a sequence involving several characters consist of several cel levels, or separate drawings on top of one another to be photographed at the same time. Each time a cel is added it affects the density of the background on which it is placed. To maintain uniform density throughout the sequence, the setup must be based on the maximum number of cels that will be needed at any point. Otherwise the background would appear to change color with every variation in the number of cels. Blank cels are used to compensate.

Because the thickness of the cel slightly darkens what is beneath it, it is wise to put what is most important (such as the product or package) on the top cel.

Limited animation does not attempt to duplicate the fluid movement of full animation. Single drawings are placed in sequence and projected for several seconds as stills. After the still, an animated transition to the next scene takes place. This greatly reduces the number of drawings required (and therefore reduces the cost). Well-done, limited animation has its own charm and will not be regarded by the viewer as a cheap substitute for full animation.

Scratch off is a method of creating animation by preparing a complete drawing, then scraping off or erasing part of the drawing with each frame of film exposed. When the film is run in reverse and projected, the drawing appears to draw itself. The use of a single cel for achieving a scratch-off effect, instead of a large number of cels which would be needed to show a similar action with regular animation, not only assures the smoothness of action, but also eliminates a considerable amount of retracing. Besides being a great time and money saver, scratch-off animation makes possible a variety of effects unobtainable with other methods.

Rotoscoping refers to a method of projecting and then tracing significant parts and elements of a frame of film (live action, usually) so that animation units can be planned to work with it. Rotoscoping may be used as a guide to action; for example, an animator may follow the movements of a human or an animal and then interpret and exaggerate the action with cartoon styling and emphasis. Or it may be used to combine cartoon and live action in the same scene. For example, the picture of a real car is projected and the animator carefully traces onto paper where the driver's seat ends, where the steering wheel is, and so on, so that a cartoon driver can be matted onto the scene.

Appendix II

Television of the Imagination: Radio

Return with Us Now to Those Thrilling Days of Yesteryear . . .

Children raised in the age of television might be tempted to write off radio as simply TV without pictures. Technically that is true. But to imply that because the listener has no electronic image to stare at he or she receives no visual impression is absurd. When we listen to radio, our imagination fills in the video. And that can be more vivid than television.

Back in the golden days of radio, before there were TV dinners, families used to gather around the Philco to "watch" radio. What they "saw" they created themselves. They pieced together their pictures out of scraps of voices, sound effects, and music. And these mental pictures were more wonderful, more amusing, more frightening than anything that could be captured on film or videotape. Radio's mental image of Jack Benny's old Maxwell automobile wheezing along the road was much funnier than the actual sight of Jack driving a vintage car in later Texaco TV commercials. There is no single stage set or special visual effect that could satisfy everyone's personal impression of Fibber Magee's closet, Jack Benny's vault, the squeaking door to the "Inner Sanctum," or the haunting presence of The Shadow. Pulses that raced to the soul-stirring sounds of the Lone Ranger's "William Tell Overture" slowed perceptibly at the sight of Clayton Moore and Jay Silverheels riding past painted backdrops and paper rocks on television. And when Superman went from radio to television, his fans went from the awe-inspiring mental image of a man of steel able to leap tall buildings at a single bound to the disillusioning realization of how silly an overweight guy can look in tights.

The classic example of radio's power to create real images was the Orson Welles broadcast of H. G. Wells's *War of the Worlds*. The poor listeners who tuned in late, after the show's introduction, were convinced they were ear witnesses to an actual invasion of Earth by aliens from Mars.

The lack of a literal picture does not limit radio's ability to communicate visually. In many cases it enhances it. It lets the listener's imagination run wild. The creative challenge in radio is to use this imagination, to choose the words, sounds, and music that will create the desired image in the mind.

This kind of radio takes more than just pounding out sixty seconds of copy to be read at top speed by an announcer in an echo chamber. It takes more than a bed of background music. It takes more than running the sound track of the TV execution. The approach to radio advertising should be visual and verbal. In radio the verbal must do more than reinforce the visual; it must help create the visual.

Radio Is Alive and Well and Moving Around

Radio did not roll over and die in the early 1950s when television burst onto the national scene. But it did change. Radio is no longer the pervasive national medium delivering huge audiences at a single sitting. This role has been assumed by television. Today radio is more like magazines than it is like television. It is personal and selective. It reaches many different kinds of people in many different situations at different times of the day and night.

Radio is now primarily a local medium. And radio is a mobile medium. This is the age of the car radio and the transistor. Radio is the medium that goes to the beach or the ball game. It can tuck into a pocket and go jogging. Radio's prime time—those hours when it claims its largest audience and demands its highest advertising rates—are the "drive time" hours between 7:00 and 9:00 A.M. and 4:00 to 6:30 P.M. when commuters are tuned to their car sets listening to music, news, and traffic reports.

Programming has changed, too. Instead of the drama and comedy shows of the 1930s and 1940s, the prevailing format is music and news. There are good-music stations, country and western stations, top forty stations. Program formats are designed to attract special kinds of audiences.

Although radio salespeople may disagree, radio has become more of a background medium. It is on in the car, in the kitchen, in the workshop. You do not have to stare at it. People usually do other things while they listen to radio. This means that the radio advertiser has to work hard to capture the undivided attention of the listener.

As an advertising medium, radio offers these advantages: 1) selectivity (It covers a certain specific geographic area and can reach specific audience segments at specific times of the day.); 2) flexibility (Commercials can be made and placed quickly and schedules can be varied market by market.); 3) intimacy (Radio's selling personality—often linked to station personalities—can be sincere, friendly, warm, and personal.); 4) immediacy (It is very often the medium turned to when fast-breaking news events occur.).

Radio's Creative Arsenal

Copywriters who sit down to create a radio commercial have many tools at their disposal: words, voices, sounds, music, silence, humor.

Words

Words to radio writers are like paints to an artist; they are used to create their pictures. But radio pictures are created for the ear, not the eye. Radio copy should be heard and not seen. The typical print writer who looks at copy on paper transmits the message directly to the brain without really hearing the sounds of the words. As a radio writer you must train yourself to hear the words. In the beginning, this often means reading them aloud or listening to someone else read them aloud.

The radio writer walks a dangerous line between simplicity and poetry. You must choose words that evoke images and combine them into enjoyable, imaginative sentences without sounding phony, flowery, or getting tripped up by alliteration or tricky pronunciations. Many listeners can be hypnotized by a dramatic reading of a Shakespearean soliloquy without understanding the content. Here are some words from an airline commercial that paint a picture of a romantic destination:

(MUSIC UNDER)

Somewhere between history and legend, stands the real Ireland. And somewhere between the River Shannon and the open sea stand the Cliffs of Moher. But for a town that was built in 1835, neither heaven nor earth has ever been able to move these cliffs. Ireland is that way. The hills are as green as they've always been. Life is as quiet as it ever was. And time has a way of standing still.

Missing, of course, is the sound of the announcer's delivery and the quiet underscoring of appropriate music. But the words do their part. Here is another example of words used to create a visual impression. The advertiser is the Fuller Paint Company and it is selling color.

(PHONE RINGS) Yello. Yes, I'll take your order. Dandelions, a dozen; a pound of melted butter; lemon drops and a drop of lemon? And one canary who sings a yellow song. Is there anything else? Yello. Yello? Yellow! Well, if she really yearns for yellow she'll call back. And if you want yellow that's yellow yellow—remember to remember the Fuller Paint Company—a center of leadership in the chemistry of color. For the Fuller Color center nearest you, check your phone directory—the yellow pages, of course!

And here is poet Dylan Thomas painting a word picture in shades of black in *Under Milk Wood:*

> It is Spring, moonless night in the small town, starless and bible-black, the cobblestreets silent and the hunched, courters'-and-rabbits' wood limping invisible down to the sloeblack, slow, black, crow-black, fishingboat-bobbing sea.

Both examples use repetition to build the sound (and therefore the picture) of the color. And both use specific associations (dandelions and bibles) to call up mental images of the color. Where meaning and emotion come from the sound of the words, radio excels. Where meaning comes from the look of words ("sloeblack, slow, black . . ."), radio loses out to the printed page.

With the usual creative proviso that rules are made to be broken (but only after they are understood), here are some generally accepted rules for using words in radio commercials:

- Use words that evoke pictures in the mind of the listener.

- Go for the simple word instead of the showy (*rain* instead of *precipitation*).

- Use words that are familiar to your audience. Write colloquially and use contemporary language. The secret is to sound conversational without making it sound the way most people really talk, which can be very boring.

- Keep the language active. Active verbs. Present tense. Remember one of radio's strengths is its sense of immediacy.

- Rhymes can help memorability, but watch out for poetry and flowery figures of speech.

- The most important thing to remember about words is that there is more to a radio commercial than words alone.

Voices

Everyone forms a mental impression of the person talking to him or her from the sound of the person's voice. Very often, when we first see people we had known only by voice, we are surprised to discover that they "don't look anything like they sound." (A switch on this was the discovery that many stars of the silent screen "didn't sound anything like they looked" and found themselves out of work when the talkies hit Hollywood.) Since the radio announcer is really the salesperson, the impression we form is likely to affect us in the same way the physical appearance and manner of a salesperson affects us in a face-to-face encounter.

Voices should be chosen carefully and should fit the message and the product. The right voice can support the emotional content of the words. There has been a trend in both radio and television away from the slick, polished delivery of the announcer to more honest, natural voices. Radio is a personal medium and you want a voice that is appealing and easy for the listener to identify with. If you know in advance whose voice you want to use, you may be able to write for that particular personality and tailor the copy to fit his or her idiosyncrasies. Lorenzo Music (the voice of Garfield the cat), for example, has a distinctive, deadpan delivery that can bring an extra comic dimension to the right copy.

To help the announcer understand the timing and phrasing you had in mind when writing the commercial, do not be afraid to overpunctuate the copy. Underlines can help indicate which word or words are to receive emphasis in a sentence. (Just do not fall into the "Blooper Soap" syndrome. In this satirical recording session, the writer asked the announcer to stress one word, then another in the sentence "Blooper soap is real good" until the hapless announcer was almost shouting the whole thing.)

Sounds

To talk about sounds in a radio commercial is like talking about pictures on television. Sound is the essence of the medium. It is through sound that radio creates its mental pictures and impressions. But as basic as sound is to the success of radio commercials it is too rarely used well. Carefully used, sounds and sound effects can involve the listener, evoke images, and even provide an audio signature for the brand or company.

If you doubt the power of sounds to evoke images, recall the last time you were alone at home or awakened at night by a strange noise. If you had seen the wind blow the door closed, you would have dismissed it easily. But with only your ear to go on your imagination takes over and a harmless slamming door becomes a sinister fiend.

The creative challenge with sounds, as with visual symbols, is to select a sound that is easily identifiable and loaded with the right kinds of associations. As always you must keep the intended audience in mind. A baby's cry would be a familiar and evocative sound to the ears of young parents, conjuring up an image quite different from that which comes to the mind of a teenager hearing the same noise.

Consider especially those sounds that are associated with the product. The sound of a can of beer being opened, bacon sizzling in a skillet, the fizz of a soft drink—advertising researchers call such things product experience cues. These sounds help get the consumer's thoughts revolving around the experience of using the product. If the experience is pleasant or appetizing, the associations pave the way for the message. It would be analogous to ringing a bell for Pavlov's dog and then reading it a dog food commercial. The bell puts it in a receptive mood.

Sounds with vivid, specific associations can be juxtaposed to produce memorable and often humorous results. In a comedy routine by Bob and Ray, we hear the familiar sound of running water in a dentist's office and the voice of the dentist informing the patient that he is going to have to drill. This is followed by the sound of a street worker's pneumatic drill hammering away at concrete. In another Bob and Ray vignette a father comes home from the dentist's office and begs his children to be quiet and stop running around. The sounds we hear are those of a bowling alley and the screams and laughter of a whole playground full of children. The imagination transposes all this bedlam to the family room. These are not commercials, but the application is obvious. Sounds can become a memorable exaggeration or analogy, producing a mental picture that television could not hope to duplicate.

Sounds, like visual symbols, depend on their context for their meaning. The same sound can produce different responses depending on how it is used. The screech of car brakes followed by a crash could be very sobering if the message were about seat belts. But it could also be funny. In a commercial for a drive-in brake service station we hear a screech and crash; then a woman gets some tips from the attendant and finally asks if she can take her car home. He answers, "Sure, lady, I'll put it in a sack for you." Sounds let the listener fill in the details, and the result is often more appealing or funnier than any single, specific visual interpretation.

Sounds can be startling and interruptive, designed to force the commercial from the background to the forefront of the listener's consciousness. They can be quiet and evocative, suggesting another time or place. They can be appetizing. They can be memorable and identifiable, providing instant recognition for the advertiser and linking the effect of messages over a period of time. They can be, as the bell to Pavlov's dog, the stimulus that triggers the response to the brand.

Music

Musical radio commercials began as jingles. Listeners who thrilled to shows like "The Long Ranger" and "The Shadow" paid for it by being unable to get ditties like this out of their minds:

> Pepsi-Cola hits the spot
> Twelve full ounces that's a lot
> Twice as much for a nickel too
> Pepsi-Cola is the drink for you.

Today *jingle* is a bad word. Jingles are sounding like singles. (Interestingly, Pepsi was one of the first to overlap from advertising into pop music when its "Girl Watcher's Theme" for Diet Pepsi became a popular song.) Today musical commercials reflect the pop sounds of the day. Chevrolet's "Heartbeat of America," Chrysler's "The Pride is Back," Levi's 501 blues, McDonald's, Coca-Cola, and Pepsi-Cola are a few of the many advertisers who have plugged into contemporary music to reach the young audiences who tune into radio to hear that very kind of music.

Besides jingles, or musical commercials in which the selling message is sung, music can be used for punctuation or background to underscore a mood. Lush strings might suggest elegance, a tuba band can conjure up an old world beer hall, a calliope brings to mind a circus or carnival, a strummed banjo can recall the roaring twenties.

Regardless of how music is used it should be entertaining. People turn on the radio to be entertained. It should be top-quality, sophisticated production because it is competing with sophisticated music (production) for the attention of listeners who, in turn, have very sophisticated sound equipment. And unlike a lot of contemporary music, it is very important to commercial music that the lyrics be understandable. Since you want people to hear the words, it puts a burden on the lyricist to make them interesting, not just selling points set to rhyme.

Although running the TV track is the radio writer's lazy way out, it usually makes good sense to use the same music in radio as you do in television. It should be arranged for the medium and the audience, but if there is musical continuity it can reinforce TV visuals that may be in the listener's mind. The success of this kind of image transfer depends largely on the memorability of the music track, the uniqueness of the visuals, and the frequency of exposure.

It is not unusual for a copywriter to start a script with the direction, "music under," and then get quickly into the announcer copy. What is unusual is for the copywriter to know what kind of music and why. Music should not be an automatic addition to every commercial. Sometimes it may get in the way of the message more than help it. Music should be an integral part of the commercial and not just an afterthought.

There is much to be said for a musical commercial that fits the programming in which it appears: a hard-rock commercial on a hard-rock station. But a musical commercial may blend in too well with the musical environment of the programming. It may slip by as a catchy tune without interrupting the thoughts of the listener enough to register a message. If the programming is music and most of the commercials are music, perhaps the way for your commercial to stand out is to not use music.

Silence

Silence is the white space of radio. Just as an art director achieves contrast in a print ad or sets off an important graphic element by framing it in white space, so can the radio writer give words and sounds room to breathe. Radio has become such a frantic, shouting medium that about the only relief the ears get is during Civil Defense tests. Listeners get so conditioned by the steady drone of sound that they are startled when it shuts up. Well-placed silence can be a useful attention getter. Once particularly relevant use of silence occurred in a commercial for Midas Mufflers in which people listening to their car radios were invited by the announcer to listen to their car noise during a long silent pause in the commercial. When the announcer resumed talking, he suggested that if the car was too noisy, maybe it needed a new Midas muffler.

Closely related to the idea of silence are time and timing. A commercial is a certain number of seconds long, and there is only so much that can be done in that time. If sound effects are to be used to build imagery, they must have time to do it. If music is to be used to build mood, it must be given time to establish itself before the announcer starts jabbering over it. If an actor or announcer is to inject any character, warmth, sincerity, or humor into the copy, he must have time to give it the necessary nuances and inflections. It is the wise writer who allows more seconds than it takes to read the copy.

Humor

Comedy dialogue is always an effective radio technique—if it is funny. Humor in advertising can go wrong in either of two ways. It can not be funny (and we have all heard jokes fall flat). Or it can be irrelevant. The joke has to come from the copy point the commercial is trying to make. But reels of winning radio commercials are rich with the humorous work of Stan Freberg, Bob and Ray, Mike Nichols and Elaine May, Jerry Stiller and Ann Meara, Dick Orkin and Bert Berdis, and Ann Winn and Garret Brown. Here is an example from Stiller and Meara's long-running campaign for Blue Nun:

HE: Excuse me, the cruise director assigned me this table for dinner.

SHE: Say, weren't you the fella at the costume ball last night dressed as a giant tuna? With the scales, the gills and the fins?

HE: Yeah—that was me.

SHE: I recognized you right away.

HE: Were you there?

SHE: I was dressed as a mermaid so I had to spend most of the night sitting down. Did you ever try dancing with both legs wrapped in aluminum foil?

HE: No, I can't say I have. Did you order dinner yet?

SHE: I'm having the filet of sole.

HE: Humm. The filet mignon sounds good. Would you like to share a bottle of wine?

SHE: Terrific.

HE: I noticed a little Blue Nun at the Captain's table.

SHE: Poor thing. Maybe she's seasick.

HE: No, Blue Nun is a wine. A delicious white wine.

SHE: Oh, we can't have a white wine if you're having meat and I'm having fish.

HE: Sure we can. Blue Nun is a white wine that's correct with any dish. Your filet of sole. My filet mignon.

SHE: Oh, it's so nice to meet a man who knows the finer things. You must be a gourmet?

> HE: No, as a matter of fact, I'm an accountant.
> Small firm in the city. Do a lot of tax work
> . . . (FADE OUT)
>
> ANNCR: Blue Nun. The delicious white wine that's
> correct with any dish. Another Sichel wine
> imported by Schieffelin & Co., New York

Comic dialogue is used to make a simple point: Blue Nun goes with any dish. Not every product lends itself to humor, but the list of those that do is longer than you might suspect. Few products are as serious to the people who use them as they are to the people who make them. What may strike the manufacturer as sacrilege often comes across to the consumer as good-natured honesty. The company willing to poke a little fun at itself can appear quite human. Here is another sample of humor by two masters of the art, Bob and Ray:

> BOB: Once again we're happy to present—"The
> Worst Person of the Week." Our scouts have
> made their worst person selection . . . and
> your name is?
>
> RAY: I'd rather not give it; you know, with the
> awful things I've done.
>
> BOB: Okay. . . . Now, you are a family man.
> Did your wife know how awful you were
> when you got married?
>
> RAY: Well, she got an inkling of it when I refused
> to say "I do" at three different wedding
> ceremonies. (LAUGHS)
>
> BOB: That's terrible. What are some of the latest
> dreadful things you've been doing?
>
> RAY: Go into a department store wearing a carna-
> tion, looking like a floorwalker. People ask
> me directions. . . . I send them to the
> wrong floor.
>
> BOB: Despicable!
>
> RAY: I like to drive on the turnpike in weekend
> traffic and purposely run out of gas in the
> middle lane. Then I get out of the car and
> just shrug a lot.
>
> BOB: I've seen you.
>
> RAY: The worst thing I do is to my own family. I
> hide the Right Guard. Just when they're all
> getting ready for a big night out.
>
> BOB: They all share the Right Guard?

RAY: That's the beauty part of it. It's a spray, see,
and they all use it. . . . So I don't leave just
one or two defenseless. . . . I leave all six
defenseless.

BOB: Six! Well, you certainly are the worst person
of the week.

RAY: Thank you. And another horrible thing I do
is leave myself defenseless.

BOB: I've noticed.

Like all good humor, this commercial has a punch line. One of the most difficult things about a humorous commercial (or any commercial) is to end with a bang. In a print ad, the headline is often the punch line. But in broadcast, the message builds to a climax. If it falls flat in the closing seconds, it can undermine the effect of everything that has gone before. Here is one last example, a humorous dialogue commercial for the Coffee Association that delivers several hints on how to make better coffee:

HE: Marilyn, do you mind if I say something?

SHE: No, Herbie, say anything you like.

HE: Your coffee'd stay fresher if you kept it in
the refrigerator.

SHE: Oh, what a good idea.

HE: Gee, I'm glad you're not offended.

SHE: Herbie, anyone with self-confidence can
take a good suggestion.

HE: Then could I say something else?

SHE: Please, Herbie, go right ahead.

HE: Always start with a clean coffee maker.

SHE: Oh, it's dirty?

HE: Ah, did I go too far?

SHE: Too far!? It's an excellent idea, Herbie. All
your ideas are excellent.

HE: And always use cold water. Very, very cold
water for the best coffee. And that's it. I'm
not going to say another word. I'll just set
the timer?

SHE: The timer?

HE: Drip coffee should never brew more than
four to six minutes. Six to eight for percola-
tor. If you care about good coffee.

SHE: Oh, I do, Herbie. And I'm glad you came over for some. Because I think you're really beginning to open up. I think we could say anything to each other. . . .

HE: We could probably even talk about your weight problem. Coffee has no calories, you know . . .

SHE: Get out, Herbie.

Summary

The guidelines for writing a radio commercial are not very different from those for creating a television commercial. Both are visual media, but radio must create the visual in the listener's mind. Both are structured in time and must flow from beginning to middle to end. Both work on the emotions as well as the intellect. Both must reward or entertain as well as inform. Both thrive on simplicity—one idea, simply expressed.

As far as radio specifically:

- Write for the listener. Radio is a personal medium. Write (talk) to the listener in his or her own language. Be direct, simple, straightforward. Reward listeners for the time and trouble they take to listen to you.

- Write for the listener's ear. Radio must be heard to be seen. Keep the words and sentences short and simple. Watch out for puns, poetry, and tricks. And remember to use the other tools—music, sounds, and silence.

- Repeat yourself if necessary, and it is usually necessary. If you have a single, important selling idea, it should be worth repeating. Do not assume that you have the listener's undivided attention.

- Do not crowd yourself. Remember to leave enough time for an announcer to get some drama and meaning out of your copy. Sound effects and music take time. Give them some. It is better to underwrite than to try to cut copy at the recording session.

- Do not die at the end. People remember punch lines, but not commercials that just seem to stop rather than end. This does not mean you have to always leave them laughing. But you should leave them thinking about the product.

Appendix III

Direct Response Commercials

Buy Now vs. Buy Later

Generations of advertising students have been raised on the short, sweet definition of advertising that John E. Kennedy passed along to Albert Lasker back in 1905: salesmanship in print. This simple notion of the advertisement as salesperson has become a bit obscured as advertising, especially television, moved more and more into image building. We have seen in the debates over what makes an effective commercial the difficulty that TV advertisers have in determining exactly what impact a specific commercial has on sales. Research journals are full of theories that try to chart the mysterious course from the exposure of a commercial through consumer memories and attitudes to an eventual influence on buying behavior. However, there is another group of television advertisers who have a much simpler method of measuring the effectiveness of their commercials. They wait for their telephone to ring. Welcome to the world of direct response advertising.

When a general advertiser ends a commercial with a call to action ("Try our brand!"), no one seriously imagines viewers leaping from their chairs and racing out to the nearest store to buy the product. At best, one hopes to have stimulated a favorable predisposition to buy, so that when a buying situation presents itself in the future, some positive feeling or memory will be triggered that may cause consumers to try the brand. But when direct response advertisers call the viewers to action, that is exactly what they expect—action. John Witek writes:

In order to sell, response advertising has to convert viewers from passivity and disinterest to active participation. It must engage the imagination to produce simple behavior shifts, such as getting up from a chair to dial a telephone. Direct response aims for positive action. And people feel good about positive action because acting gives the impression of being in control. Thus the act of buying through direct response television is accompanied by positive associations that do not accompany general consumer advertising.

The slickest, costliest general agency productions cannot make a prospective customer get up and do something *now*. Consumer advertising seeks to leave its audience with a simple impression that influences their behavior at some time in the future. But direct response advertising works immediately. It takes customers by the hand and leads them every step of the way up to and through the final sales transaction.[1]

Direct response is John E. Kennedy's kind of TV advertising: salesmanship on television.

Although direct response advertisers remain true to their salesmanship function, many would like to shed their blatant salesperson image. Early TV standup pitchmen set a style and tone that still survives in the fringe viewing hours when fast-talking heads demonstrate amazing vegetable slicers and kitchen knives. As television matured, slick pitchmen gave way to smooth-selling celebrities, but the style of those early direct commercials remained basic show-and-tell. And, unfortunately, many of the offerings were not as amazing as represented.

Abuses were rife in the early buccaneering days. Products sold through television might arrive months after they were ordered, while others never arrived at all. A lot of merchandise that did show up was third rate. Some commercials were vicious come-ons for shark toothed salesmen with shady real estate deals, phony freezer food plans, overpriced house siding, fake diet pills, and junk encyclopedias at premium prices. The principles of truth in advertising and a full disclosure of terms of the sale were often disregarded. The TV audience was finding out the hard way that an offer that sounded too good to be true really was too good to be true.[2]

Since the early 1970s, the medicine-show mentality of these early direct commercials has been replaced by the more sophisticated, viewer-rewarding techniques that characterize the most creative general consumer commercials. Today many can be distinguished from glossy general commercials only by the inclusion of their toll-free 800 number at the close. Specialists in direct response advertising justifiably resent having their work stereotyped as crass, tasteless, and void of production value. Al Eicoff pointed out:

Does this mean that direct-marketing commercials are dull, drab, unimaginative? No, it means just the opposite. A direct-marketing

---

1. John Witek, *Response Television: Combat Advertising of the 1980s* (Chicago: Crain Books, 1981): xxi.
2. Witek, 8.

commercial must simply present the benefits of its products or services in the most informative and interesting way. Notice that I use the word "interesting," as opposed to "entertaining." Effective television advertising often is interesting rather than entertaining. In the early days of television, "interesting" 30-minute sales pitches were the norm. Though they aired constantly, viewers responded positively to them. In fact, they created as much discussion as the "hot dog" commercials did.[3]

Uses and Types of Direct Response Commercials

There are three basic uses for direct response commercials: 1) selling products or services directly to consumers (records, books, magazine subscriptions); 2) generating leads (Armed Services, financial services, schools, tourist boards); and 3) supporting other sales activities (watch your mail, look for this ad or display).

Direct sell commercials may be one-shot offers or they may sell a continuity program, such as a collection of Time-Life books. One-shot offers are usually sixty seconds long; the more complicated continuity offers tend to be two minutes. Lead-generation commercials, which invite viewers to call for more information, and support commercials, which simply sell the piece of advertising that will do the real selling, are usually just thirty or sixty seconds long.

The advent of cable TV has also opened opportunities for longer infomercials. *Infomercials* are detailed product demonstrations or presentations lasting from three to fifteen minutes. They are often presented in conjunction with some kind of interactive system that allows the viewer to order directly.

Creative Considerations

The reminder to include an 800 phone number or an address that enables the viewer to respond is probably the only guideline to direct response commercials that would not be equally appropriate for general commercials.

- Talk to individuals. Television is a mass medium, but every copy writer has been told to write to one person, not a mass. Direct response advertisers ask for an immediate decision from the viewer so their appeal must be even more personal than general commercials. In fact, they are more apt to liken their commercials to direct mail than to ordinary commercials. As one writer put it, ". . . Your opening is like the direct mail outer envelope (or headline/graphics in a print ad). The

---

3. Al Eicoff, *Eicoff on Broadcast Direct Marketing* (Lincolnwood, IL: NTC Business Books, 1988): 51.

spokesman and approach from your letter become the audio dialogue of your commercial. The brochure becomes your audio visual story with dramatizations of benefits and exposition of features. Your nuts 'n' bolts, the other card or coupon becomes your ordering information at the end."[4]

- Keep it simple. This is sage advice for any kind of commercial, but when you have only a minute or two to close the sale, it becomes critical. All the information that is presented should be clear and relevant. You cannot afford to get bogged down in details. On the other hand, neither can you afford loose ends. You must include all the information you need so that the viewer is not left with unanswered questions.

- Be believable. The shady history of TV pitchmen is bound to have left a residue of skepticism. The name and reputation of the advertiser, the careful choice of a spokesperson, the use of testimonials, demonstrations—all these things can help build credibility, as can, of course, a money-back guarantee.

- Grab attention—another basic rule for advertising that takes on additional significance in direct response. The viewer's interest must be hooked very early if there is to be time to make the sale.

- Motivate the viewer. Remember you are trying to change a couch potato into a customer. According to one expert, the secret is *"momentum—*a flow of vivid rhetoric that sweeps viewers away on a tide of words and images. Momentum is not information, it is style; it is a way of presenting information that turns passive TV watchers into active, telephone-dialing, letter-writing customers."[5] Finally, a use for time-compression.

- Make it easy to order. Alert the viewer that an address or phone number is coming. And keep it on the screen long enough for viewers to get it. The basic rule of thumb is fifteen seconds in a 60, twenty seconds in a 120.

Here is a typical format for a two-minute direct sell commercial:

5 to 10 seconds. This is the attention step, which may include exciting visual material or compelling copy. ("In the next two minutes, I want to tell you about something that may change your life.")

65 to 75 seconds. In this portion the product or service is described, with benefits, features, demonstrations, and testimonials. There is a complete arsenal of persuasion packed into a fast-paced pitch.

15 seconds. Next comes an action device to motivate the consumer immediately. (Procrastinators tend to lose interest and never order.) Premium offers often increase the response. Usually free, these premiums are designed to win over the half-hearted consumer.

---

4. Joan Throckmorton, *Winning Direct Response Advertising* (Englewood Cliffs, N.J.: Prentice Hall, 1986): 326.
5. Witek, 1.

20 to 30 seconds. Finally, ordering information, including the terms of the offer and the telephone number or mailing address, is given. If the product or service is not available through any other means, this is the place to hammer home that information. Ordering information must be repeated.[6]

The Rosy Future of Direct Response

Retailer John Wanamaker (1838-1922) once said, "Half the money I spend on advertising is wasted, and the trouble is I don't know which half." The direct marketer would have a simple answer: The money spent talking to people who are not prospects for your product is wasted. This is the basic appeal of direct marketing—its ability to single out prospects and talk to them one-on-one. The most direct medium is mail. It knows the prospects by name and address. Magazines have become increasingly selective, attracting prospects by tailoring editorial material to very specific interests, such as running, or backpacking, or gardening. Television, on the other hand, has been a mass audience medium ever since it seized that role from radio. As television attracted the huge national audience with mass appeal programming, radio became more localized and specialized, designing formats that would attract smaller but more specific audiences. Television was *broad*casting; radio became *narrow*casting.

But television is changing, and as it does, direct response advertising can only grow in importance. The three major TV networks are battling for shares of a dwindling national audience as television viewers see their viewing options expanding with the spread of VCRs and cable. "Cable TV finally arrived in the eighties (it 'arrived' when it reached a circulation of over 30 million homes). This opened special-interest channels to direct marketers—sports channels, music channels, ethnic channels, financial and news channels."[7] Cable subscribers have dozens of choices as they curl up on the couch in front of their new large screen stereophonic TV sets. Instead of "The Cosby Show," they could watch a weather channel. And if you were selling barometers or tornado detectors, where would you put your commercial?

The late 1980s also witnessed another phenomenon: home shopping. "No other TV business has had as rapid a rise, and subsequent consolidation, as home shopping. And no home shopping service better illustrates the industry's many contortions than Home Shopping Network (HSN), the service that started the frenzy when it went national in '85 and public in '86. . . . It rose from its roots as a regional Florida shop-by-TV channel to become the hottest new programming idea to hit cable—and the hottest new issue to hit Wall Street."[8]

---

6.   Elizabeth J. Heighton, Don R. Cunningham, *Advertising in the Broadcast and Cable Media* (Belmont, Calif.: Wadsworth Publishing Co., 1984): 260.

7.   Throckmorton, 317.

8.   "A Year after the Frenzy, Order Starts to Set In," *Channels* (December 1987): 111.

Things began to go sour for HSN (its stock declined, stockholders sued, competition increased, revenues dropped) and the industry has toned down. "Now, with major retailers like J. C. Penney, Sears Roebuck and K-Mart investing heavily in services of their own, home shopping has moved out of the sole domain of TV and into the even bigger world of retailing. Even TWA has gotten into the act with The Travel Channel, which sells international goods during World Shopping segments."[9]

The immediate significance of home shopping is the indication that viewers are taking on a more interactive role with their TV. This can only bode well for direct response advertisers who depend on motivating viewers to act at that moment. "Interactive video services, linking home computers and telephones with the TV screen have been in a testing mode for nearly ten years, and every year we get a little closer."[10]

Television may soon cease to be the medium for just the national advertiser or mass appeal products. It may become more segmented, more selective. And it may become more action oriented than image building. Direct response, now a footnote to the general topic of creating television commercials, may become the primary focus of advertisers in the 1990s and beyond.

---

9.   Ibid., 114.
10.   Throckmorton, 317.

Index